D1446857

the paranoia of *everyday* life

the paranoia of *everyday* life

escaping the enemy within

gerald alper

Prometheus Books

59 John Glenn Drive
Amherst, New York 14228-2197

Published 2005 by Prometheus Books

Inquiries should be addressed to
Prometheus Books
59 John Glenn Drive
Amherst, New York 14228–2197
VOICE: 716–691–0133, ext. 207
FAX: 716–564–2711
WWW.PROMETHEUSBOOKS.COM

09 08 07 06 05   5 4 3 2 1

Library of Congress Cataloging-in-Publication Data

Alper, Gerald.
    The paranoia of everyday life : escaping the enemy within / Gerald Alper.
        p. cm.
    Includes bibliographical references and index.
    ISBN 1–59102–345–9 (pbk. : alk. paper)
    1. Paranoia. 2. Delusions. I. Title.

RC520.A46 2005 2005
616. 89'7—dc22

                                                                    2005013879

Printed in the United States of America on acid-free paper

For Anita

contents

preface

"Y ou talking to me? . . .

"You *talking* to me? . . .

"You talking to *me?* . . ."

With those four words, repeated like a mantra, Robert De Niro—concealed deadly handgun at the ready, eerily fantasizing and rehearsing before his bedroom mirror what he will soon carry out in real life—burned his way into contemporary consciousness. His portrayal of Travis Bickle, the psychotic, vigilante taxi driver, quickly became a cinematic existential, inarticulate icon of paranoid rage against an unjust, evil world. So electric was the performance that years later it would be reprised in the equally legendary *Raging Bull.* This time as Jake LaMotta, the uncontrollably violent middleweight boxing champ, Robert De Niro, eyes balefully unmoving in a face drained of human emotion, sinisterly queries his profoundly insulted, incredulous brother, again and again, as to whether the brother slept with Jake's wife. In contrast to *Taxi Driver*, there is now no pretense of existential angst at the moral iniquity of the human race. In its stead, we are treated to one of the creepiest and least sentimental expressions of brutish, paranoid jealousy ever depicted on the screen.

In the new millennium, our fascination with the dynamics and cinematic iconography of paranoia has hardly abated. In *Kill Bill, Volumes 1* and *2*, we have Quentin Tarantino's long-awaited homage to kung fu movies and their exuberant celebration of over-the-top, revenge-driven, ritualistic bloodletting. While in *The Panic Room*, there is the other side of the coin: the abject fear of a woman and her daughter scurrying like rodents for a safe hiding place from the malevolent trespassers who have broken into their newly purchased home.

Although the scenarios may vary, the underlying themes of either unbridled hatred of a persecutory enemy, real or imagined, or the runaway terror in the face of being mercilessly, diabolically stalked, remain constant. What Tom Wolfe prophetically once called the "culture of violence" has now been with us for many decades. Its dual aspect—murderous rage or craven panic—continues to be cinematically portrayed, explored, celebrated, exploited. At times there is the pretense that an honest attempt is being made to penetrate to the root of these twin faces of violence. The link, however, that is supposedly being sought, as I hope to show, is paranoia. Not the global kind, the September 11 kind, but the mundane, soap operaish, everyday garden variety that is regularly featured on daily TV.

This may become clear if we step back for a moment from the hysterical, hyperbolic images of rage, violence, and panic that routinely inundate us. Consider, for example, the rather innocuous ad for Brink's alarm systems that (as I write this) is currently being aired on television. A wholesome-looking woman, presumably a contented homemaker, is glimpsed in the comfort and safety of her cozy little house. She is startled by a sudden noise—the Brink's alarm system has just sounded. She rushes to investigate and to her horror sees a burly man in a black ski mask about to smash through the glass paneling of her downstairs patio. Without missing a beat, she gathers up her two small children, retreats to an anteroom, and dials what seems to be the ever-alert command headquarters of Brink's security system. We see a worried-looking man snatch up the telephone and then this exchange:

"Is everything all right?"

"No. Someone is trying to break into the house."

"I'll call the police."

The ad ends happily as the woman, drawing her frightened children protectively to her sides, announces to the camera, "We'll be safe now!"

The ad quite obviously is selling fear—fear of housebreaking, burglary, possible rape, even murder—in order to sell Brink's alarm systems. But it is hardly scary. The man in the ski mask looks oddly clumsy and even faintly ridiculous. The mother seems much too predictable, unconvincing, and bland in her reactions. The Brink's security contact seems more anxious than concerned and his concluding response—"I'll call the police"—is not particularly reassuring. But it is on the psychological plane that the ad is most deficient. Almost certainly, a mother who has just seen an ominous-looking man on the brink of violently entering her home would be terrified as she waited for the police to respond to the Brink's SOS. Could she possibly not be worried that the man in the ski mask, perhaps a dozen or so yards away from the tiny anteroom to which she has fled with the children, might just possibly get there before the rescuing police do?

It is helpful at this point to remember the average American's famously low threshold for tolerating uncertainty and frustration. All the ad wants to do, after all, is modestly whet our consumer curiosity while alerting us to the dramatized benefits of its product. It no more truly wants to disturb our sleep than does the life insurance salesman, whose stock in trade is the threat of bereavement, want his prospects to authentically face up to the existential trauma of death. Movies, by contrast, which increasingly do not pretend to mirror reality and therefore do not have to be taken seriously, have the luxury of truly terrifying us. Consider the cornered kidnap victim in *Fargo*, another wholesome-looking woman ludicrously entangled in her own bathroom shower curtain, grotesquely scampering and hopping around like a headless chicken as she attempts to elude her now-laughing kidnappers. Or Jodie Foster's riveting portrayal of mind-numbing fear in *The Panic Room* as she is hunted down in her own home by predatory housebreakers.

Although devoid of apparent entertainment value, the ad for Brink's alarm systems is an accurate and useful reflection of that vague but pervasive uneasiness I am calling the paranoia of everyday life. Compared with what is termed clinical or psychotic paranoia, this everyday version may be considered normal. Perhaps no homeowner has ever been entirely free of a passing thought, suspicion, or fear that his or her house may one day be susceptible to unlawful entry. Indeed the whole point of the Brink's ad is to construct a plausible scenario with which the average person would find it impossible *not* to identify. If someone, for example, who found himself in the real-life equivalent of the scene depicted in the ad did *not* feel some terror, it could be argued that he was not in touch with reality. By contrast, someone who manifested the same degree of terror dramatized in the ad when there were absolutely no discernible signs of housebreaking would be clearly paranoid in the clinical sense.

I use the bland Brink's ad as an illustration, although plenty of others abound, because there could not be a more straightforward appeal to a very basic, universal dread. We all fear, each in our own way, that our most prized possessions, our most guarded, physical boundaries—our home, our car, our very bodies—can at any time, especially in a dangerously over-crowded urban area, be brutally violated. But simultaneously while being alarmed, we are reassured. It is normal to be frightened by an intruder in a ski mask. It becomes abnormal only if and when we begin to imagine an intruder in a ski mask who is not there. The ad, thus, by neatly tying up our fears in a self-evidently situational paranoia subliminally congratulates us on our normalcy (while urging us to buy its product).

Imagine someone now, uneasy about one thing or another, often unaware of just what it is that is frightening her, out and about in the real world. The everyday world where anything can happen, where there are no unmistakable alarm bells warning us of encroaching dangers, where there are no hotlines to trained watchdogs who will ensure our safe pas-sage. Understandably, it is then difficult to accept that we are indeed fair game for whatever is cunning enough, strong enough, or just plain irre-sistible enough to harm us. It is natural to want a substitute of sorts for the Brink's alarm bell, an efficient internal warning system perhaps or a patch-work equivalent of it, to shore us up in times of peril.

A paranoid point of view develops when our natural desire to protect ourselves crosses an invisible line, which varies immensely from one person to another, and begins to become unconsciously irrational. It is character-ized by a kind of runaway vigilance, an increasingly pointless and debili-tating around-the-clock guardedness that can be maintained only at a steep psychological price. R. D. Laing once brilliantly and succinctly described this peculiar perspective as being the result of a *failure of feedback*. He meant a failure of positive feedback. That there is no resting place, no sanctuary from whatever is chasing you, no means of preparation and defense that can exclude the possibility that you have unwittingly overlooked some fatal chink in your armor, some telltale loophole in your chain of deductions, left some window of opportunity open for your enemy to slip in. And Franz Kafka in *The Burrow*—the journal of the never-ceasing labors of a small, partly human animal to construct a secret nest impregnable to the nameless but increasingly audible predators that never stop stalking it—uncannily evoked the spellbinding power of full-blown paranoid thinking.

It is the nature of true paranoid fears that they are unspecific, arriving from the blue without the fanfare of Brink's alarm bells. This, of course, is in contrast to the conventional or situational paranoid triggers upon which the media and culture at large are fond of dwelling. Typical, approved-of paranoid triggers are characteristically concrete: An alarm bell sounds; an infant cries; a small child is endangered and in need of protection. Paranoid triggers can be biological: Ethologists categorize these as separation calls of distress, such as a lost duckling or a hungry one crying out for attention from its mother, and believe they are programmed into the genome. On the more complex psychological level, paranoid triggers can be implanted in the psyche—working their way into the unconscious—by the ambient culture, one's peers, and especially one's parents. According to current attachment theory, for example, a person who is unexpectedly cut off from his or her required field of safe human contact, at whatever distance deemed necessary—which, based as it is on very early, formative dyadic experiences, can vary greatly from one individual to another—will be susceptible to bouts of paranoia.

Because they are unspecific, however, true paranoid fears will often have unconventional, idiosyncratic, and personalized triggers. Someone, for example, may dread being perceived as or feeling powerless, in turn fostering an obsessive and impossible quest to always be in control of one's self and immediate surroundings. Or someone may fear being abandoned, or humiliated, or narcissistically injured. Typically, such a person will be ignorant of the provenance, the incubation period of his fears. He will not understand that what he is experiencing, though it often will impress him as strangely novel, is but the end of a characteristically long, convoluted chain of dynamic associations.

When a paranoid point of view reaches a certain critical intensity, the person can achieve a kind of altered consciousness. She may then become so strikingly irrational in her thinking that she can be said to have crossed an invisible line and entered a paranoid world. And this is exactly what she means when, having restored herself—remember, the everyday paranoia we are considering here invariably is of limited duration—she looks back and, with relief, exclaims, "I was paranoid!"

What is a paranoid world? It is, in many ways, a melodramatic, suspense-filled world, not unlike a living soap opera, that is anything but boring. It is a perception of one's life that veritably cries out for immediate action, that self-evidently justifies a rigidly defensive self-armoring and closing off of reality. It is clear that here there can be no place for those linchpins of intimacy—trust, collaboration, and mutuality. Here, ordinary values of relating are turned upside down. In such a dire place, communication with the other is not only inappropriate but irrational. In its stead, there is the covert interpretation of codes, signs, clues, innuendos—the grim acceptance that almost nothing means what it says, that true meaning is hidden beneath the surface or obliquely signaled, that messages when they arrive as often as not are cast in the form of threats, that understanding, when it comes, is achieved by doggedly deconstructing what everyone else seems to take for granted.

Not surprisingly in such paranoid ideation, in the narratives and scenarios it endlessly weaves, there will be secrets, plots, and counterplots galore. The characters who people it, especially those designated agents of persecution, will typically be shrunken, hatefully reduced to one-dimensional, cartoonish caricatures. The focus of attention will not be on human emotions or feelings but on strategies, the more seemingly objective the better. The emotions that do filter through will tend to be polarized around issues of dread and suspense or, mercifully, a fleeting relief (often from a momentary sense of triumph). An occasional feeling of security is derived not from human contact but from the perception that one's defense system is in fine working order (the key message in the Brink's ad). Although from an existential point of view this is a profoundly solitary position to be in, the undercurrent of suspense and excitement mixed with dread can serve as a buffer against the realization of one's loneliness. Nevertheless, in what might be called the downtime of paranoid thinking, when nothing much is happening, the pathos of this way of being may surface. Such moments of self-doubt typically do not last long. Paranoid thinking, in contrast to what Harry Stack Sullivan sometimes called the perplexity of the schizophrenic, stubbornly will not settle for a puzzle. It demands answers, solutions.

David Shapiro in his classic *Neurotic Styles* masterfully noted that paranoid ideation is characteristically noncontextual. By focusing so narrowly on details, objects, and signs, contextual richness is lost. Emotional clues in particular, subtle underlying meanings that might well mitigate the harshness of the paranoid point of view, are often grievously missed.

With that in mind, early in my career I developed a method—which I called *the paranoid companion*—for working with my more paranoid patients. The basic idea was to find a benign way to enter their paranoid world no matter how bizarre. I could do this, of course, only with patients who already trusted me as much as they could trust anyone. I would begin by tentatively accepting the fundamental paranoid premise of their system as being at least worthy of our joint examination. I would patiently, as non-threateningly as I could, follow the chain of their inferences one to another. Inevitably, I would very quickly arrive at the gaps, the discontinuities, if not blatant contradictions, between one thought and the other. Pointing this out, I would wonder aloud at the strangeness of the connection. I would begin to hint at alternative, perhaps equally plausible, interpretations of the same facts under scrutiny. My hope was to slowly, incrementally demonstrate at least the possibility of the relativity and relevance of different perspectives. By thereby introducing complexity into our discussion, I wanted to highlight the narrowness, rigidity, and rule-governed nature of the claustrophobically restricted, self-referential world they had constructed. With my more seriously paranoid patients—those who seemed convinced they were the target of some orchestrated, Machiavellian conspiracy—I would, at some critical juncture, after a painstaking groundwork had been laid for the need for more expansive thinking, quietly ask them, "Do you really think you're *that important* to them they'd go to this much trouble?"

Given the massively entrenched, rigid nature of paranoid thinking, I had limited but encouraging success with this method. I realized that when it worked, it worked because my introduction of the principle of difference and subjectivity served to erode the tyranny of their fundamental paranoid premise. And that proved liberating. Once freed from its oppressive grip, they could begin at least to consider the underlying subjective and emotional foundations of the ironclad system they themselves had constructed.

Playing the part of the paranoid companion made me conversant with the inner world of the paranoid. I began to see how the paranoid point of view works by fantastically reducing the range of real possibilities, while simultaneously elevating to a spurious hegemony the dominant paranoid fantasy. By thereby ousting all other legitimate contextual candidates, it forcibly conspires to make the unreal seem real. This may be why when someone emerges from a bout of paranoid thinking, having at last gained the necessary distance from it, a very typical response is to feign surprise at how one "was taken in" by the now-discredited paranoid fantasy. Because paranoia is still regarded as a cultural stigma, there is an invariably pejorative connotation to the attribution in "You're being paranoid"—or the admission "I was paranoid!" The implication is that paranoid moments, or episodes, are viewed merely as disjunctive breaks in normal functioning, isolated aberrations. In other words, it is not seen, as I believe it should be, as a process. From that standpoint, "I got paranoid" is intended to temporally distance oneself, putting it safely in the past. Meaning: "I'm not paranoid anymore. I'm myself again."

By contrast, I hope to show that the paranoid point of view is considerably more normal than given credit for, is going on all the time, and what are called paranoid moments, or lapses, are simply the tip of the iceberg, the crystallization of a process, hitherto beneath the radar of consciousness, but now so pressing it cannot fail to draw attention to itself.

Part of the reason it is hard to accept the prevalence of the paranoid point of view is that, as mentioned, it is so devoid of the conventional, situational paranoid triggers that make the Brink's ad so instantly and reassuringly recognizable. By contrast, the triggers of genuine paranoid fears are buried in the unconscious. The encapsulated idea that sets the process in motion is repressed. When it does emerge, when the trigger reveals itself, its urgency will often serve to mask the obvious dissociation from the context in which it arises.

When therapy works with such a patient, it works by exposing the hollowness of its insistence on infallibility, the imminence of personal catastrophe, and the conspiratorial, self-referential nature of its universe.

As I have mentioned, the greatest protection I know against the pernicious spread of paranoid thinking is a lively, healthy, and reality-based trust of the other. Unfortunately, as most of us recognize, there are many factors in our contemporary culture that mitigate against this kind of benign trust and therefore unwittingly contribute to what I am calling everyday paranoia.

Why everyday paranoia? Because the subject needs to be liberated from the chains of clinical diagnosis and psychiatric classification in which it has been safely incarcerated. By no means do I deny such syndromes exist. But after all, syndromes begin, take root, and grow up some place, and that place is the real, mundane, everyday world.

In the book, I explore as graphically, narratively, and profoundly as I can the many faces of everyday paranoia. I conclude with a major clinical study of a patient (whom I call Becky Jamison) who vividly personifies my principal themes.

The people portrayed, howsoever briefly, are based on actual patients I have known and worked with. They are presented as they were originally seen by me through the prism of psychoanalytic psychotherapy. The names, of course, have been changed and circumstantial details have occasionally been altered so as not to betray the confidentiality to which they are entitled. But the incidents that are described and, especially, the psychological dynamics that are depicted are as true as I can make them.

chapter 1

the terrorist within

A telltale characteristic of paranoia is the primitive defense mechanism once designated by Melanie Klein as splitting of the object. It refers to the basic psychic failure to tolerate and process the intrinsic complexity, ambiguity, and ambivalence of objects of our affection. Someone under the sway of this defense mechanism will tend to love or hate whatever it is that captures its fancy. Emotions will be expressed in a binary way, black or white, either/or. Internal contradictions, inconsistencies, qualifications that crop up are regarded as impurities that must be purged away.

We immediately see that what we are calling paranoid triggers are split off, all-bad, hated aspects of something that is threatening the person, something that has considerably more dimension and subtlety than is being admitted. To see this clearly—the amazing fascination this undeniably primitive defense mechanism continues to hold for us—we need to go no further than our decades-old, ongoing romance with gangsters, crime families, and violence. I begin with the current rage, HBO's beloved Tony Soprano.

THE SOPRANOS—
AMERICA'S FAVORITE DYSFUNCTIONAL FAMILY

In a memorable scene, teenaged Meadow, enraged by her father's bullying control, dares to call him a hypocrite. In a manner she certainly does not expect, and has apparently never witnessed, Tony gets in her face and snarls, "You trying to tell me something?" Unknowingly, she has touched a nerve, hit a paranoid trigger in her father, that for a moment threatens to push him over the edge. We see Meadow viscerally cringe, as she never has. "N-no," she whimpers.

The fear she palpably feels (and we in the audience feel for her) is far more than the fear of a father's wrath; it is the fear of subhuman violence exploding in her face. For just a moment, she has glimpsed something subterranean from which she has up until now been scrupulously protected. For, over the years, the series has made a point of demonstrating that Tony Soprano, serial-killing mob boss of New Jersey's largest crime family, never lays a finger on either Carmela, his wife, or his daughter, Meadow. (Although occasionally, when he deems it necessary, he is not above mildly cuffing Anthony Jr., his only male heir, for what are considered unacceptable upstart remarks.) We are meant to believe that this shows a radical and near-perfect split between how Tony behaves to the two families that dominate his life. To make the point more forcibly, it portrays Carmela as the physical aggressor in the relationship, someone capable, when sufficiently provoked, of throwing objects, even occasionally swinging out at her husband.

Throughout it all, Tony as the supposedly nonviolent husband and father, grits his teeth and bears his wife's endless stream of put-downs. It is only when she taunts him with being secretly in love with his underling Furio, a stone-cold killer, does Tony aim a vicious punch in the direction of his wife's face (only managing at the very last second to divert it into the wall where it leaves an immediate, gaping hole). For crime family aficionados, the scene is reminiscent of Michael Corleone in *Godfather II* who—his wife taunting him that she has willfully aborted his son because "this evil must stop"—for the very first time savagely slaps her. It could be said, up until this point, that neither Carmela nor Meadow and Anthony Jr.—who both tease their father but only go so far—have ever in the slightest tested his boundaries. We see why now.

To reinforce in yet another way the magnitude of the split between his two families, we are repeatedly shown how at one Tony Soprano is with the Mafia code. At a blink of an eye, he will order to be killed—sometimes personally doing it himself—whoever needs to be eliminated. The illusion cherished in pop culture is thus dutifully upheld that even the most vicious gangsters when at home can be truly as loving to their respective families as anyone else.

It is characteristic of paranoia that, denying complexity, it approaches matters of the heart in a binary fashion: There is to be absolute loyalty or absolute betrayal. To fantastically narrow the range of options in this way, to brand anything less than unbroken fealty as tantamount to treason, is to create a false sense of omnipotent control.

In this *Sopranos* gangster version of a supposedly American family, the split between loyalty and betrayal could not be more dramatic. Loyalty of a family member is repaid by a fiercely jealous, vigilant protectiveness. Betrayal, especially if by a trusted member of one's crew, results in near-instantaneous murder. In perhaps the series' most gripping scene, we see this Mafia code of ritualistic murder graphically enacted when Tony Soprano discovers, hidden in the dresser drawer of his best friend, Big Pussy (whom he "loves"), the smoking gun–wiretap he has been looking for.

Nowhere is the profundity of Tony's splitting shown so clearly as in this climactic episode. For he has been tormented for a very long time by a dawning suspicion that (unthinkable as it is) his friend has turned FBI informant. Somehow he has managed to rationalize away or outright deny the telltale signs that he is being betrayed: the startling tip by the crooked detective who works for him that Big Pussy, to avoid prosecution on a heroin charge, has actually turned informant; the months-long, sudden disappearance of Big Pussy that was never satisfactorily explained; the mounting evidence that someone in his innermost circle is leaking information to the feds. But it is only when Tony, who dreams often throughout the series, meets up one night with a seemingly dead fish—who, addressing him in the unmistakable voice of Big Pussy, says, "Come on, Tony, you know it is me. I had to do it"—does he finally admit what he has just been told by his oracular unconscious. For Tony does not need a dream interpreter to tell him that "sleeping with the fishes" is the Mafia term for ritualistic murder.

The transformation that follows is chilling to see. Almost the moment upon waking up, we see that quiet, fixed, stone-cold killer look with which the audience is well acquainted. Although not yet morning, Tony hastily gathers his crew and rushes to the home of Big Pussy. Under pretext of urgently needing to go to the bathroom, he goes upstairs, stealing into his friend's bedroom, and carefully begins searching. When he discovers the wiretap hidden in the dresser drawer, he knows he has the smoking gun he needs to justify to himself and his crew what he is about to do.

The actual execution scene takes place in the isolated cabin of his private yacht far out into the ocean. The moment of truth—when Big Pussy realizes the real reason for what he thought was an innocent outing—is horrible to watch. We cannot help but be sympathetic to the poignancy of his terror as he stares childishly, beggingly, but hopelessly at his former best friends in the world and comrades-in-arms now transformed into a deadly firing squad.

There is only a single occasion in the entire series when this split between Tony's two families is not upheld. In a very early episode, he is driving his daughter, Meadow, clearly the apple of his eye, to an out-of-state prospective college she wants to scout. Perhaps warmed by the coziness of the trip, Meadow decides to pop the $64,000 question, "Are you in the Mafia, Dad?" After the reflexive, awkward denial, followed by some moments of palpably wrestling with his conscience, Tony admits, "Well, some of the money I make does come from illegal sources." Grateful for the first crumb of honesty she has ever received in her life from her father, Meadow beams. "Thank you for your honesty."

This father-daughter moment, to say the least, is short lived. For, in a matter of minutes, stopping at a gas station, Tony, to his utter disbelief, catches sight in another car of a very old "rat": someone who once betrayed a man very close to him and who for many years had safely disappeared into the hated witness protection program. In spite of the fact his daughter is sitting by his side, Tony simply cannot resist the chance to settle an old score. Crazily he swerves through traffic in pursuit of the suspected informant. Lying clumsily to his daughter as to why he is acting so bizarrely, he stalks the man until his suspicions are confirmed. Then, with Meadow tucked away in a motel, he steals to the man's home, sinisterly waits for his chance, and the moment arriving—fierce, pleasurable, sadistic rage contorting his face—garrotes one more rat who thought he had gotten away.

The Sopranos works hard to make this incredible split—between loving, tender feelings on the one hand and murderous, psychopathic, criminal impulsivity on the other—plausible to the viewer. It succeeds in part, but only in part, by showing every other character in the series to be similarly divided—although not nearly as radically and pathologically as Tony Soprano—each in his or her own way. Thus we see Carmela, Meadow, and Anthony Jr. having to deny over and over again the shocking truth that Tony Soprano, in addition to being the devoted, traditional family man they know so well, is also, when it is necessary, an unrepentant, calculating killer.

So staggering is their collusive denial, a kind of collective family brainwashing, that it is painful to watch. As viewers, we have been made privy from the start as to Tony's real nature. We understand that when insecure Anthony Jr. bravely announces he has become an "existentialist" who does not believe in God, it is his childishly ineffectual way of standing up to his father. We wince at how pleased with herself Meadow appears to be as she teases her father for not being as cool and up-to-date as her friends' dads. We suffer in silence as Carmela flirts with her seductive parish priest, experiences her first extramarital kiss with a house painter after almost twenty years of faithful wedlock, and fantasizes about making love to the Italian assassin Furio, whom she pathetically takes to be the first authentically sensitive man she has ever met.

Even Dr. Melfi, Tony's psychiatrist who is treating him with Prozac for his panic attacks, seems to join in the group denial. Upon learning what her new patient really does for a living, she informs him that under law, and by the ethical canons of her profession, she is bound to immediately report any revelations whatsoever of ongoing or imminently impending criminal activities. So the rules of the treatment are that she cannot under any circumstances be placed in a professionally compromising position. Incredibly, she somehow thereby convinces herself that this makes it permissible to turn a blind eye to what she surely knows—that the man she is treating with Prozac is a psychopathic, homicidal mobster.

It is characteristic of the paranoid to hate the object of their persecution. In the gangster psyche, such hatred is taken to a heart-stopping extreme. There is the unforgettable scene in *The Sopranos* in which ten-year-old Tony accompanies his father, a loan shark and enforcer, to the neighborhood grocer. Although instructed to wait in the car, Tony, sensing something is up, sneaks into the store. In the tiny doorway of a back room he witnesses his father—as punishment for having fallen into unacceptable arrears on a gambling debt—chop off the little finger of the hysterically screaming grocer.

Unexpectedly needing to explain to his visibly terrified son what he clearly was not meant to see, his father, appearing wild-eyed and psychotic-looking, justifies his action by underscoring the degenerate nature of the gambler's addiction and the necessity of never being disrespected. He concludes his lecture to his son pleading, "What else could I do?"

Throughout the five-year run of *The Sopranos*, this pattern of rationalizing acts of unnatural violence by expressing outright contempt for their hapless victims is repeated. In every one of the many scenes of graphically depicted, explosive violence—for which the show is both famous and notorious—we are treated to this sneering sense of sadistic self-satisfaction. Each character, when forced to act as an enforcer, is shown as almost viscerally enjoying the beating he is administering. For the impulsive criminal who must act out his murderous paranoid rage, splitting of the object is a desperate but perhaps necessary defense. It may be—by so thoroughly discharging his savage impulses within the confines of his secret, ritualized criminal life—he is unconsciously helping preserve a comparatively safe venue for the personal expression of his more tender, sentimental side (which, according to Mafia lore, has always been channeled toward parents, family, and especially children).

How different this is from ordinary, everyday paranoia, in which objects of persecution tend to be kept under tight wraps, internalized, sublimated, or acted out in obsessive ways. Here, there is precious little real-life drama. Here, by contrast, it will be the tiny details in our life that seem most to torment us. Here we move from fighting crime families and the federal authorities to fighting something that can even be as small and unheroic as a mouse.

A BETTER MOUSETRAP

George had not thought of himself as phobic in any way, and certainly not in regard to rodents. After all, he lived in New York City, and what were there, supposedly eight million of them? Like everyone else, he had seen his share. A rat moving about or sometimes even strolling along the tracks of a subway station. A mouse darting from a sidewalk bush. On each such occasion, he would shudder for just a moment, stare transfixed at the spot from which the creature had materialized, and then quickly look away.

But George had never seen one up close. The most vivid personal experience he could conjure up went back to his childhood, when he was nine years old and living with his parents in a small but comfortable two-story house in Hartford, Connecticut. The first thing he remembered was his mother screaming and his father almost simultaneously jumping up from his kitchen chair. Although he had been fortunately looking the other way, he could have no doubt that a mouse had just raced across the kitchen floor and disappeared somewhere beneath the large refrigerator that stood in the corner.

Even more startling to George than the sound of his mother screaming was the panic that contorted the face of his father. Not only had he never remembered seeing his father acting that scared, but up until that time, he had never been aware of him looking nervous or worried about anything. Although his initial reaction had been to disbelieve his own eyes, he was unable to discredit his ears as well. For in the dead of night, in his bedroom on the second story, which abutted that of his parents, he had been awakened by an odd metallic scraping noise that seemed to be coming from the downstairs kitchen, and he had realized, almost immediately, that the trap that, earlier, his father had baited with a sliver of American cheese and then cocked, had been sprung. *It must be the mouse,* thought George, *squeezed in the trap, yet desperately trying to squirm free, that was producing the noise.* His mother thought so, too: Through the thin wall separating their adjoining bedrooms, he could hear her strident voice: "Joe, it's caught. Go downstairs and get rid of it." Yet, even more tellingly, was his father's cowardly rejoinder. "I'll wait until the morning, when it's dead."

Thirty-odd years later, it was still not dead. George had come to me for therapy in order to exhume the state of his late marriage to his former wife of ten years, so as to better understand it, to come to grips with the appalling loneliness of sudden bachelorhood in a Queens apartment, and to divine, if he could, a more sanguine path that his life might take. Furthest from his mind (as he would later explain) was a need to confront a morbid anxiety concerning a possible inhabitation by rodents.

Yet, three months after I had first met George, when I believed that we had settled comfortably into a fruitful exploration of his postmarital, post-traumatic syndrome, that is exactly what happened. Visibly upset, George had arrived at his appointed time and promptly announced that something totally unexpected, something truly horrible, had just occurred. At about

eleven in the evening, while he was lolling in the TV room adjoining the kitchen, he had seen something small and dark begin to flash from the border of the kitchen stove in the direction of the refrigerator, a distance of about five feet.

Instinctively, and instantly, as though to communicate his refusal to be visited by a rodent, George, jumping to his feet in the manner of his father years before, had yelled, "No!" And indeed, reacting to either the movement of his body or sound of his voice, the mouse, reversing its path in an incredible, seamless U-turn, had returned to the vicinity of the stove. But that, as George would tell me, was only "the beginning," the crystallization of the first moment of terror occurring seconds after the sighting when, looking at his bare feet and realizing at some point he would have to cross the TV room through the kitchen in order to go to bed, it dawned on him that no longer was he the sole occupant of his apartment. Like it or not, he had been joined by a repulsive visitor.

After more or less standing frozen in his tracks, and increasingly feeling that at the age of thirty-nine he was behaving like a ridiculous coward, he suddenly made a dash across the kitchen floor to the safety of the far side of the room. Turning to survey the territory he had just covered, George, out of the corner of an eye, saw a gray spot (which he presumed was the head of the mouse) cautiously advance from the bottom edge of a small garbage pail standing by the kitchen stove and, almost instantaneously, retreat.

Alternately frightened and then infuriated, George, arming himself with a broom from a hallway closet, proceeded to deliver a series of ear-splitting whacks to selected targets in the kitchen area in the faint hope of terrorizing the rodent into returning to wherever it had originally come from.

It would not be enough, George realized (noticing that he was actually pacing in small circles as he was thinking), to provide the security of the knowledge that there was no creature prowling the premises, which he would need in order to fall asleep. He would require traps for that. So, although it was late in the evening, he hastily dressed and headed for the all-night corner supermarket and bought every rodent trap it carried: small glue traps for mice, large ones for rats, and, for good measure, some old-fashioned spring traps.

Returning to his apartment, just in case the mouse was freely and over-

confidently wandering around, George leaned on the front doorbell to announce his arrival. He then opened the door, cautiously and carefully scanned the visible floor space, reentered the apartment, banged around some more with the broom, and immediately set to work deploying his arsenal of over half a dozen guaranteed traps.

That night George slept fitfully at best, but at least he wasn't awakened by the odd metallic noise that had long ago roused him from his sleep. When he did awake in the early morning hours, he was by no means sure what he hoped he would find: a caught, half-dead, or dead rodent that needed to be disposed of or an assortment of untouched traps that perhaps suggested the intruder had vacated the premises. When, fearfully padding from room to room, he ascertained that his fate was to be the latter, he felt relieved. Clearly he had overreacted and, given the unholy din he had angrily created with his broom, it made sense to think that the solitary mouse had been put to rout.

So, from that point on, a routine was established. George would return from work to his residence in Queens, lean on the bell just in case, and then compulsively check the contents of each and every trap. After four consecutive days in which nothing was discovered that he did not want to be discovered, he concluded that the scare, at bottom, had been only that—a scare.

But on the sixth day, relaxing after dinner in his bedroom with a book, George became startled by the nonimaginary and indisputably concrete sound of a trap being sprung. Impulsively leaping from the bed, he raced to the kitchen area, the site of the two spring traps that days ago had been carefully cocked and baited with American cheese and that so far had been unmolested. After first determining that the trap behind the wastebasket by the kitchen stove was intact, George then saw, beyond doubt, that the spring trap that had been set by the baseboard next to the sink had been not only sprung but also completely flipped over onto its face.

Something had not only totally eluded the snap of the trap but had knocked it silly. But what? In order to find out, George called up an old friend, Will, who knew so much and talked so much about the rodent problem in New York City that he was jokingly nicknamed by his friends "the exterminator." (Years ago, as a poor young actor living on the Lower East Side, Will had been visited and eventually infested by rats, so much so that he had been forced to vacate the premises and to move in with a friend

until workers from the health department had at last grudgingly come, trapping nine rats in all and locating and removing three nests that had actually been built in the temporarily deserted apartment. And even after Will had nervously returned, there had been the time when he had woken up in the morning to discover a very much alive rat stuck in a large glue trap: one that had squealed and "gone crazy" as he lifted it with a shovel and then dropped it in a bucket of water, where it quickly drowned.)

Even though it was a late evening call from a friend whom he had not heard from for over five months, Will grew instantly attentive and totally serious at the mention of a mouse in the apartment.

"Are you sure it's a mouse?"

The question made George uneasy. "What do you mean?"

"Well, a mouse looks small, kind of round and gray. Rats are dark."

"Well this was dark, I think. But small."

"Did it have a long tail?"

How long is long? thought George, who was sorry he had called Will after he hung up, but reminded himself that the tail did seem somewhat long. Shuddering at the thought that his visitor might be a baby rat after all (which might explain why it was strong enough to knock over a spring trap without getting caught), he got dressed and made a return visit to the corner supermarket for some fresh supplies.

Back in the apartment, George deployed another six traps in new locations, and, reassured that no rodent could possibly avoid all of them, he went back to his bedroom. During the following seven nights, buoyed up by the fact that his morning inspection continued to reveal no unwholesome surprises, he managed to regain his normal pattern of sleep.

By then he had convinced himself of a new theory: Whatever had knocked over the kitchen trap had undoubtedly been startled by the vicious metallic snapping and therefore had fled. Mercifully, the thought of a rodent living in the same apartment with him had begun to fade from his mind when he awoke in the middle of the eighth night, cognizant only of an urge to urinate. As he was a light sleeper, accustomed to many such urges, he knew his way by heart through the ten feet of darkness separating his bedroom from his bathroom.

As soon as George had let himself in the bathroom, even before he had switched on the light, he had heard a rustling. And when he had occupied the bathroom, closing the door behind him, the rustling grew unmis-

takably louder, and he could no longer ignore it. Although nauseated at what he might see, George glanced at a corner of the bathroom, from which the rustling seemed to be emanating. He saw a mouse two to three inches in length, grayish in color, with a medium-sized tail, begin to scoot parallel to the door frame, across the width of the tiny room, to the shelter of the nearest corner and then, as though equally miserable to be closeted within sight of George as he with it, try to hide behind the base of the bathroom sink.

Conscious of his naked feet, and the distinct possibility that at any moment the mouse, in its panic, might scamper over them, George retreated to the wall furthest from the sink. With his left arm, so as to provide a means of escape, he slid the bathroom door open a few inches (enough for the mouse to get out in a direction away from his bedroom) and proceeded to bang on the wall with his fist. Within moments the tactic had worked, the mouse scurrying through the window of opportunity provided by George, down the hallway and into a nearby closet.

Having bolted from the bathroom almost as quickly as the mouse, George had been able to see it in the act of disappearing into the closet, and, determined that this latest hiding place would be its last, he frantically created an impassable line of glue traps along the outer edge of the closet door, which he now firmly closed. Only two choices awaited the rodent: It could discover, within the confines of the closet, an egress leading out of the apartment, or it could endeavor to squirm its way back into the hallway corridor, where it would surely be trapped.

Still, it was not enough. Although he was as certain as he could be that what he had seen had been a mouse and not a baby rat, the experience of being closeted with a mobile rodent had done serious damage to his already fragile confidence. From such a perspective, a dozen traps were insufficient protection. In what was becoming a late-night ritual, George got dressed and paid another emergency visit to the corner supermarket where he discovered that only a single, large spring trap designed for a rat was available. Better be safe than sorry, thought George, who purchased it.

Back in his apartment, knowing there was at least one live rodent on the premises, he decided, for good measure, to add the forbidding new trap to his arsenal before returning to bed. It was already, according to his kitchen clock, three in the morning. Exasperated that so much time and energy were being devoted over a period of weeks to a disgusting and ongoing pest-control problem, George baited the trap with an extra large chunk of American cheese and then tightened the spring.

He was amazed at how much more powerful this trap was than the (by comparison) diminutive ones used to kill mice, for it took both his thumbs to pull the rectangular frame all the way back. The problem was he needed to free one hand so he could connect the bar that held down the lethal spring at the far end of the trap to the tiny bait with American cheese at the other end. To do that it was necessary to carefully slide the end of the bar through a hole in the bait.

So, pressing his right thumb as hard as he could on the taut frame, he slowly lifted the bar in his left hand. And suddenly George completely lost control of the trap: the frame slipping from under his thumb and then violently snapping shut. He could barely comprehend what had happened and certainly could not react. He saw the spring trap seemingly catapult itself about six inches from his right hand into midair, and almost simultaneously he felt a sharp pain on the side of the pinky of his left hand, as though it had been struck by a hammer.

George instantly realized that somehow, as the trap was springing shut, it had caught the side of his finger with a glancing blow. Had it trapped it squarely, judging from the fearsome impact from only a glancing blow, George did not doubt his finger would have been amputated. As it was, it seemed to be rapidly turning partially blue and swelling up to nearly twice its size before his very eyes. His first thought was, is it broken? And he wiggled it to see if he could move it (indicating it was not broken), which he could do to a limited extent. His next thought was, what would his former wife, who had been so indispensable in emergency situations such as this, have told him to do? And remembering what she undoubtedly would have said—make a compress of ice and press it against the injury to reduce the tendency to swell—George did just that. For the next hour, standing alone and miserable in the center of his kitchen, he extended his little finger, which, fortunately, did not continue to swell and, more and more, did not appear to be broken.

The following day, George made a point of visiting two new grocery stores and purchasing an additional ten traps, running up his total to over twenty. He was aware that he derived malicious pleasure, as well as genuine comfort, from the extent to which he had booby-trapped his apartment. And when five more days had passed without so much as a sign of disturbance in a single one of the multitude of traps, he began to believe that the rodent had most likely evacuated the premises through some aperture it had discovered within the recesses of the hall closet.

But on the sixth day, George finally caught a mouse. Almost immediately upon opening the front door, he saw it, squatting motionless on a small glue trap set by the base of the kitchen stove not far from the locus of the original sighting. As George entered the apartment and moved slowly forward to examine the dead-looking mouse, it moved. As he took another step to make sure that what he had seen had been more than a last-gasp death rattle, the mouse began to palpably squirm in the trap and to squeak. It was gray, fat, with a medium-sized tail, and very much alive. Suddenly George understood why the instructions on the back of the glue trap were devoted exclusively to the preferred means of deployment.

As George began once again pacing the floor, he realized that the means of actually killing the filthy rodent that had been plaguing him for nearly three weeks, lay squarely in his hands. Should he bash it with the broom? He imagined squishy insides staining the floor. Should he flush it down the toilet? What if it couldn't flush and just stayed there? The method he settled on (suffocate it), although equally repulsive seemed the safest.

His heart palpitating, he positioned a large glue trap over the head of the squeaking, mired mouse, and carefully dropped it, creating in effect a glue trap sandwich. Hoping his work was done, George quickly stepped back to survey the damage he had wrought. To his amazement, the large upper trap that was almost a foot in length, in testimony to the rodent's will to live, started slowly to wave. Knowing now he had no choice but to get his hands dirty, George, using the handle of the closet broom as a lever, began pressing the two glue traps together. His aim, as he told himself, was not to crush the mouse but to force glue up its nose, so as to asphyxiate it.

And, after a respite of about fifteen minutes, gritting his teeth and forcing himself to peek between the sandwiched glue traps at the inert, gray, pancaked body, George was satisfied that it had worked. Lifting a corner of the upper trap with his forefinger and thumb, he slid the remains into a plastic bag, which he then carried to the incinerator in the outside corridor and deposited in the dump chute.

The following Sunday, at Will's behest, George arranged to meet his first professional exterminator, a friendly, efficient man who conducted a thorough tour of the apartment: searching the kitchen area for telltale droppings, examining the pipes, radiator, the base of the plaster wall, and plugging with plaster or steel wool whatever holes or crevices he encountered. Forty-five minutes later, he announced the results of his investigation. "I don't think you have a mouse living in the apartment now. And we got all the holes so nothing that isn't here already will be coming into the apartment for a month, that's guaranteed. There is always the possibility, of course, they might create a new hole."

Before leaving, the exterminator presented George with a supply of traps preferred by professionals, but not readily available in local stores, and explained: "These yellow glue traps are more reliable than the big black ones, which mice seem to be able to slip through. The boxes here with holes in them contain poison. The mice play around in the poison, and then die. I like the old-fashioned snappers [meaning the kind of trap used by George's father thirty years ago] except today, you know, we find peanut butter works better than American cheese."

George shook hands and received a final reassurance, "You should have no problem."

In regard to real rodents, the exterminator was right. But as George was to bitterly learn, from the day that he had first sighted the mouse, and throughout the year that he continued to see me, he would be tormented by the mouse that was running around in his head. The mouse in his mind that he could not exterminate, "my internal mouse," as he called it. It had become from that first day a permanent part of the repertoire of images populating his dreams: usually appearing as a grayish substance that would begin to expand, move, and eerily assume an unmistakable mouselike visage. It was even more troublesome in the daytime when, fully awake, a sudden play of light and darkness, a flickering shadowy motion, a faint unexpected noise, could make him instantly, fearfully alert. And it was no surprise that the twenty-odd traps remained a fixture in George's apartment and that each evening, returning from work, he would lean heavily on the doorbell in spite of the fact he knew perfectly well that there was at least no human occupant within to hear it.

It was a rare opportunity as his therapist to witness the startling power of something that had begun as an ordinary paranoid thought—the uneasy fear of a small, scurrying animal that had so inexplicably frightened his parents and had taken hold in his nine-year-old mind. Thirty-odd years later, surprisingly transformed, it had reemerged with the force of a full-blown trauma. From the moment that George laid eyes on the mouse, an experience that lasted about a second, it preoccupied his mind. By his own reckoning, he must have invoked the memory of that initial sighting hundreds of times in the months to come and if he were to tally the instances of all mouse-related thoughts and associations, the number would be in the thousands.

Such abnormal monopolization of thinking is all the more extraordinary when it is considered that it is almost primarily devoted to negative psychical qualities. Although the classical idea that the person by repeating the trauma is endeavoring to master and undo it is applicable here, a question arises: How is this to be accomplished? And one answer, suggested by George, is through desensitization: to literally grant the object not only a second chance but as many opportunities as are necessary in order to be revisited and reexperienced in a less disturbing and more humane fashion.

Viewed that way, what the traumatized person such as George is really trying to do when he repeats a trauma is to experience its absence of affect: that is, to encounter the original threatening object without being subject to an involuntary turbulence of emotions. By invoking the traumatic object on his own terms, through willfully orchestrating the timing of its arrival and departure, the person hopes to desensitize some of the affiliated noxious memories.

It is, of course, in the nature of a trauma to resist such efforts at containment, and one of its most terrifying aspects is just this capacity, in spite of an array of psychic forces to suppress it, to return. In this regard, it is obvious that the phenomenal agility and elusiveness of the mouse (taking George almost three weeks to capture it) is an important reason it is such a universal object of phobic dread. The fact that the mouse is alive, has mobility and intentionality, and, so to speak, pursues you by actively invading your turf and doing everything it can to resist expulsion all contribute to the uncanny impact it is capable of producing. This can be better understood if it is compared with a traumatic object that is inanimate: a stretch of deep water, for example, in which one has nearly drowned; a diving board one cannot jump off of; a knife that one has cut oneself badly with; a flight of stairs down which one fell. It is not insignificant that such objects are inanimate and, in the manner that dead things can be banished at will from one's personal space, can be obsessively avoided.

But the traumatic idea that has moved inside one's psyche cannot be banished. The traumatized person, who has painfully learned that he cannot prevent its recurrence, therefore repeats the traumatic event as a defense against the unbearable suspense of having to anticipate the moment of its return.

The intentional repetition effectively neutralizes the element of malign surprise that characterized the original trauma and is also an attempt to arrange a showdown with the traumatic object—but once again on his own terms. In this sense, desensitization begins to look suspiciously like calculated psychical combat training: The person revisits the unsoiled state of mind that antedated the inauguration of the traumatic event, superimposes the psychological minefield that unfortunately developed, and doggedly tries to familiarize himself to the new reality and present danger.

The person mentally rehearses the traumatic scene in order to more comfortably occupy it, much as an actor practices on an empty stage in the hope of one day commanding it in earnest. Until that day arrives, and it rarely does, he feels persecuted and abused by the trauma that holds him in its grip and alternately belligerent and determined that there is no other recourse but to fight back.

As Adam Phillips has noted, a phobic symptom, such as George deploying more and more traps in his apartment, may be viewed as an attempt to slow the march of time and freeze the possibilities of action. When there is a need to control the specific source of dread (e.g., catch the mouse) that cannot be met (the mouse is too frisky), it becomes apparent how powerful is the drive and why it is that it dominates the psyche. The greatest freezing of the traumatic object occurs when one can actually kill it, as George was eventually able to do with the mouse in his apartment. By contrast, the least freezing occurs when the object is literally alive and on the loose, as the mouse was for several weeks. Since most traumatic objects were never alive in the first place, they cannot be killed. The best one can do, then, is to deaden their impact.

The relationship between the originating traumatic event and the individual psyche upon which it impinges can be likened to a master/slave, sadomasochistic dynamic of power. Normally, being controlled feels like being puppeteered. Being controlled by a trauma, however, especially in light of its irrationally repetitive and unrelieved persecutory aspect, feels like being sadistically enslaved. In such circumstances, there can be no hope of appeasement through reason or cognitive working through. The only resort seems to be that of violent revolt, radically turning the tables and enslaving the tyrant, which is why the initial phase of the self's attempt to desensitize the newly acquired traumatizing affects can be comparable to the experience of being forced to undergo combat training. By contrast, when someone perceives himself to be enmeshed in a nontraumatic but nevertheless controlling situation, there is always the chance of either finding a way out or, if one cannot, of ingratiating oneself with the controlling agency (e.g., a boss) and thereby loosening the coercive pressure. When the control originates from an internal traumatic object or affect, however, it is obvious that there is no directive, intelligent agency with which to bargain and the situation, accordingly, feels more hopeless.

Because a trauma is so unnaturally frightening, it is not sufficient to call it oppressive: It is more apt to compare it to an alien entity (like a multiple personality) that somehow has lodged itself in the psyche. When the object is another human being—as so often is the case when someone psychologically, physically, or sexually batters another person—to the degree that the experience is traumatic, a nonhuman alien identity will be unconsciously projected onto the perpetrator. For all of these reasons, a trauma represents the most direct experience a person can have and perhaps the clearest example that a pathological process or a pathogen is at work. From an experiential, phenomenological standpoint, a trauma is tantamount to an infection of the psyche.

Because of this, a common fear is that as one progressively succumbs to the spell of a trauma, one is either beginning to break down or may already have lost one's mind. There is a basis to such fear: When the so-called normal person has been traumatized, in view of the radical loss of ego boundaries that is entailed, he has probably come closer than he ever has to the experience of being mentally unbalanced. (Although cognitive functioning generally remains intact, the characteristic profound emotional fluctuations are difficult to distinguish from a clinical mood disorder.)

It is easy to see how ordinary paranoid fears—their runaway nature unchecked—can become phobic, traumatizing thoughts, thoughts that, assuming a life of their own, begin to prey upon their unsuspecting creator.

Much of the maddening frustration one feels in such a situation derives from the depressing realization that there is now absolutely no court of appeal. Whatever is persecuting you does this so mercilessly that it seems to be an alien presence.

This, of course, is clearly seen when the persecuting object is authentically alien (e.g., deep water or a mouse). It is then frightening because, given that it is so unempathic and impersonal, once such an object begins to silently invade, control, or even kill (e.g., deep water), there is nothing, no brake, to stop it.

There is no contingency of everyday life that is more unempathic and impersonal than the inevitability of our own death and the death of those we love. There is nothing more alien than the presence of someone we love, who happens, however, to be dead. There is no more fertile soil for the paranoia of everyday life.

"I SEE DEAD PEOPLE"

Haley Joel Osment's famous line from *The Sixth Sense* sent tingles down the spines of millions of spectators. It is especially terrifying to see dead people—seemingly dissatisfied and unwilling to accept their fate—return to visit the living. What could they want from us? What could we possibly do for them? There is the creeping suspicion that, envious of everything we have, they wish to steal something from us, perhaps a little of our life. It may be that our natural survivor's guilt, a lingering unconscious feeling that we might not after all be worthy of being alive, that perhaps the wrong person is dead, taps into this. By a simple process of projection, we may begin to imagine that the dead feel this way also and want us to join them, suffer with them, or offer reparation for the undeserved extension of the life we have been granted.

For a long time, popular culture has notoriously fed off our myriad paranoid fears about the dead. The media is replete with sweet-faced psychics who profess to be in communication with those who have departed long ago, who, with apparent ease, seemingly before our very eyes, regularly cross over and back again. It is noteworthy that these adored New Age psychics bear only glad tidings. The dead, it turns out, want only to meet our needs, assuage our fears, put to bed all our past guilt, and assure us that they still think about us, love us, and, of course, in their own special way, continue to exist.

Movies, of course, by contrast, wanting only to entertain us in frightening new ways, are more than willing to push the envelope of our paranoid fears. Not surprisingly, cinematic dead people are anything but the warm, fuzzy creatures eager to make contact with television's avuncular cross-over psychics. Thus, in *The Sixth Sense*, they are clearly hostile alien presences, caring nothing for us, demanding angrily that we do their bidding. While in *Ghost* there are both good and evil spirits (mirroring our ancestral paranoid fears that when we die we shall be saved or damned, rewarded or punished, for the life we have lived): Patrick Swayze as the beatific, protective lover heroically trying to warn and rescue Demi Moore from the murderer who murdered him, and a legion of troll-like, black, diabolical, chanting shapes streaming from sewers eager to drag their latest victim into the infernal depths below. Perhaps most terrifying of all is the vengeful ghost, the drowned girl in *What Lies Beneath*, who waits and waits for her chance to pull Harrison Ford, her murderer, to the watery grave he richly deserves (reflecting a very deep paranoid fear that among the dead who have known us are those who loved/love us and those who hated/hate us).

By comparison the ordinary imaginings and perceptions of the dead are quite different: less dramatic and more convoluted, ambivalent, and characteristically unresolved, as I think the following case vividly shows.

Of all the patients I had ever encountered, Sandy was the most involved with death, with people she had loved who had died, and, especially, with the prospect of either dying or killing herself. There was a history to her morbid curiosity. When she was eight years old, she handed a note to her teacher that simply said that she wanted to die. She was promptly referred to a school psychologist who compelled her, against her wishes, to confide in her once a week her most troubling thoughts and feelings. When she was twelve, Sandy heard, read, or perhaps learned from the movies that a certain critical loss of one's blood would cause death. Fascinated, she stole into the family bathroom and began shaving her right shoulder with her father's razor until, at last, blood began to faintly seep down her arm.

At sixteen, Sandy accepted her first lover—a reckless young man, five years older than she and already married and separated, who had a habit of getting into bar fights and then getting arrested when he wasn't cracking up his motorcycle. For Sandy, the romantic highlight of her year-long passionate adolescent infatuation came on the evening she visited her lover in the hospital, twenty-four hours after he had nearly died. Inexplicably, a van, failing to see him, had collided head-on with his motorcycle, sending him flying about thirty feet through the air. It was a miracle, the doctors said, that it had been only his right leg, and not his neck or spine, that had been broken. But Sandy was hardly interested in what the doctors had said. Was it true, she breathlessly wanted to know, that his whole life (as she had often heard) had flashed before his eyes in the few seconds he had been catapulted through the air when he had to believe he was about to die?

When she was eighteen, she attended her grandmother's funeral, someone she had loved since childhood far more tenderly than her own mother. After that, there was barely a day in her life that passed that she did not think about the nature and meaning of death. And since she was already a firm believer in the existence of the spirit world, she never doubted, six months later, that the old woman sitting in the foyer with a peculiar black shawl wrapped around her—whose image had startled her by appearing and disappearing in the space of a minute—had been a visit from her dead grandmother and not a hallucination.

From that point on, proofs of the existence of another world began to accumulate for Sandy. When she was twenty, she visited her first psychic who predicted that within the next three years she would meet a man, fall in love, marry, give birth to a daughter, all the while continuing to commune with her dead grandmother—all of which came true. And when her daughter shyly confessed when she was eight years old that she had been feeling a presence in her bedroom for some time and had actually awoken one night to see a smiling old woman in an enormous black shawl sitting by her side, Sandy was thrilled that seemingly her daughter had been blessed with the same power to receive benign spirits.

Shortly thereafter Sandy came to see me. She did not come because of her ongoing contact with the dead, which she considered a positive feature of her life and in no way as evidence of a tendency to hallucinate on her part. It is worth noting that in the three years I worked with her—outside of my natural skepticism vis-à-vis the epistemological status of her presences and visitations from the dead—I found no instances of what I regarded as delusional thinking or examples of thought disorder. On the contrary, as Sandy saw it, her problem was not her communion with the dead but her contact with the living. Crippled by abysmally low self-esteem, terrified of the disapproval of her intrusive mother and of nearly everyone else, and convinced that no one had ever really loved, respected, or listened to her—other than her grandmother who had died when she was eighteen—she yearned to escape from the prison that was her life.

She was not afraid of death; she was frustrated that she could not embrace it, for she was morbidly frightened of an excess of pain that might be the price she would have to pay for the release from her present torment. Although she could not therefore seriously contemplate the act of killing herself, and never once made even a token attempt on her life, she could spend hours a day for weeks on end envisioning the details of one suicide plan after another. She would go to the library and leaf through books on toxicology, curious if she could find a poison that was painless, fast-acting, lethal, and easily purchasable. She would stand before the bedroom mirror, when her daughter was safely in school, and draw lines with a scissors, a nail file, or a razor blade up and down her arms or across her wrists until she was satisfied she could at least see the blood beginning to well up under the surface of her skin. And she would sometimes walk onto the balcony of her second-floor apartment, lean over the railing as far as she dared, and wonder what it would be like if she found the courage to jump and go flying head first through the air, as her lover once did?

When Sandy was not imagining the act of suicide, she was bemoaning the bad fortune of those who were doomed to occupy the land of the living. To die was not only to escape, it was to find nirvana, and, transferentially, therefore, more than any patient I had known, Sandy brought the presence of death into therapy. Her obvious morbidity, hopelessness, and clinical depression aside, she showed me in a unique way the rich phenomenology, the range of meanings open to someone who invests in relating to the dead. It was interesting to me that psychoanalysts who explore just this subject—following Freud's seminal *Mourning and Melancholia* (1915)—have tended to focus almost exclusively on the myriad reactions to loss. But relating to the dead is also an object relation in its own right, and, from an object relations standpoint, therefore, it is a good question to ask what kind of object relation it is when the object is dead.

Although obvious, it is important that it is static, does not move, and cannot be dynamic. It tends to be thought of sentimentally, in terms of nostalgia, and, therefore, one must invoke the relationship before one can reexperience it. In this sense, there is an analogy to the earliest object relations, before object constancy has been established and when the infant needs to perceive the object in order to believe in its existence: The dead object in order to be really believed in as a reliable object of memory that can be faithfully reexperienced has to be first internally perceived (remembered). Put another way, object constancy for the dead object has necessarily become problematical, and memory is often employed solely as an antidote to a pervasive ambivalence as to its existential status.

Object relating as such usually comes down to a short-lived evocation from the dead. Poignancy is added, not so much because one is reminded of the original death of the person who was loved, but because one senses that the instant one stops remembering, the person, in effect, dies again. This may be a reason there is sadness even at the end of an especially joyful remembrance: the loved one returning to the limbo of the dead with the difference that this time it is the mourner who is directly responsible for their disappearance and the reestablishment of their nonexistence. (It is important to note the mourning I am basically referring to is not the primary and necessary reparative work that the person undertakes after a significant other dies, but a nostalgic, defensive grieving that could and often does occur, sometimes pathologically, years later, as in the case of Sandy.)

To remember the dead is to relate to two objects: the one who appears to be alive in memory, as she once was, and the one who has died and is now assuredly an inert corpse. It is the dynamic tension between these intertwined, but radically contradictory, ways of thinking about the other that makes such remembering not only poignant but effortful. Compounding the matter is the major difference that exists between the immediacy of experiencing and the retrospective act of recollecting. Regardless of how vivid and stunningly accurate the recall of the past may be, in the back of the rememberer's mind is the added perspective of something only she can know—the future or fate of the particular memory. When the object of memory is a dead beloved, then knowledge of the future will include many details of the precise circumstances of the person's dying, funeral, and so on. The mourner, in other words, cannot forget that in addition to what she fondly, sweetly remembers, she also knows something that the other was profoundly concerned with, yet profoundly ignorant of: the occasion of her death. It follows to be a mourner is to be simultaneously a clairvoyant in regard to the future death awaiting the person who is being lovingly evoked, and to thereby assume an oracular perspective, engendering a survivor's sense of guilt, with which few people are comfortable. Thus, a specter of death hangs over even the most joyous of memories. And the death that one knows of applies not only to the physical existence of the person who was loved but also to all the psychical futures that were being invested in at the time. To remember a dead other, therefore, is to be privy to many deaths: of all the hopes and dreams that were also once vibrantly alive.

The dead other—no matter how ardently evoked—can live only in the past and cannot talk back or interact in the present. To the extent, however, that the immediacy of memory brings the dead other back to life she can seem alive in a ghostlike way. It follows relating through memory—remembering as an object relation—is profoundly nonreciprocal. The person being remembered cannot experience the rememberer in any form, and it may therefore be that part of the intensity of mourning derives from a frustrated unconscious demand for reparation for an unacceptable lack of reciprocity: from an object of adoration who is insensate enough not to remember, to recognize, or to empathize in the least with the present pain of the act of mourning. It may also be that by obsessively recollecting shared mementos from the past, the mourner is unconsciously saying, "See how well I remember you? Do you remember me, too?"

From that standpoint, mourning and afterward reminiscing can be an unconscious strategy for determining the comparative aliveness or deadness of the being that is evoked: Analogous to the animal who pokes and prods a fellow creature who has died to see if it will move, mourning—as a primitive way to reassure oneself—may be an attempt to shake up a memory to see if it responds with a show of independent life. Accordingly, in the context of nostalgic reminiscing, the accessibility of especially comforting, cherished memories of a beloved decedent can be unconsciously equated with the responsiveness of the dead to the rememberer. By contrast, a memory that does not come can seem like a rejection, a refusal to relate, while a memory that not only comes but also surprises the person with serendipitous reassurance can seem to be the result of a secret intent to nurture on the part of the dead object (a ghostly wish to relate).

As another consequence of the nonreciprocity between rememberer and remembered, the person may often feel—particularly in regard to precious memories—guilt at being a kind of voyeur: That she can look back at someone who can no longer look into the future can seem like a one-way relational mirror. Over time the complete absence of any contact, especially at moments of the greatest memorial tenderness, can feel almost sociopathic. When the act of remembering is unattended by actual reciprocal experiencing, it can then represent a desecration of what was once ¯profoundly intersubjective, as though the rememberer, greedy to gratify herself at any cost, will exploit the best of what was and even settle for a one-dimensional facsimile of the real thing (remembering becoming a profane exhumation of a past life).

Although taken for granted, it is worth noting that mourning comforts only the mourner and does nothing to nourish the decedent. However lovingly intended, the retrieval of a memory, in comparison to the primary experience upon which it is based, can only be a gross caricature and reductionistic travesty raising nagging doubts as to the depth of the original object relation. Unconsciously, to mourn may be equated with being a memorial necrophiliac. Reminiscence, therefore, no matter how nostalgically gratifying, always contains a deprivation. Invariably, to a greater or lesser degree, there is resentment. Memory itself could then serve as a psychic death certificate: a means of retaliating for the lingering deprivation stimulated by persistent intrusions of the dead object by officially placing it in the past tense.

A mourner's memories can be passive or aggressive. A passive memory is easily available. It is there ready to gratify. It can be invoked or controlled seemingly at will. An aggressive memory, by contrast, arrives on its own terms, often intruding at times when we are distinctly not ready for it. Instead of being invoked, it invokes a mood or something in us. By seemingly wanting to be revived and nourished by our reminiscing, it creates in us an uncanny sense of a solicitous mnemonic presence: as though our collaborative remembering is needed by the decedent in order to return to life. Yet, whether passive or aggressive, memory can be experienced as an invitation to be a psychic revisionist of one's personal history. And although one may not be cognizant of the constructivist aspects of recollections, there is usually an awareness that memory, by being able to arbitrarily collate, edit, and select what it chooses to elaborate, is necessarily a revisionist.

One of the reasons for obsessional mourning, therefore, may be guilt that memory, even at its best, is so incomplete and biased: the sensory data emanating from an actual, historical transaction being so vastly greater by comparison with the experiential skeleton dredged up by the most potent of memories. Seen this way, obsessional mourning may be in part a futile attempt at reparation for the sensory absence of reality. In short, to mourn is to make contact with two major areas of deprivation: psychical (intimacy) and sensory (reality).

It is obvious that the psychic deprivation will center on the memorial object, which being scripted, cannot change, and therefore has no autonomy. To remember is also to destroy the illusion of free will. From the lofty vantage point of hindsight, the person feels privy to all the forces of social history that the other could not foresee. It is as though, assisted by mnemonic retrospection, the person can grasp how completely fate shaped and dominated the other's life course. Put another way, memory, inasmuch as it is primarily a record of what did happen, not what the protagonist wished, wanted, or imagined would happen, tends to nullify the existential sense of psychic freedom that typically informs present experiencing.

A memory can be viewed as an ambivalent experience and the act of remembering as intrinsically ambivalent. At one and the same time, it is alive and it is dead. Everything about it belongs to the past, but its most crucial function—its ability to be resuscitated—belongs to the present. On the one hand, memory makes the past present, but, on the other, it lacks the qualities that in essence define animate experience: the undecideability of a future that cannot be predicted, the tension and dread as to what will be the outcome of what is being transacted, the hopes and dreams in which one has invested, the anxiety over expectations that have not been realized. (Although, of course, there are anxiety memories; they tend, unless traumatic, to be muted.) All of which can be summed up by saying that there is little suspense or excitement engendered by even the most lively objects of memory. Generally, they do not frighten one. While there may be triumphant memories, there is scant triumph in the experiential act of remembering.

This may be why the typical setting for nostalgic reminiscing seems to be one of inactivity or at least subdued action, matching the muted affect of most memories: an armchair, for example, a quiet contemplative moment that can occur while walking, sitting, or thinking. Memories are triggered during pauses, the moratorium between stretches of goal-directed behavior, downtime, and rest periods. They are products of after-thoughts, ruminations, musings. And since they lack the impact of imme-diate reality, people do not go out of their way to avoid encountering them. (Of course, we are talking about conscious, whether voluntary or involun-tary, remembrance—not repressed memories, which by definition cannot tolerate revival.)

To rekindle an attachment to a dead other is to also raise questions as to where one's heart lies. In which interpersonal world—the past or pre-sent—would one rather be living? Either way issues of loyalty are impli-cated. But it is undoubtedly part of the pleasure of reminiscing that one is free not only to be uncommitted but also to betray one's memories—by behaving now in ways that would have been utterly unthinkable in the past—knowing full well decedents must be blind, deaf, and dumb to their posthumous betrayal. Furthermore, if one wishes, one can become the director of one's own memory script, orchestrating the sequence of actions and events as though puppets, which means deciding whether to allow the next puppet memory to occupy center stage or whether to cancel the entire memory puppet show (by, for example, willfully dis-tracting oneself).

So what kind of object relation is it when the other is the remembered dead? It is obvious the relationship is not interpersonal. In fact, there is no real relating at all. The person simply identifies, loses, and immerses her-self in what is most compelling about what is being remembered. That is more difficult than it sounds because the object relation we are describing to a certain extent is schizoid: As you actively recall the past, you cannot help but be aware of the many incongruous features of your present sur-roundings, and accordingly, you try to drown yourself in the content of the memory so as to blot out the totally alien world from which you are psy-chically spectating (analogous to the celebrated willing suspension of dis-belief by audiences at plays). Memories, however, unlike plays, are dra-matically incoherent and do not hold their audience. Instead, there is per-ceptual blurring, fostering the ability of the person to withdraw with comparative impunity from the memory experience—a cardinal feature of the schizoid relationship. By contrast, immediate reality, no matter how detached you are from it, grips and holds you more.

There is an important difference between relating by identification, as one does with one's memories, and doing it with a live other. Since there cannot be spontaneous engagement, there is only (uncontested) identification with one's memorial object. It is another matter when one wishes to relate, by identification, with a live other who is present and who may or may not welcome such an aim. In that case, there is often an unconscious strategy to reduce the tension of any incongruent differences that may arise so as to pave the way for the continued internalization of the other, in addition to allowing the internalizations that already exist to remain in peace. The other, however, may not be invested in the unconscious need of the person to identify with him—may even interpret such behavior negatively as overly propitiating, deferential, and cloying—and can easily therefore react in ways that directly challenge or at least do not facilitate straightforward identificatory processes (which may have something to do with the wisdom of the saying that it is better never to meet your heroes).

Identification can be secondary or primary. Secondary identifications, which are far more common, tend to work best from a distance: where, like memory, they can function without being disturbed by the demands of interactive intimacy. By contrast, primary identification (in the sense of Fairbairn 1952 based on the infant-mother paradigm) appears to have at least two phases: an initial defensive need that arises interactively (based on the helpless infant's total dependence on an all-powerful, life-sustaining mother) and a subsequent solitary period wherein the unconscious process of identification can find the solitude it needs to sort out what pieces of the other (mother) will be accepted, modified, or abandoned. Put another way, the identificatory process of both secondary and primary identification, like editing, entails revisioning of the persona of self and other.

Such a process requires considerable solitude because whenever you identify—no matter how positively—you are simultaneously editing and deleting everything with which you do not identify. It is understandable there will be a paranoid fear of retaliation upon the other's perception of the inevitable distortion and deletion of the identificatory process. Distance is therefore needed to preserve one's identifications. Although it is true people often seek out those with whom they identify in order to recharge their identifications, there is also an awareness that they are quite likely, should they spend too much time with those with whom they most identify, to be disappointed. Even when identification with an aggressor is in full force, the chances that there will be real congruence between the identificatory process of each party are slight.

Ironically, therefore, when there is identification, there is also a need for interpersonal distancing. One of the reasons it is so easy to treasure the memory of a beloved decedent is that the person, in the course of reminiscing, will have so little actual contact with all the negative, hate-engendering aspects of the dead other that existed in the past, and—should their memories intrude as occasionally they must—in most cases she will be able to block their further elaboration.

When I was seeing Sandy, an icon of the entertainment industry, Dean Martin, someone who has been in my consciousness since childhood, died. As I listened to and then reflected on the announcement of his death, I could not help but note how it is taken for granted that we can immediately intellectually know, accept, and react to the sense of the sentence "Dean Martin died today at ——" even though every one of our thousands of media-driven associations to him has, in effect, overwhelmingly contradicted that statement: He has always been alive. Furthermore, and even more strangely, it is matter-of-factly assumed that we can so quickly transform our object relation from one involving a live person to one involving a dead person that the now-appropriate feelings of mourning, loss, and shock can be in place almost by the time the announcement ends. And because it is so taken for granted, it is hardly looked at, phenomenologically, the remarkable thing that happens when a live object becomes a dead object. Consider the following.

Reminiscing over a decedent may not only be a denial of the fact of death, as is often thought, but, more significantly from our viewpoint, a refusal to relate to the dead person in the present. One has only to pose the question, What is the status of the person who is being devoutly remembered right now? to realize the enormous difficulty this entails. If the deceased is believed to no longer exist and has been reduced in the psyche of the survivor to a pure nothingness, how does one relate to an other as nothingness (for which there is no human precedent)? If the deceased is believed to have been somehow transmuted into an amorphous afterlife form—what is it and how does one relate to it? Does one talk to the dead spirit and risk raising doubts in the eyes of others or of oneself as to the stability of one's mind? Or does one blithely deny the facts of medical science; gratify oneself with New Age miracles, angels, and assorted spiritualistic assuagements; and thereby risk the attribution of being at least soft-minded?

It is important that even traditional religions that heartily subscribe to the existence of an afterlife stress the rituals for remembering and paying homage to the dead through praying and attending church or synagogue rather than attempting to specify direct contact with the deceased in the present. Understandably, it is easier to return through memory and the ritual of mourning to a familiar relationship with a person who is now dead than to squarely face that one has an entirely new postmortem relationship with the decedent. Put another way, one often remembers the dead as a diversion from having to deal with whatever may be alive in the new relationship. And it may be preferable to face the narcissistic injury and traumatic abandonment at the hands of a loved one who dared to die than to try to seriously relate to the bizarre, nonexistential status of the present dead person: that is, to contend with such painful sentiments as, "If only you were here," "I miss this about you so much," and "Your spirit lives on in so many special ways," rather than with the much more relevant and awe-inspiring, "Where are you now?" "Who are you now?" and "How do I feel or you feel about the horrible fact that you do not seem to exist in any palpable, recognizable form?"

Adam Phillips (1996) has shrewdly noted how mourning reassures us of how much we are attached to our objects by effectively dramatizing the withdrawal pain we suffer upon their loss. From our standpoint, I would add that mourning, reminiscing, and relating to the dead in all of its myriad guises also helps us not to see the various ways we did not relate to the lost or dead person when he or she was available and do not relate to comparable others who are present. Typically, the one who mourns or nostalgically reminisces is granted a dispensation from reproach by both self and other. The fact that such admittedly soothing intrapsychic relationships almost never seem to develop and go anywhere—a natural, dynamic outcome in light of their peculiar, partly schizoid character—makes them blind alleys as well as seductive consolations: obstacles to intimacy that have been granted psychic immunity from inner scrutiny.

Ironically, in addition to fearing death, there are those like Sandy who *embrace the dead in order to escape from a paranoid dread of living in the real world.*

THE SECRET SHAME

Paranoid thinking is often regarded as a stain, a deficiency, a blemish on a person's character. It seems shameful to be so afraid of what one does not know, so consumed with secrets, so hidden in one's innermost being. Not surprisingly, someone being paranoid does not want to admit what he or she is really doing. Instinctively he will try to cover it up in the same way that someone with a visible stigma will go to great lengths to disguise his defect. But before depicting the reactions of paranoid patients to stigmas, I would like to present some relevant personal experiences and history.

Although I have memories going back to when I was three years old or earlier, I cannot ever remember not being able to talk. Yet I have been told many times by my mother that I was not known to have uttered a single word prior to my third birthday, that I had been pronounced most likely congenitally deaf by several doctors, and that she could never forget the day that—behind her back, as she walked with me in the street—she heard, like a judgment, the Yiddish word for mute whispered by a neighbor. According to my mother, it was Dr. Sharpe who proved our family's savior and upon examining me just did not think I had the look or behavior of a deaf child, who noted instead I had uncommonly large adenoids, which just might be blocking my hearing. It was his recommendation that my adenoids be removed.

Three weeks after the operation, I approached my mother carrying a large piece of twine and supposedly uttered—not my first word ever—but my first sentence, "Ma, tie this!" A day of indescribable joy, announcing that at long last I could be fully admitted to that class of people known (in Erving Goffman's wonderful but chilling phrase) "as normals."

I don't know to what extent the story is apocryphal and can only guess as to how it shaped me. But I am aware that from an early age I was sensitized to the manifestation of stigma. When I was five, living in the Bronx, I would feel an eerie sensation whenever I walked with my older sister past the special yard attached to the clinic in which it was said the "Mongolian idiots" (the usage at the time for Down's Syndrome) played. From afar their heads seemed melon-shaped, weird, and distinctly nonhuman.

Several years later, when we had moved to Connecticut, I accompanied my mother to the home of a neighbor and listened once again to the tale of the miraculous rescue of my hearing powers at the hands of Dr. Sharpe. This was the first time, however, that the story was told for the benefit of a stranger, a nervous-looking woman who kept one eye on her ten-year-old son who had been diagnosed as incurably deaf—who stood statuesquely in the middle of the living room—and one eye on my mother. She seemed hopeful as she carefully wrote down the name and address of Dr. Sharpe, and she seemed startled, as I was, when my mother, administering an improvised hearing test in a none-too-subtle fashion, deliberately let her house keys fall noisily to the floor. What I remember most vividly was the disappointment in my mother's eyes as the boy failed utterly to respond to what sounded to me like a thunderclap and her subsequent poignant realization that perhaps, unlike me, he would never be admitted into the world of normals.

Although my mother was painstakingly polite in the company of cripples and the palpably deformed, she invariably would inwardly cringe. Over time I became attuned to her cringing, and if, perhaps walking in the street together, we would encounter a strange young girl, her face indelibly, horribly burned, we would in unison, when safely out of earshot, sigh our commiseration.

As Goffman pointed out, the formation of prejudices to stigmas of various sorts begins early and casts a long shadow. Twenty years later, when I was working as a volunteer counselor in my first mental health agency, I could confirm for myself the shaping influence of my childhood. A particular moment of truth that arrived when I happen to be walking directly behind a fellow counselor, a young woman with whom I had enjoyed numerous friendly conversations over the past two months. Not for a moment did it occur to me that my unsuspected vantage point of walking behind her should reveal to me anything that I did not already know about. Yet it did. Uncannily, as my heart missed a beat, I saw clearly that she was entirely without a left hand, a fact she had been amazingly adept at concealing. When I guiltily shared my revelation with a mutual friend, he immediately shook his head in sympathetic bewilderment: "I knew her for six whole months before I realized she had only one hand!"

Twenty years later, as I write this chapter in the Manhattan office where I practice my craft as a psychotherapist, I have lots of reminders, if I need them, of my abiding sensitivity to stigma. If not the mecca, then New York City is a favorite home for the homeless, the disabled, and the misfit. I cannot walk several blocks without being accosted by a panhandler who may be either mentally or chemically unbalanced. In my daily commute to and from my office, when I change trains at the populous Lexington Avenue station, I encounter a familiar although eccentric cast of characters: a short, obese, drooling, profoundly retarded man who stares stonily ahead behind a cardboard placard hanging from his neck, which asks for leftover food; a somewhat distinguished-looking blind accordion player who sits endlessly on a tattered cushion on the platform and plays for some change; and a psychotic saxophone player who generally boards the first arriving train and promptly announces to the startled passengers that "I AM DESPERATE. DO NOT BE CHEAP, OR I WILL PUNISH YOUR EARS AND NOT GO AWAY!"—a threat he seems to enjoy carrying out.

On my way home, should I spot in advance a certain panhandling one-armed self-proclaimed Vietnam vet, I am careful to cross to the opposite side of the street. I know from bitter experience that were I to inadvertently walk within a five- or ten-foot radius, he will wordlessly expose, slowly raise, and point the remaining stump of his amputated left arm in my face—a ritual he carries out with nearly every passerby (an enraged attempt, as I imagine it, to extort what he considers long-overdue reparation for his condition of agonizing deprivation). To balance the record and by way of contrast, I should mention two characters with whom I most sympathize: a cadaverous-looking man and woman who often board the train that I take at Lexington Avenue. They take turns informing the indifferent passengers in barely audible voices that they both are afflicted with AIDS and are homeless and in need of some food or change. In recent months, I have given this woman a dollar or more on twelve separate occasions, and each time she receives it with a heart-wrenching look of seemingly profound gratitude. Yet she never remembers me from one time to the next.

These random experiences and floating impressions were given some coherence last fall after a friend and colleague had nonchalantly remarked that some of my writings reminded him of no one so much as Erving Goffman. While I had not up until then read Goffman, I did vaguely recall from the sixties a front-page review in the *New York Times* Sunday Book Review section proclaiming that, although comparatively unknown, Erving Goffman "was one of the most intelligent men alive." It was an offer my narcissism could not refuse, and I systematically began to read him, starting with the classic *The Presentation of Self in Everyday Life* (1959), then on to the wonderful *Interaction Ritual* (1967). Not surprisingly it was *Stigma* (1963) that most moved me. And in the library in my mind I place Goffman alongside Franz Kafka, Samuel Beckett, Nathaniel West, R. D. Laing, Harry Stack Sullivan, and other poets of despair. One can only speculate that somehow Goffman's own life experience sensitized him (as did mine) to the torments of the socially stigmatized.

Nevertheless, as a psychoanalytic psychotherapist, the patients I see have two hands, two arms, two legs, two eyes, a nose, and an intelligence that typically ranges from normal to above. Although it is not uncommon for a homosexual, a Jew, or a black to walk into my office—all of whom were nominated by Goffman in the sixties as members of a stigmatized class—it is rare to hear one's minority designation presented as the problem. On the contrary, today you are not supposed to feel bad if you are a member of an ethnic minority. If you happen to be politically discriminated against, you are encouraged to identify the prejudices and possibly illegal actions of your oppressors and to at least rationally fight back. A contemporary attitude of ethnic assertiveness that owes something to the effort of pioneers such as Goffman.

Although the patients I see would virtually all nominate themselves, in Goffman's terms, "as normals," they are not immune to the torments of the socially stigmatized. They see social stigma, such as being homeless, as an unconscious invitation to treat the other as an outright lowlife, someone not entitled to social privileges who may, on occasion, be even treated as a criminal. From such a person you can move pointedly away and do not find it necessary to extend basic social courtesies. There is incomparably greater freedom to ventilate contempt, irritation, even global criticism. You are released from the customary burden of empathizing with the pain and distress of a suffering fellow human being. One of the reasons, therefore, that the thought of being socially stigmatized is so terrifying—as one particularly desolate patient wailed, "What if I become a bag lady!"—is that observation of the treatment of blatantly stigmatized persons, such as the homeless or the visibly mentally ill, teaches us how easy it is to withhold fundamental social validation without ever having to resort to legal restrictions.

Furthermore, it is possible to exercise not only social but existential invalidation. A prostitute who brushes by or, worse, accosts someone in the street can be treated as though she does not exist. To deliberately withhold social deferences by pretending to be oblivious to her presence is to demote a person to a nonperson and is intended to strip away a core of dignity. There is a difference, however, between treating an adult stranger whom one passes by in a crowd as though one does not know him or her (although we typically see considerably more than we care to acknowledge) and pretending that someone does not exist.

The main way someone pretends the other does not exist is to act as though his or her expressed needs carry no weight. Thus it is common, socially acceptable practice to behave as though one has not heard the perfectly audible request of a beggar on the street for "some change," but it is considered an unthinkable insult to feign a similar deafness to an anonymous traveler who suddenly approaches and asks for help in locating a certain nearby address or simply requests the correct time of day.

Even more painful for the social outcast is that the inner qualities of the person, what D. W. Winnicott (1965) has referred to as the true self, are judged to be almost exactly proportionate to one's social rank. Thus, if one happens to be grossly unkempt, without visible means of support, and perhaps homeless, one is assumed to be comparably bereft when it comes to psychic value. To comprehend just how staggering a reductionist evaluation this is, imagine a society in which a person's entire existential worth as a human being was judged according to the status of his bank book or his active income—so that if someone's balance was to dip to zero or he should become temporarily unemployed, he could expect to be treated as utterly without value. Another way to say this is that persons who are socially stigmatized are often looked upon as though they never had a past and have no future—only a timeless and degraded present.

As a psychoanalytic psychotherapist, however, I am concerned mainly with the psychic stigma (deformation of the true self) that can develop without ever incurring the slightest social sanction. Ironically, a principal way this can occur is when a person is treated with customary social amenities, but only social amenities: that is to say, when—beyond an interest in not creating unnecessary antagonism by withholding normal social deference—there does not seem to be any apparent desire to make contact with the person as someone who is obviously more than just a social entity. From such a perspective, behavior that is welcome and even soothing the first time one encounters a neighbor, say, on an elevator in the building in which both live, can become galling if repeated unchanged several dozen times.

Part of the reason for this may be that, according to the dynamics of intimacy, if there is to be any prospect for intersubjective closeness, the relationship must over time, howsoever incrementally, developmentally move forward. The fleeting social paranoia that anyone is subject to, no matter how gregarious, upon meeting another person for the first time can therefore be viewed as having distinct stages: an initial relatively innocuous stage wherein each party pays deference to the presence of the other, and a much more telling second stage, arising after sufficient time and a certain number of encounters have been registered, during which there is the expectation that purely ritualistic, social deference will naturally evolve into a more personally textured interaction. When this fails to occur, as is frequently the case when, say, after running into a neighbor on the average of once a week in the elevator or on the street with nothing more significant exchanged than a perfunctory comment on the weather or some such like, then sooner or later there will be a suspicion that the deferential treatment being accorded is purely social and, furthermore, that there must be some hidden barrier, something unspoken going on interpersonally between them that is somehow turning the other off from pursuing even an incipient nonsocial relationship. Should even more time elapse and the pattern of random and meaningless social encounters continue unabated, what began as suspicion may give way internally to frank paranoid denunciation, for example, "I've known her seven months and all I get is a smile and a nod?"

This is because whatever a person's level of self-esteem or lack of self-esteem may be, no one can really accept that all that there is of him, all that meets the eye, is only a social self. He must also be manifesting a nonsocial real or true self, and while the other may be intensely critical, bored, unimpressed, or repelled by this actual nonsocial self, she cannot be totally indifferent to it. By such unconscious logic, a person often decides that the only explanation for a complete refusal to explore a more authentic relationship that transcends the merely social must be a negative one: Somewhere there exists a powerful dislike that is masking itself behind noncontroversial decorous behavior (instilling a paranoia that the other has not been taken in by a safe social persona but has succeeded somehow in penetrating to the worst aspects of the hidden self).

Another way to say this is that there is such a thing as an *intimacy hunger* that, after a sufficient period of deprivation, cannot be satisfied by a simply social substitute. Each person has a threshold that varies widely, beyond which he or she will not tolerate being treated as a merely social being. Although such intolerance tends not to be directly expressed—it is not uncommon for couple interactions to be sustained over a period of years with only the most meager of social exchanges—it is typically accompanied by a covert decision that it is pointless to either expect or to invest anything in the other beyond the grossly superficial. Viewed that way, social deference is not simply showing respect for the public impression the other has made (as Goffman ingeniously points out) but on another level is an acknowledgment of the significance of the other's intimacy potential. Thus, the statement "It was nice seeing you," when it is sincere, is not just the required validation of a person's social prowess but a declaration that one has appreciated, was touched by, engaged by, howsoever briefly, the impact of a genuine, nonreplaceable true self. And for this reason, after certain social time has passed, there will be an expectation that an intimacy stroke will be forthcoming, even if it has to be simulated (giving rise to Holden Caulfield's [1951] famous lament that he is forever saying "nice to meet you" to people he never wants to see again). One could say in the latter case that the deference that is being paid, even if ritualistic and artificial, is really being paid not to the social self but to the psyche of the other.

For all of these reasons, it is probably true that most people will become sooner or later increasingly frustrated, unconsciously or consciously, if someone continues to treat them socially as though they are not also imbued with an irreducibly singular psyche.

If anything, Erving Goffman's ideas on stigma are as alive today as they were in the sixties, but the stigma he talked about has insidiously spread deeper—into the self.

Disconcerting as it may be, however, to treat someone only as a social self, it is even more so to treat them as a nonexistent social self. I am referring to the almost universal phenomenon wherein a person who has known another will, for any of a number of reasons, begin to withhold customary social deference to the point, finally, of not even bothering to say hello or—having encountered the other more than enough times for social courtesies to be exchanged—will refuse to do so, seemingly pretending as though he had never met the individual before and accordingly is under no obligation to signal recognition. (I am reminded of one man who bitterly complained in sessions about a Chinese cashier, who on nine separate occasions continued to act each time as though he were a total stranger. When the cashier declined to recognize my patient on a tenth visit, he made a conscious decision never to frequent the store again.)

When such is the case, and assuming the neglected person manifests no outstanding stigma and is a member in good standing in the social order, the conclusion is inescapable that the other is expressing some unambiguous contempt for the imagined underlying true self by refusing to show deference to the social self. There is a sense in which that is even more humiliating than the nonperson status accorded the officially stigmatized, such as the homeless, prostitutes, the conspicuously mentally ill—who can rightly say in their defense that they are being dismissed without being given the chance of showing who they really are—because in this instance, the discrediting is clearly of the self and not of the lack of social status.

In this light, we can see how the paranoid who typically is bedeviled by the details of life—who has a perverse gift for thinking small, who can be traumatized by a mouse, who can become spellbound by the ghostlike memory of a departed grandmother, who can be morbidly sensitive to any conceivable shaming or stigmatizing of the self—can, in a final twist, even be paranoid about being paranoid.

paranoid interludes

C onsider Richard, a patient.

As precise in his habits as in his dress, he waits patiently for the train that will take him to his Manhattan job. Although the subway platform is rapidly becoming congested with commuters in the early morning rush hour, he knows that Continental Avenue in Queens is the very first stop for his train. The thought that he cannot fail to have his pick of preferred seats comforts him, as does the fact the car that he enters is for the moment predictably devoid of passengers. This feeling of temporary exclusiveness is enjoyable because Richard is aware that in a matter of seconds he will be joined by a swelling trickle of incoming passengers, some of whom will no doubt savor a similar illusion of starting their day with as many choices as possible.

But something is different this morning. When, after several minutes, absolutely no one comes into the car, Richard becomes suspicious. Craning his neck, he glances into the car on his immediate left. Perhaps awash in his frequent early morning reveries, he has absentmindedly wandered into a train that is in the process of being taken out of service. Yet people seem to be taking their seats and settling into their ride in the adjacent car. Perhaps inadvertently he has selected the very last car of the train. Once, shortly after relocating to New York City from Virginia, someone warned him about the potential danger of isolating himself in this way from the other passengers. Too tempting for prowling wannabe muggers. Now, remembering this, he is thankful to see a second car slowly filling with people on his right.

Is it possible there can be just one car in an entire subway train at the height of rush hour that will transport a single passenger? Richard, who loves puzzles, wonders if he has stumbled on something interesting. For a few seconds he tries earnestly to deconstruct and analyze his own question. But when another minute passes this way, Richard, aware he is much too nervous to pursue such idle thoughts, abruptly stands up and gets off the train. Like a conductor looking to pinpoint the source of a malfunction, he walks quickly along the platform, making rapid surveys of each car he passes. Although embarrassed to admit it, he can no longer deny he has become exceedingly anxious over the possibility of being mugged. Irrational though he knows it to be, Richard cannot help appraising each passenger in every car that he sees in terms of his private rating system. Knots of unruly teenagers, capable of spinning out of control at any time, are, of course, to be avoided. Elderly people—the more elderly, the better—are the safest. Train drunks are the worst. Suspicious-looking characters, the plainly psychotic, are always a threat. But the greatest danger, the mere thought of which can still unnerve him, is the unexpected. What is most to be feared is, unfortunately, that for which you are least prepared.

Richard, for example, can remember, shortly after coming to New York, sitting or rather daydreaming in his customary seat, waiting for the subway train, which had just stopped, to start up again, when he was startled by a sudden, heavy thud resonating a few inches from his face. On the other side, the platform side of his window seat, a lean, young, black man, who had obviously delivered the blow with his hand, was pausing to look at him. The murderous stare sent a message far more menacing than the actual blow itself: a warning that seemed to say, "Anytime I want, I can kill you." Yet more than the blow, the message, it was the randomness of the event—a vicious, young black man walking along a subway platform had spotted a passenger's face, a white face that had triggered his hatred—that most terrified him.

Although crazed as Bernard Goetz undoubtedly was, Richard could understand the vigilante state of mind that could take root in a festering city such as New York. How different this place was from the South, where he had been raised, from the years he had spent at elite boarding schools, where his youthful idealism, his sense of camaraderie, of honor, of family had first been awakened. As a teenager, he proudly remembers, he had once challenged the class bully, broken his nose with a single clean punch, earning for himself, like a badge of honor throughout his remaining school days, the nickname "one-punch Richie."

But what would he have done, what could he have done had this sinewy subway killer, instead of passing on, had chosen to enter his car and physically confront him? What would he have done had he been the actual target of the sordid abuses he kept seeing in the streets and subways of his adopted city?

In therapy, Richard has slowly become aware of a variety of paranoid triggers that can instigate questions such as these, but as yet he cannot sense the connections as they occur. His experience in the oddly lonely, unoccupied subway is a good example of how paranoid thoughts can blind-side their victims: pulling them into a convoluted maze of irrational thinking from which—once in—it is almost impossible to escape.

Sitting in the subway car by himself, Richard is therefore at first unaware of what is beginning to make him anxious. What does capture his attention seems to be only a transit system glitch, a problem perhaps of logistics. Why is only one person in the crush of the early morning rush hour allowed to sit all by his lonesome in a huge subway car? It is an abstract puzzle needing to be solved. When time passes, however, and the conundrum remains, Richard in an epiphanic moment realizes his com-parative isolation has thus unwittingly made him a prime target for prospective muggers. Both intensely anxious now and keenly cognizant of it, he gives himself over to a flight of insistently paranoid ideation.

Here in a nutshell, then, is a basic dynamic of everyday paranoia. Someone, cut off from the true source of his uneasiness, notices something that is awry in his immediate surroundings. What begins as an impersonal investigation becomes personal. A suspicion grows that what seems coinci-dental is perhaps intentional. Something, a malign fate, a perversity of nature, is afoot. In a second insidious transformation the malign fate assumes the face of a human persecutor.

Uncannily, such a person, scarcely understanding what has happened, has become paranoid. Through the mechanism of projective identification, an unbearable anxious field of unspecific threat has been personified. What a moment ago was amorphous, without boundaries, has been radically pared down, made concrete, and precisely positioned in space-time. There is a place now to which the paranoid can point accusingly from whence the felt anxiety seems to be emanating. No longer is it necessary to wait helplessly in the dark to see whether one's terrors will materialize. One knows where to look and what to do. From that perspective, Richard's car-by-car inspection of the subway train is a vivid example of how a paranoid point of view is simultaneously a defense strategy, a survival map and a battle plan.

But the paranoid solution is at best a shaky one. Invariably there is a persistent dynamic tension between the person's residue of undischarged nonspecific anxiety and the grotesquely specific danger that now seems to be looming (e.g., the burglar in the ski mask). This oscillation between the two poles of global threat and traumatic specificity is a characteristic of the paranoid process. What before was unconscious has now become conscious, but in a grossly distorted fashion.

Paranoid narrativizing can therefore be viewed as a kind of abortive short circuiting of a more organic processing of unconscious anxiety that has yet to run its course. It is an urgent attempt to prematurely freeze, bind, and hold in place something that is very much in dynamic flux. Underlying the familiar characterization of paranoid thinking as weirdly illogical may be our intuitive sense of just how much has been amputated from the normal process of reality testing. Looked at this way, a paranoid episode—such as Richard's car-by-car inspection of a rush-hour New York City subway train—is a flight from the dread of experiencing a much more intense anxiety, the true meaning of which it does not understand.

There is therefore another kind of tension and oscillation in the paranoid world: between flight and fight impulses. To a certain extent, the rigid thinking and insistent air of certainty so typical of the paranoid mask a profound ambivalence over whether to stand one's ground or run. The soap-operaish, hyperbolic, cinematic nature of even ordinary paranoid ideation also serves to cover up this intrinsic ambivalence, something Hollywood long ago recognized and has never been shy in exploiting. Who, for example, has seen it just once can ever forget the great white shark in *Jaws* or the shower scene in *Psycho*? (Two classic instances of paranoid triggers being shaped and inculcated courtesy of popular culture. What is overlooked is that the archetype for each of these triggers existed in the unconscious long before the making of these movies: the fear of being devoured live by a monstrous predator is no doubt an evolutionary one, going back to our ancestral beginnings; the fear of being murdered in the act of bathing ourselves taps into our earliest memories of being maternally protected and tenderly nurtured at the times of our greatest helplessness.)

Richard's experience in the subway train shows how a paranoid trigger, once it is tripped, assumes a life of its own. The ordinary world one moves about in can then seem electrified with tension and fear. Things speed up. Time itself becomes like a ticking bomb counting down to the fantasized moment when some imagined terror might explosively materialize. When a commonplace fear has mushroomed into a paranoid trigger, it becomes overloaded with the affect of dread, in turn wiping out the normal associative links that compose the complexity of everyday life. In its place are the links that lead only to escape or defense.

From this perspective, being a paranoid companion is the therapeutic attempt to restore these missing links, to hopefully reinstate the healthy skepticism of basic reality testing that has been temporarily lost. It follows that for a patient such as Richard, it can be especially helpful—and eventually a great relief—to realize it is the patient himself who has constructed his paranoid world.

Nearly a century ago, Sigmund Freud in *The Schreber Case* laid a cornerstone for the modern dynamic understanding of paranoia with his concept of projection. It is generally agreed, however, that he too narrowly restricted the paranoid process to being simply a defense mechanism against unacceptable, repressed homosexual impulses.

By contrast, as already mentioned, numerous triggers in our complex everyday world can set this process going. There is the paranoia of dying and the paranoia of living. There is sexual paranoia. The dread of being humiliated. Of being bullied. Of being competitively beaten. Of being powerless. The paranoia of being abandoned and the paranoia of being engulfed.

As already mentioned, one of the great linchpins against being susceptible to the paranoia of everyday life is a basic trust: a primary readiness to engage in an intimate connection with another human being. But, also as mentioned, many factors in our contemporary world actively mitigate against such requisite trust, thereby unwittingly contributing to a pervasive paranoia: the relentless consolidating of political, corporate, and media conglomerates, all of which take for granted the powerlessness of the individual. The increasingly addictive glorification of stimulus gratification with its conception of the person as a unitary receptacle of myriad, tantalizing consumer options. The corresponding conception of satisfaction in life—endlessly promoted by popular culture—as being about the politics of gratification rather than the achievement of meaning and connectedness. The corrosive effect of America's capitalistic emphasis on strategic manipulation and opportunism as a way of life. With the result that competing begins to replace relating and there is the elevation by our current culture of narcissism of a feel-good, custom-made lifestyle as our ultimate goal. Arriving at the reductionistic binary depiction of relationships as being about grandiose betrayal (e.g., *The Sopranos*) or the narcissistic ecstasy of self-fulfillment (as in the Oscar-winning film *American Beauty*).

The example of Richard is a graphic illustration of the barriers to feeling safe and connected in an increasingly high-tech, alienating world. Finding a safe place means finding a safe distance between yourself and the stranger you are going to encounter. What is a safe distance? Although everyone will have her personal idiosyncratic yardstick, it means finding that intermediate space where you believe you are least likely to be threatened by the other's encroachment (and vice versa). And perhaps the first, most fundamental, and universal way a stranger may enter, intrude upon, and disrespect our personal space is with her eyes.

THE STARE DOWN

In the two years that I had known him, Dean had shown no instances of undue shyness, painful self-consciousness when out in public, or nagging suspiciousness as to what others secretly thought about him. So I was somewhat surprised when he spent an entire session obsessing as to why a woman on a subway train had been staring at him.

As a highly successful stockbroker who prided himself on his expertise in handling people, Dean was not one to engage in staring contests with strangers. And in point of fact he had not been looking at the young woman who was seated in front of him and who, from the moment he caught sight of her, seemed to be quietly and unquestionably staring up at him. Caught off guard and made more uncomfortable by their proximity—he was standing directly above her, holding onto the handrail of the subway car, with perhaps not more than twelve inches of space between them—he had instinctively edged sideways. When he quickly glanced downward again, to his dismay, she was already staring up at him.

For the five minutes they rode together in the subway train, there seemed to be nothing that Dean could do, or not do, that could put an end to this woman's insolent staring, and in the session he ruminated aloud as to how it had happened. Had he, lost in his own thoughts, unknowingly stood too close to her and thereby threatened and angered her? Was he, perhaps, completely mistaken, even paranoid? Had what he had been certain had been a bold, unblinking, penetrating, confrontational stare in reality been an absent-minded, harmless, aimless gazing? Or had his own eyes—as he mulled over the various thoughts that were preoccupying him—been guilty of unconsciously roving and of at least (inadvertently) appearing to be actually staring? Or, as he secretly suspected, had he done nothing untoward—neither in the manner that he stood nor in the way that he looked—yet, nevertheless, been irrationally accosted by this woman?

When I asked Dean what he thought the reason might be that a strange woman would choose to stare him down, a number of causes immediately sprang to mind: She was a militant feminist who relished turning the tables on men who were accustomed to making women demurely hide their eyes; she was a woman who had been molested on the subway in the past and was therefore determined to defend herself; she was neither—just an ordinary woman who happened not to like or respect the way he presented himself.

By no means had Dean been the first patient I had encountered who had been profoundly disturbed by the glance of a stranger. In *Portrait of the Artist as a Young Patient*, I had described how a craving for attention coupled with a dread of intimacy can foster an obsession with a world of staring eyes that, under sufficient stress, can culminate in a full-blown clinical paranoia. Such defensive and dramatic distortions of the real world, however, are not confined to unrecognized, marginal artists, and, as I was to realize, there is an ordinary suspiciousness, mistrust, or paranoia, if you will, so widespread in our present culture as to be taken for granted. Because of this climate of mistrust, there are few things more effective— from the vantage point of the person who wishes to control—than to put the other on trial.

Putting the other on trial means endeavoring through the use of (either direct or indirect) aggressive, accusatory behavior to tap into the sense of alienation and state of intersubjective suspiciousness that, to a greater or lesser degree, exist in everyone. Accordingly, someone who is put on trial perceives himself as being regarded as a suspect.

It is easy to see in our society that the stare is a peculiarly potent means for achieving this. There are a number of reasons why this is so. Perhaps foremost is that, of the five senses, sight seems to be the most comprehensively incorporative: It takes in the widest range of phenomena, and since the stare fundamentally implies that something is disturbingly wrong, someone who has been ocularly accused, and who wishes to exonerate himself, is automatically faced with the daunting task of defending himself on the most general possible basis (e.g., wondering, "What on earth could be the problem?").

Compounding the difficulty is that the stare is particularly hard to challenge: By already assuming that the person has committed some gross impropriety, it leaves room for little else except the acceptance of just desserts. And, finally, in such a climate of stern accusatory indignation, the puzzled protesting of one's innocence ("Why are you staring at me?") is likely to be greeted only as a provocation to an altercation.

Typically, someone who, like Dean, finds himself unexpectedly stared at views the other as inexplicably and totally out of line, or even outright paranoid. Moreover, the person, realizing that the decision to stare generally indicates the time for civil discussion has passed, feels annoyingly put into the uncomfortable position of having to act quickly in order to prevent an already manifestly volatile situation from further escalating. And, of course, this may come at the time when he may be preferring to do just the opposite—be dreamy and introspective.

A stare, therefore, unequivocally demands (and almost always gets) a response: from the aversion of one's eyes as an act of submission or gesture of reparation to the willingness to stare back and engage the other in a combative test of who can outstare the other. Often, in recognition of the interpersonal danger lurking in the air, the person will attempt to answer the accusing stare but in a deliberately inquisitive manner, calculated to deliver one or more of the following messages: that one has nothing to be afraid of, does not intend to be bullied, is only innocently looking, and therefore hopes the other will understand this, stop staring, and allow the person to once again resume the status of an anonymous object.

In addition, the person answering the stranger's stare may be endeavoring—by adding just a little bit of one's own pressure to the situation—to ascertain whether (hopefully) only a mistake has been made: either that the person erroneously attributed a stare to the stranger who was merely staring vacantly in his general direction or who, perhaps, was indeed angrily staring, but at someone else. Usually, if no mistake has been made, this will be immediately shown by an intensification of the original staring, at which point the person will unhappily conclude that he has to deal, one way or another, with a paranoid other.

The power of the stare to intimidate, however, by no means resides solely in the eyes. On a deeper level, it is derived from its capacity to foreclose any possibility of free expression of the self, to almost instantly back the person into a corner and to force him into a power play of one kind or another in order to survive, and to riddle him with pervasive self-doubt through the act of wordlessly accusing, while simultaneously infecting him with a dread of the threatening stranger that can be tantamount to temporary paranoia.

This kind of ability to put the other on trial—of which the stare is only one example—can therefore come in many forms: from a questioning tone of voice, a quizzical expression, a mysterious refusal to interact with or to acknowledge the being of the person. What they all have in common is that they manage, through the device of withholding basic existential affirmation, to place the other in a quandary as to how to proceed.

The person who experiences himself as being put on trial also realizes he has been put into a box and that all at once the manifold richness of life has collapsed into just two possibilities: either to stay in the box or to try to get out. Since the dilemma seems to have been imposed externally, arbitrarily, unfairly, and perhaps even sadistically, it is almost impossible not to resent it and to feel that somehow whatever effort is invested will only be in the service of the other's needs (who, typically, is perceived as secretly wishing to see the person defensively squirm).

Compounding the insult to the true self is that the attribution of defectiveness is usually unnamed. The person has been accused, clearly, of something—but what? And why? Most terrible of all is the realization that the accusing other feels so disconnected and indifferent that she apparently feels free to neither consider nor articulate the dilemma that she herself has gratuitously fashioned.

Seen in this light, Joseph K's plight in Kafka's *The Trial* is only a grand metaphor—surreal, political, and existential—for a type of interaction that probably occurs millions of times daily in our contemporary culture.

Both Richard and Dean in their own ways, then, became obsessed with finding a safe distance from a potentially threatening stranger. It is obvious, however, to do that it is first necessary to appraise the intentional state of mind of the other, especially in regard to you. But paranoid encounters notoriously are brief affairs, often beginning and ending in a matter of moments. Understandably, a feeling of urgency can arise, a sense that nothing less than instantaneous action is called for. Although on some level the person will know he is scarcely prepared to make such a vitally important decision, he is likely to think it may even be more dangerous not to act.

If overcrowding means, by definition, there are already too many people for optimal living, it is hard to believe your added presence, to a greater or lesser degree, will not also be regarded as intrusive. It follows that the paranoid quandary of insufficient spacing will often seem to spontaneously arise in tight quarters: in subway cars, elevators, narrow passageways, congested street corners, traffic intersections. No small part of George's obsessive quest to catch the mouse in his apartment was a desperate need to prove that his personal space was impregnable to the invasion of loathsome alien presences.

Paranoid encounters fall naturally into two broad categories: those that threaten the body and those that threaten the psyche, or self. It is obvious that the outward presentation of the person, the body, will be the first and easiest target for the encroachment of hostile strangers, while the self—being far more inaccessible and therefore needing to be probed—will be most vulnerable to those who know us best. Although the differences are enormous, all paranoid threats to the self, as the following examples will show, in some way involve a dread of being invalidated in the core of our being and of sustaining a lasting narcissistic wound.

The great psychologist David Rapaport, in presenting his concept of the projective hypothesis, tried to elucidate the common underlying mechanisms of the various projective techniques: Each individual presumably will have a distinctive way of organizing her personal perceptual environment in accordance with her unconscious needs. Often, however, because we have been socialized to react similarly to familiar perceptual signs and cues—so we may arrive at a consensus of a shared reality—our individual organizational styles will be obscured. By contrast, unfamiliar, ambiguous stimuli—which, by their nature, lend themselves to multiple interpretations—will far more successfully flush out the hidden organizational principles of the individual personality.

When, for example, confronted with a Rorschach inkblot, as Rapaport notes, "the subject faces something new, something to which he *has to give meaning by organizing it.* The process of organization proceeds from those features of the inkblot which induce in the subject a meaning" (1967). Since, however, not all of the features of the inkblot will seem to fit the particular meaning that has been assigned to it by the subject, there will have to be modification. A dynamic process, often unconscious, ensues in which the subjective meaning and the objective features of the stimulus begin to mutually modify one another. The eventual verbal response of the subject will then be studied and interpreted by the experienced tester, who will look for telltale signs of the underlying organizational style.

I suggest it is a short step from this to the mechanism of paranoid projection. The paranoid will also have his distinctive organizational style. Unlike the subject being presented with a Rorschach inkblot, however, he will be encountering the real world. The ambiguity he experiences, rather than issuing from amorphous stimuli, will be the result of a profound emotional and relational deficiency. The deprivation will be one of connection, a failure to make and sustain contact with the interpersonal world of self and other. Although there is invariably, to a greater or lesser extent, a factual distortion of the ambient real world, the primary, originating distortion will be the inability to experience and perceive the human presence of the imagined persecutory other. Viewed this way, what fundamentally drives the paranoid projective distortion of reality is what I have elsewhere called an *intimacy panic* (1992).

Although David Shapiro rightly stresses the cognitive rigidity and obsessive detail orientation of the paranoid style, my focus will be on the radical loss of a meaningful human context. If the characteristic conspiratorial, persecutory nature of paranoid thinking shows anything, in my view it shows the desperate need of the paranoid to construct a world in which someone or something at least is paying close attention to what he is doing. The incredible hostility typically attributed to the persecuting other—itself a projection of the paranoid—masks an underlying and unacknowledged craving for nurturance and a bitter rage at not being able to receive it. The ambiguity that fosters the projection is the result of the disturbing impoverishment of emotional clues. Being unable—because of an anxious panic that is soon to escalate—to sense the contextual animated presence of the human other, the paranoid is free, for the duration of his episode, to resurrect familiar demons from the past and to concoct imaginary arch enemies of the future.

In the examples that follow and throughout the book, ordinary people are seen to lose their way and become alienated from reality. Although the emphasis is on how this happens—the evolution of the baffling mazes they unwittingly construct for themselves—their stories are presented against a background of social alienation, a world in which any meaningful sense of community seems to have vanished: a social and cultural paranoia, then, that unfortunately is all too real and objective.

THE POSTER

I was annoyed. Why was that man sitting there on the sidewalk anyway, fifty feet from my stoop? He didn't look homeless or anything. Actually, his face was rather interesting... sensitive, poetic looking, and I could see that he was very troubled by something. He kept muttering to himself, every once in a while glancing up and down the street as though he were waiting for someone. But I knew that what he really wanted was the chance to catch the attention of a pedestrian, any pedestrian, and hand them one of the fliers that were always stacked by his feet.

That person, I was determined, wasn't going to be me. I developed a technique of walking rapidly to my door, with my head slightly turned to the right as though I were looking at something across the street. Even though it always worked, I couldn't stop myself from getting more and more anxious as I drew closer to him. What if he accosted me? What if he completely saw through my little ruse of pretending not to see him? What if he were slowly becoming enraged with me for refusing to acknowledge his presence, which is exactly what I was doing? How would I handle it?

Although Michelle has lived in New York City for the past four years since relocating from Minnesota, she knows she has hardly adjusted to the carnival of human suffering and broken lives that sometime seek shelter or lay claim to the streets. She may be an accomplished social psychologist by profession, someone who has just published a book, but while it is one thing to empathize with the heartache of another in the comfort of your office, it is another to have it waved in your face by your doorstep. I ask Michelle, what did she imagine was on the flier?

> I keep asking myself that. A half a dozen times I've seen him hand that flier to someone polite enough or curious enough to take it. He starts talking to them right away very calmly as far as I can tell, and his apparent sincerity seems to hold their attention at first, but quickly I think I see them back off and shrink away. I find the interaction fascinating. I assume he is delusional, paranoid about something that he has become obsessional about. But why on my block, why fifty feet from *my* doorstep? My guess is that someone on the street, a neighbor, a landlord, did something to him, or he thinks they did, something so terrible that he is willing to spend a good portion of his life protesting it.

A few weeks later, Michelle has her answer. Flushed with her discovery, she can't wait to tell me about it. I suspect she realizes her narrative gifts have by now hooked me as to the contents of the mysterious flier. But I also see she appears quite embarrassed about what she is about to say:

> I guess... well, I must have been really paranoid last Monday. For about a week, he had been sitting everyday in his favorite spot on the sidewalk. But instead of his customary stack of fliers, he now had a very large poster, over a foot wide, two feet high, laid out in front of him. It had a big photograph of a face in the center of it. Whenever he managed to stop someone he would raise the poster, point to it, and start talking a little bit more excitedly this time. I could not help becoming more and more curious as to the identity of the face that he was undoubtedly denouncing. That face, I told myself, was of someone who lived on my block.
>
> Maybe I had a premonition, I don't know. But when I stopped at the corner grocery store to get my morning coffee, I was startled to see, not two feet ahead of me in line, this very man, clutching his poster, getting his coffee just like me. I saw he was already in the middle of an animated conversation with the Korean owner, who was handling the cash register and at least listening politely. I listened too, his voice oh so soft and barely audible. All of a sudden he said a name that began with an M. That is all

I could make out. I didn't understand then why my heart seemed to skip a beat when I heard that M.

As I was paying for my coffee, the idea popped into my brain that I should ask the owner, with whom I was friendly, what the man had been talking about. It seemed a tempting, simple way to put an immediate end to my interminable questions as to what this man was up to on my block. But it seemed like a strange, paranoid-sounding thing to ask and I just couldn't think of any plausible way to start the conversation. So I just paid for my coffee, watched him out of the corner of my eye go to that same spot fifty feet from my doorstep, and settle down with his poster, coffee, and fliers.

When I actually had to cross to the parallel block, before crossing back over to my building so as to completely circumvent having to directly pass him, something I had never done before, I knew something was wrong. No sooner had I got in my apartment than I raised the possibility for the first time whether the name I had heard beginning with an M had been Michelle. It was a crazy idea, I know, to think this man whom I was certain I did not know had begun a campaign to expose, embarrass, and denounce me. Instantly I dismissed the idea, telling myself that the face on the poster had been that of a man. But was I really so sure? And even if it was the face of a woman, how could he possibly have gotten hold of *my* photograph?

And then a really horrible thought came into my head. My book! In the back of my book is a clear photo of my face. The book is in a Barnes & Noble store not two blocks from my apartment. It is entirely possible someone from the neighborhood could have identified me from that photo. But big deal. So what? Denounce me for what?

It was spooky, how instantaneous, how ready-made, the answer and the plot came to me. For months, as you know, I've been paranoid that the new landlord-owner in my building, who's been handing out subpoenas to tenants left and right... to get them out so he could raise rents... would come after me too... for using my studio as an office in which to see patients, which I suppose I'm technically not supposed to do.

What was the plot, you're probably asking yourself?... [*laughs nervously*]... It was this. This crazy man had found out somehow that I was seeing patients in my apartment... and was very upset by it... Why?... Well, maybe he himself had been unfairly harassed by his landlord, evicted even... and didn't like the fact I was getting away with something in his mind scot-free. Maybe he had been a patient himself, had a really bad experience, and now hated therapists with a passion. That's not so far-fetched, I don't have to tell you.

What were the odds, a thousand to one...no ten thousand to one...that I was the face on the poster? It didn't matter, I had to find out. Afterwards, I knew I would feel like an ass for caving in so totally to such a paranoid fantasy...but I told myself the relief I might feel would be well worth it.

I put my coat back on and left the apartment. At the front door, after making sure the man was still there with his poster, fliers, and container of coffee, I turned left in the direction away from him. My idea was to circle the block slowly, as though I had an errand to run, and then nonchalantly reappear at the opposite corner, as though I was merely returning. This time I made up my mind I would be looking not to my right, but straight ahead, so that I could more easily and casually peek at the poster as I passed by. But I would do whatever was necessary...even if it meant stopping and talking to the man...to find out whose face was on the poster.

Here Michelle pauses dramatically, having reached the end of her narrative: "Up close, without breaking my stride, with a single, brief glance I could readily see what the poster said in a glaring banner above and below the head of our mayor of New York: 'IMPEACH MICHAEL BLOOMBERG.'"

We exchange wry smiles. Michelle knows I would whole-heartedly approve of any simple test that might conceivably nip in the bud a runaway paranoid fantasy. She knows I am aware how terrified she has been that the aggressive, seemingly vicious, new landlord might seize on any pretext for driving her out of the comfortable home she has managed to make for herself since arriving in New York. How anxious she therefore is that someone in the neighborhood might stumble upon her first book—as proud as she is over its publication—recognize her photo, put two and two together, and realize she has been seeing patients in her apartment. How lonely she has felt, in spite of her success, since coming to New York. How even more unloved she feels now than in the bitter cold marriage she at last managed to leave behind her in Minnesota.

The more you know about someone, the more you see how far back the antecedents of a paranoid episode reach into the roots of her life history. Although these antecedents will vary immensely from person to person, the emphasis here, my emphasis, will be on the universal dynamics and phenomenology of the typical paranoid episode, that—once hammered and tortured into a life of its own—take wing.

THE DEAF GIRL

Although nearly thirty, Arthur wanted to think of her as a waif, a chubby, round-faced innocent who seemed to thrive on attention. She would manifestly beam whenever his wife, the irrepressible extrovert, greeted her in the elevator. If only Arthur could speak to her like that, comfort her like that, but he knew he was much too self-conscious. How do you speak to a deaf girl anyway? Do you mouth the words slowly so she can read your lips, or does that insult her? Do you pretend you do not notice, do not care, or are not bothered by her deafness? Or do you make a point subtly of showing you are aware of her handicap but more than willing to offer the extra nurturance she requires? Or do you just try not to think about it and treat her, if you can, like anyone else?

Because, fortunately for him, Arthur always seemed to encounter her only in the elevator with his wife by his side, Arthur felt safe to do what he does best—observe. And slowly over the months he would gather bits and pieces of biographical information regarding the deaf girl. She lived, it turned out, right on his floor with a roommate, a large, fortyish, aggressively vocal, nondeaf woman whom he would see occasionally in the building, but always alone. Possibly the deaf girl had a boyfriend, too, for once his wife had seen her late at night in the basement saying good night to an attentive young man and then kissing him very warmly on the lips.

Whenever she spoke, in long, labored, high-pitched, drawn-out syllables that, while painfully audible, hardly sounded normal, Arthur would listen intently. Her name was "Shuuurleey." It seemed important to share this with his wife, to whom she had quite obviously taken. Recently he had seen Neil LaBute's famously cruel movie, *In the Company of Men*: the unvarnished story of two corporate yuppies who, solely for power kicks, sadistically plot to jointly romance a lonely, deaf, sensitive office temp, Christine, before simultaneously dumping her. Although he tried to put it out of his mind, Shirley's squeaky voice, to a degree that always made him uncomfortable, kept reminding him of the sound of Christine's—likened mockingly in the movie to that of a dolphin.

What difference did it make anyway? Did she even notice his existence? Had he made any impression at all on her? Or had he once again paled by comparison next to his wife's social exuberance? Arthur, who fashioned himself a shy but secret humanist, made up his mind to befriend this girl. He would come out of his shell for once. He himself would at last dare to speak.

But the words? They had to be crafted carefully and rehearsed. Not too friendly or formal but genuine, simple, considerate, thoughtful, and appropriately attentive. To prepare himself as best he could so he would not be taken by surprise, Arthur grilled his wife as to Shirley's habits: her comings and goings, the times he was most likely to bump into her alone, her moods, what seemed to hold her attention, what she might like talking about.

Then this happened. Arthur, having come home later than usual, was standing by the basement elevator door, waiting impatiently for the notoriously slow elevator to make its descent from the top floor. Was he absentmindedly standing too close to the arriving elevator door, which had an annoying habit of being suddenly pushed open? Having seen no one inside when he peeked in the small oval window, Arthur didn't think so, but as he reached for the doorknob, to his great surprise, the door flew open and nearly cracked him in the face.

In an obvious hurry, Shirley emerged from the elevator, brushed past him with scarcely a nod of recognition or word of apology, and headed for the basement exit. Too flustered and irritated to react, think, or speak, Arthur stared unhappily at her, retreating before starting to enter the car. He was more than startled, however, when she abruptly stopped and began screaming: growly at first, then guttural, hoarse, increasingly loud, and eventually surprisingly audible—"J-JUST S-STANDING THERE... N-NOT FUCKING MOVIN'...G-GET THE FUCK OUT OF... T-THE F-FUCKING WAY!"

Stunned, Arthur saw her half whirl around and furiously, unmistakably glare in his direction. By now halfway into the car, he nervously pretended not to see this and was more than relieved to close the door behind him.

Incredible though it seemed, his sweet, innocent, deaf cherub had metamorphosed before his very eyes into a fulminating virago with a mouth like a sewer. He could hardly wait to tell his wife, a committed optimist who insisted on seeing the best side of people.

Appropriately surprised, his wife listened carefully before presenting her customary forthright appraisal of the situation: "Well, I admit I would never have expected her to react that way... She probably just didn't recognize you... didn't know that you didn't see her... and I think she's very insecure anyway about how people regard her because she's deaf."

None of that mattered. Although often curious as to why people behaved the way they did, Arthur's overriding concern now was simply whether he had suffered one more social humiliation, whether—unlike his wife, who, despite her relentless cheerfulness, when the situation called for it, could be as combative as was necessary—had failed to stand up for himself.

So, timidly, dreading the answer, Arthur put the question to his wife: "How would you have handled it?"

Without missing a beat, the answer was supplied: "I would have confronted her. I would have said, 'Is there a problem?'"

Exactly! In her overly direct way, which Arthur alternately so admired, envied, and resented, she had put her finger on it. It was not what Arthur had done—what could he have possibly done that could ever justify Shirley's vile outburst?—it was what he had *not done*. Without a murmur of protest, he had allowed her to publicly degrade him, had shamefully even used the elevator's arrival as a pretext for miserably slinking away.

Knowing he had been humiliated, he had to prepare himself for the next encounter. Should he completely ignore her, treat her as a nonperson, someone beneath contempt? Should he go with what his wife suggested, that she did not recognize him—and therefore would not possibly link the man standing next to her in the elevator to the man in the basement—and just wipe his hands of the matter? Should he confront her instead? Quietly look into her eyes, force her at last to notice him, make her search her memory for clues as to his identity? Or should he come right out with it? In a calm, authoritative way, remind her who he really was, how, not seeing her in the basement elevator, he had in no way disrespected her, how, instead, in a horrible misunderstanding, it had been *she* who had disrespected him? Or was that just asking for trouble, opening up a Pandora's box?

In the weeks that followed, Arthur entertained contingency plan upon contingency plan, scenario upon scenario. Nothing satisfied him. He hated the fact he felt driven to think these thoughts. Even more, he hated the deaf girl who was the cause of it. To imagine, he had once felt warmly toward this person, had once wanted to befriend her, had once seen her as a pitiable innocent. And he hated his wife, too, for the ease with which she had won the deaf girl's heart, realizing now it had been his envy, rather than his misguided humanism, that had gotten him into the mess in the first place.

His thoughts turned ugly. Sadistic fantasies in which he exacted his just revenge by turning the tables and shaming the deaf girl began to proliferate. No longer did he see the incident in the basement as the product of a single terrible misunderstanding, an aberration of sorts. No, it went much deeper than that. There was something *wrong* with the deaf girl. It was more than her handicap and understandable insecurity stemming from it. There was an aggression, a rage in her that the more Arthur relived the incident in his mind, the more unnatural it seemed. Why, it had not been inconceivable that she had actually been on the brink of physically attacking him. A new, strange thought crept into his brain. Could it be that Shirley, despite the evidence of the kiss, was really a dyke, a dyke capable of real violence? Was she perhaps psychotic, too? His thoughts began to fixate on the strange roommate, the big, boisterous woman he would sometimes see. Was she a dyke also? He hadn't thought so and when he asked his wife, who did not share his interest in pursuing such homophobic inquiries, it turned out neither did she. Nor had his wife ever suspected the deaf girl of being a dyke, either, although she had to admit their roommate situation had always struck her as, well, "peculiar."

There was to be no simple experiment for Arthur with which to resolve his paranoid quandary, as there had been for Michelle. He was not to encounter the deaf girl again during the time I continued to see him. Although I suspected that, far from a quirk of fate, this had been unconsciously arranged by Arthur (dreading he would not have been capable of coping with the enormous tension of such a meeting), neither did I think such an encounter could have done much to alleviate his tormented state. He lacked, for one thing, Michelle's sophistication, who intuitively recognized the importance of nipping in the bud a burgeoning paranoid fantasy. Far more likely was it (as is the case for most paranoids) he would have succumbed to R. D. Laing's failure of feedback: There was nothing that could have been sufficiently reassuring so that he could no longer wonder if he had somehow overlooked, or been tricked into, not seeing a hidden trap.

Arthur did, however, have one minor epiphany that afforded him at least a brief measure of relief. Waiting in the basement one evening, it occurred to him as he hurriedly reached for the arriving elevator door that he was standing, as he now realized he always stood, to the *left* of the tiny oval car window, and that meant that any occupant of the elevator standing to the right of the portal would not be able to see him. So Shirley, most likely as eager to get out of the elevator as he had been to get in, and not seeing him as he had not seen her, but assuming he had seen her as he had assumed she had seen him—had understandably been convinced that Arthur had deliberately disrespected her.

Although he cogitates endlessly, what is poignant about Arthur, what he unfortunately does not see, is how further and further his ruminations take him from any contact with his true self. He does not see how the more he elevates the imagined persecutory threat presented by the deaf girl, the more he disempowers himself. That the more he embraces the role of victim, the less chance he has of achieving a satisfying, personal mastery of whatever is bothering him. That the more energy he invests in thwarting or countering the encroachments of his designated oppressor, the less will be available for the pursuit of his own best interests. Arthur's dilemma is characteristic in that it points to a central distortion of paranoid thinking: that somewhere, outside of themselves and beyond their grasp, lies the solution to their troubles, if they could only reach it.

DR. FRANKENSTEIN

Jennifer could not remember when she had formed such an immediate, instinctive dislike for one man. That he was supposed to be her doctor, someone in whose hands she might one day be entrusting her life, made it that much more unbearable.

She had little trouble, when I tried to explore this, in articulating her grievances:

"First, I didn't like the office. A schlocky-looking waiting room with a lot of depressed people sitting around. Even before I got there I had a bad feeling. When the receptionist told me he was only in his Queens office two days a week, I thought, what kind of real doctor has two offices?"

"It sounds like you already distrusted him even before you met him."

"You can tell a lot about a doctor by the receptionist he hires. This woman could not have sounded more businesslike and obviously not interested in me as a person at all. And the office was just like that. Cold and impersonal. I should have walked out right then...."

Jennifer's previous doctor, against whom she is measuring the man she is now calling Dr. Frankenstein, is a sainted figure in her mind, someone she believes once actually "saved my life." She has yet to recover from the shock and deep frustration when soaring malpractice costs and perhaps personal health problems—"he just didn't look well to me"—drove him to an early retirement. While her own concern for the escalating costs of health care, and that she has no one to look after her since her husband died, that she is suffering at age forty-two from the hormonal curse of an early menopause, persuaded her for the first time in her life to select—from the anonymous provider lists of a major insurance company—a brand new gynecologist.

Just thinking about this, reliving her initial encounter as she tells me about it, persuades her again that she should have trusted her first impression:

"I just wish I had walked out when I had the chance. As soon as I went into his private office to meet him and saw his face, I knew it was a mistake, but it was too late then."

"What was it about his face you didn't like?"

"I don't know.... It was cold and mean.... I remember thinking... I'm going to be internally examined... in the most delicate part of me... by a mean old man.... It's one of the worst experiences a woman can go through. Dr. —— was always considerate. If I ever expressed any discomfort, he would immediately stop and ask me about it. It was obvious he cared. So I was really surprised that this new doctor... Dr. Frankenstein... was hurting me so much. I mean it never feels good... it's like having metal hardware put up your body... I didn't want to complain.... I wanted to make a good impression, you know, on my first visit....

"But when it kept hurting I figured I should speak up, so I said, very nicely.... 'It's hurting me, doctor.'... And without stopping he said, 'You haven't been examined for a while and you're kind of dried up inside,' and he just kept going without changing anything as though he were in a hurry to finish.... Then, I tried to joke with him... you know, when I get insecure I try to get people to like me by kidding around... so I said, 'In other words, the patient will live.'...And there was this pause...during which he looked at me in this odd way as though he were trying to understand just what kind of person he was dealing with, and all he said was, 'What?'...and I saw, of course, that he hadn't thought what I said was funny at all, and I felt even more insecure...so I thought I'd better forget about the jokes and show him that I'm a serious patient, so I said, 'I mean you're saying that it is a normal reaction to feel the pain that I do.'...And, with a frown, he immediately corrected me, 'I didn't say that!'"

Seemingly pleased, Jennifer paused to reflect on all she had been saying. I could see giving free reign in this way to her enormous disappointment and rage over the visit was both clarifying and cathartic for her.

"He was putting me in my place....It wasn't that he didn't understand me, he didn't want to....I could see he had other things, more important things, on his mind than me. I got the impression that no matter what he said or was doing with me, his attention was already on the next thing that needed to be done....

"He had no patience for me, my comments, my asides, my jokes. My questions in particular seemed to annoy him....I guess I was just supposed to accept everything he said at face value and do whatever he recommended....When he looked at my blood work and thought I might benefit from the new bone density treatment...I told him I had been reading up on that and would prefer to treat it in a more natural way.... He really didn't like that...he called in his receptionist and, as though giving dictation, said, 'The patient refuses treatment.'...

"When I began telling him about my laser surgery ten years ago with Dr. ——, the condition that had led up to my cervical dysplasia, he snapped, 'I *know* what causes dysplasia.'"

Needless to say, I am surprised to learn Jennifer plans at least one more visit to the repellant doctor. She wants to get the results of the Pap smear that was administered to her, obtain a copy of the lab report for her private records, and gain the necessary time in which to find another, hopefully much more empathic, gynecologist.

My sense that this is a rationalization and perhaps a mistake is confirmed when I next see Jennifer, who is visibly distraught. The Pap smear, it turns out, showed she has some "atypical squamous cells" while noting that the test sample was "limited" due to "excess of blood." Both revelations seem to strike terror in Jennifer's heart. She cannot forget that ten years ago it was a similar showing of some atypical cells that had led her and Dr. —— down a trail that would culminate in laser surgery: from the freezing of the cells so as to prevent them from developing into a pre-cancerous condition, to an assortment of experimental treatments, none of which, unfortunately, managed to work. The laser surgery that was the last resort was the first surgery Jennifer had ever undergone. So traumatic did this experience prove to be that the mere fact that she survived, that it was successful as well was indisputable evidence, if she needed any, that Dr. —— was a caring and wonderfully skillful professional, someone, as mentioned, who she came to believe had truly saved her life.

So I could see Jennifer had decided she was in a trap. She dreaded that ten years later, in the worst-case scenario, should a second laser surgery be required, she would find herself in the hands of a doctor whom she increasingly loathed. But she also dreaded the alternative that—to change doctors in mid-treatment—might be risky and quite dangerous: "Crumbs, after all," as Jennifer liked to say, "are sometimes better than nothing."

To help her, I tried to suggest to Jennifer, as I often do to patients who are beginning to panic, that her options are not necessarily so binary. It may not, for example, be the case that changing doctors this early would have an adverse effect. As a matter of fact, given the intense level of her dislike for her current physician, it was hard to imagine that a new doctor would not be a distinct improvement. It was even possible over time she might grow to trust him in the manner she had once trusted her former gynecologist. Yet all such efforts to contain, if not modify, her incipient paranoia were to fall upon deaf ears.

As I feared, then, when I next saw Jennifer, she was manifestly worse. In her hand she clutched a lab report for a follow-up Pap smear. But the report had erroneously been sent to the wrong doctor who had, in turn, forwarded it to Jennifer. Not only that, it appeared there was a slight discrepancy between the two tests, a discrepancy that necessitated a *third* Pap smear be administered. And furthermore, with time to study the report that had been mailed to her, she could see that the laboratory upon which her doctor apparently relied was one she had never even heard of.

All of which not only enraged Jennifer but also served to fuel her paranoia, which was now in full flight. Although she was relieved that the new lab to be used would be Quest Diagnostics—the very same Dr. —— had always dealt with—she was seized with a horrible premonition. What if the report that came back confirmed her growing suspicion that all of the past tests administered by Dr. Frankenstein had been somehow botched and misdiagnosed? What if the atypical cells had already advanced into a pre-cancerous condition? What if, worse, she actually had cancer? What if she immediately needed a second laser surgery, as she dreaded, and it had to be done by the hands of Dr. Frankenstein? Would she be so fortunate this time as to survive it? For the first time, Jennifer began to seriously imagine this worst-case scenario. She tried to picture his hands silently at work on her in the surgery room, those repulsive hands, messengers of pain, that struck her as so creepily clumsy, unfeeling, and mechanical. The phrase "excess of blood" then popped in her brain and lodged there. Had those mechanical hands been the one and only cause of that surplus of bleeding? Had her doctor actually committed the one unpardonable sin, the one inexcusable breach of the sacred Hippocratic Oath—"Above all, cause no harm to the patient"?

It is painful as a therapist to witness a patient who has succumbed to a paranoid panic. Yes, I could point out the irrationality of imagining the worst, instead of just waiting out the return of the test results when every one of her questions in one fell swoop would be answered. I could call her attention to the important fact that so far all the objective evidence, the hard data of the lab reports, had seemingly pointed toward a positive out-come. I could remind her that, when all was said and done, her entire impassioned depiction of the monstrous incompetence of Dr. Frankenstein seemed to rest on her perception of his singularly unfeeling, self-involved bedside manner—a trait that, unfortunately, is pervasive among contem-porary physicians. While I could do all of these things (and did), I also knew how easily my best efforts could be wiped out by an ordinary imper-sonal piece of paper bearing bad news from a scientific laboratory.

It is in the nature of a paranoid episode, however, that the worst rarely happens. When the test results came back indicating that her blood work was "normal," Jennifer now at last found the strength to sever her relation-ship with her frightening doctor. To her enormous relief, she believed she had narrowly escaped the clutches of two monsters: of Dr. Frankenstein and of the specter of an invisible malignancy that silently was poised to invade her body.

Like most paranoids, Jennifer possesses the perverse talent of pulling monsters from her hat: from the world without and the world within. From the teeming carcinogenic macrocosm illuminated afresh each day by our death-denying, hypochondriacal popular media—and from the giddy imagination of an oversensitive soul, to whom the profound absence of empathy characteristic of our culture can indeed assume the shape of a Frankenstein.

THE BLACKOUT

On Thursday, August 14, 2003, at 4:11 p.m., life seemed to stop in New York City and throughout much of America. At that moment, I was on the long-distance telephone speaking to my editor when the lights dimmed. The air conditioner went off, the fan stopped turning, the refrigerator stopped working, and my answering machine clicked off. Anxious to investigate the extent of the power failure, I quickly got off the phone and went into the hallway. As though on cue, doors of other apartments opened and curious tenants began milling about in the hallway. It was obvious that whatever had happened to me had happened to everyone else in the building. But it was only when I reached the street and saw a similar outpouring of tenants from assorted buildings on both sides of the street and up and down the block that it became apparent that an electrical shortage of unprecedented scope had occurred.

Throughout the late afternoon and into the stifling night, people congregated in makeshift groups and swapped the latest bulletins concerning the extent of the malfunction, the ongoing efforts to repair it, and the prognosis as to when full power would be restored. If anyone was in need of a reminder of how vitally important electricity is to our daily lives, this was it. Trains and buses shut down almost completely. Countless thousands of suburban commuters were helplessly stranded in an unaccommodating city. Traffic ground to an eerie halt.

Slowly and palpably, as the night wore on with no relief in sight, the level of anxiety climbed. What if the grocery stores, the supermarkets, the restaurants remained closed, how would one get food? What if the food in the refrigerator all went bad, as it surely would? What if people could not get to needy family members who crucially depended on them? What if—

for those New Yorkers like myself who remembered the last blackout—there was to be a similar outbreak of random citywide vandalizing? And what if, in the worst-case scenario imaginable, the power failure had not been an accident at all?

Although rarely voiced, conspiracy theory, child of the events of September 11, 2001, hung in the air and insidiously did its work. For after all, even if a subsequent investigation should discredit each dark suspicion, as the media would subsequently claim, there was always a next time. And hadn't the paralysis and incipient panic that had indisputably touched millions of Americans during that long, agonizing weekend been proof of just how vulnerable to strategic attack we could be? Had it perhaps planted the seed of a diabolically ingenious idea in the brain of just one evil terrorist?

Although the blackout, of course, would pale by comparison with September 11 in its impact on the national psyche, there is a sense in which people would not have reacted as they did had not the former catastrophe occurred. From that standpoint, in addition to whatever else it stands for, September 11 has become an iconic trigger in our time for paranoid behavior of all sorts. It hardly mattered that resemblance between the two events was shadowy at best; it was more than enough to jolt millions of involved spectators to an alert standby as the ramifications of the enigmatic power failure continued to reverberate.

As already noted throughout, how different are the everyday paranoid events chronicled here. With little fanfare and no warning, they arrive. No one cares, except those who are affected. No one knows what sets them off, what the particular paranoid trigger happened to be, least of all those who are its victims. There is something convenient, even reassuring, to be able to assign an astounding welter of paranoid thinking to the events of September 11 or to a much lesser extent to the recent blackout. It is handy to have a well-publicized diagnosis like post-traumatic stress syndrome at the ready to explain what seems at first a disturbing and chaotic diversity of irrational behavior. It is practical to have a DSM-IV psychiatric diagnosis of clinical paranoia to tell us how to react to a friend or a loved one whose mind has apparently gone around the bend.

The experiences of Richard, Dean, Michelle, Arthur, and Jennifer all fall far short, slip well beneath the radar of such officious-sounding classifications. Not a single one of the countless paranoid thoughts they were prone to can remotely qualify as being clinically psychotic. The closest was perhaps Michelle's obsession with the thought of her own face appearing on the deranged man's protesting poster, but she had the presence of mind to immediately put it to a critical test so as to nip it in the bud. What they do share in common, however, is that, each in his or her own way, they are highly susceptible to the paranoia of everyday life. As already mentioned, the causes of their vulnerability are twofold: A unique constellation of life experiences has sensitized them to an imagined radical loss of a meaningful human context, and a very real, objective surrounding world in which any true sense of authentic community seems to have disappeared. Two powerful forces, then, that in combination make for a dynamic but toxic duo.

There is something sad and pathetic in the way the paranoid, drowning in a sea of alienation, will grasp at any straw, no matter how bizarre, how inhuman, of possible connection to something. Because such episodes can occur in one form or another millions of times daily, because they tend to be automatically overlooked or trivialized, often most by those who undergo them, I believe, as was once famously said of Willy Loman, "attention must be paid."

chapter 3

the dread of being powerless

To be powerless is to feel like a human puppet—the slightest push, pull, force, or leverage can send one this way or that. It does not matter whether the strings are believed to be pulling from the outside or from the inside. To such a person what counts, then, is a preoccupation with issues of control, an anxious need to gain power over oneself and others, or a dread of failing to do so and of being irresistibly manipulated. This, of course, is not control in the adaptive sense of healthy defenses and autonomous self-regulating: Rather it is the compulsion to get the upper hand that often results in human behavior becoming so stilted that it can be seen essentially as a technique or a strategy rather than a process (perhaps best typified in our contemporary corporate culture by such mainstream professional roles as selling and advertising).

Not surprisingly, when personal behavior is thought of this way, as a technique, a strategy, or the product of puppetry, it is often conceived of as a discrete unit: something that is indiscriminately pushed or pulled along, like cars on a train, by a unitary force. It is characteristic of such behavior that there is neither time nor inclination to contemplate multiple-level causation or overdetermination. It is characteristic of this frame of mind that it feels goaded by urgency and crisis and views motivation as a kind of trigger: there is only one button to press, and it is a question of finding it. Behavioral puppetry resting on an unconscious perception that one is being controlled or dominated by a dammed-up excitation (analogous to a pressure cooker) that must be released will often appear simplistic, and this is because psychological pressure, paralleling bodily pressure, does not allow the leisure or mental space in which to ponder alternative and more complex courses of action. For someone who feels, therefore, under the gun of a pressurized motivation, as the person preoccupied with issues of control almost always does, the most compelling impulse will be to find the most expedient way to relieve the obsession.

Behavioral puppetry can be divided, roughly, into feelings of dominating or being dominated (much more common). Feeling controlled from without is almost always preceded by projection; in other words, first there is an introject of primitive control, which subsequently is mapped onto another suitable person.

Although there will be the expected range of variations, when a person feels controlled, manipulated, seduced, or overpowered, whether from within or without, there are often some recognizable and consistent reactions. Such a person, as indicated, may regard his own behavior as relatively simple, comprising a small range of motivations and entailing few options. There will invariably be hostility toward the self, especially whatever is perceived as controlling the self, resulting in a compulsive tendency to divide oneself up into parts that are controlled and parts that are autonomous. The philosophy that is compatible with this perception of the self is of life as a Darwinian power struggle: A good life is one that masters the tasks and musters the forces necessary to achieve satisfaction.

Someone who feels controlled by something or someone else feels abused. He harbors the *paranoid suspicion* that if he were more respected, he would be granted more space. Feeling controlled can become confused with being intruded upon. It is as though there were a telephone or doorbell ringing in the mind that won't stop. The implication is that one cannot fight off the intruder (and make it stop ringing) and is therefore weak. Or maybe the voice that is insistently calling knows something, and the message that is begging to be delivered is one that should be listened to.

Feeling controlled, therefore, feels like being pressured. Feeling pressured feels like being badgered. Feeling badgered feels like being punished. And feeling punished feels like being bad. It is easy to believe that if only one had more self-control, there would not be this need for an outside agency (or an accusing inner voice) to take over.

And it is because such a person experiences the controlling influences as a kind of low-grade alarm that is constantly going off, it is almost impossible to feel that it is safe to leave well enough alone and allow one's life to unfold spontaneously (and, as they say, smell the roses). Nothing seems more obvious than that there must be activity and change and that life is a matter of push and pull, of levers and manipulation, of cause and effect, of whether you wind up as puppet or puppeteer.

No one therefore who feels continually harassed can avoid feelings of being deprived, unloved, and unfairly taken advantage of; they go with the territory. The suspicion grows that life is unfair, that there is little real mercy, and the lesson to be learned is that whenever there is power, it will be used. Sooner or later the cynical belief grows that relief from pressure will come only from meeting force with force, controlling what controls. It all leads to the demoralizing conviction that you will never be nurtured, that nothing will ever be given to the self when you are perceived as victim.

Feeling excessively controlled, therefore, breeds a survival psychology and automatically reinforces existing narcissistic tendencies. Behavior is perceived as effortful, since effort is needed to overcome whatever is holding one back, and accordingly cannot be easy or fluid. Instead, there is the pragmatic sense that what happens is the product of dynamic forces and conflicting strategies. And not surprisingly, it is difficult to feel creative when feeling controlled if only because the required space and freedom for creative play are painfully absent.

Still other characteristics accompany this state of mind. There will be a need to predict the outcome of events so as to eliminate surprise. Since the only outcome that can be tolerated is relief from pressure, waiting can entail only unwelcome suspense and anxiety. There will be an irresistible tendency, therefore, to try to orchestrate the situation, to eliminate undesirable variables, and to oversee the process. It all adds up to what classically is called rigid behavior.

The underlying feeling of being controlled often results in defensively trying to produce behavior that may be perceived as a performance, package, or product. It is a corollary of this eventually to have the sense that one is somehow being objectified, behaviorally mechanized, emotionally pared down, and existentially reduced so as to better be controlled.

And in the final analysis, it is the prospect of winning that may be the greatest allure of behavioral puppetry. For there are undeniably many short-term benefits from believing that control has been won, and there is no doubt as to who is in charge. Now one can concentrate exclusively and comfortably on outcome, dispensing entirely with development and process, which means that a great deal less has to be contended with. Since the goal of interpersonal relationships is now clearly nonreciprocal, this means sooner or later there will be an expectation of resistance. But this also means that one will be struggling only with defense mechanisms: Experience of the other is therefore irrelevant, except as it impinges upon operational defenses. Part of the security of being in control is that one also has control over who does the rejecting and does not have to worry about abandonment. To the extent that the person in command can orchestrate and dictate the tempo of a relationship, there is even partial control of time. And last, there is the belief that one is autonomous because empowered—yet another illusion, inasmuch as real freedom is freedom from the need to control.

We seem to live, in short, in an intensely competitive time, when people are obsessed with issues of control, with game playing, power plays, power operations, and the like. If this is so, by the law of averages, many will fail to thrive in such a pressure-cooker culture. No one, of course, will come out on top all the time, and everyone, sooner or later, will succumb to the humiliating feeling of watching someone gain the upper hand over them. It is a short step from this to the realization that we live in a culture that is prone to the paranoid dread of being manipulated, that our defenses may not be sufficient to stave off unsuspected attempts to encroach upon what is rightfully ours. That in ways we cannot yet conceive, in one situation or another, we may be on the brink of becoming dangerously powerless.

There are thousands of power plays, power games, and strategies or control that have been designed to forestall just such a catastrophe of the self. What follows are some of the principal ones. Although there are many differences, all of them have been so seamlessly woven into the texture of our contemporary culture that they are taken for granted. What makes them important to my mind is their devastating ability to nip intimacy in the bud.

It is the unconscious recognition that power plays are games that no one can win that make them such sinisterly fertile soil for what we are calling the paranoia of everyday life.

A BLUEPRINT FOR CONTROL

One of the leitmotifs of therapy is the patient's fear that he or she will forever be unable to escape the clutches of an especially controlling parent, spouse, lover, friend, or boss. Compounding the issue is that often the person—through the mechanism of identification with the aggressor—will have unconsciously internalized selective attributes of the dominating other. I am reminded of a patient, a very sensitive, insecure, aspiring young actress who spent hour after hour in therapy lashing out at a mother who she believed would thwart her at every turn; who did not seem to hide the fact that she preferred the older sister, whom the mother unabashedly praised in her daughter's presence; who hardly listened when they spoke on the telephone and almost never made mention of any of her accomplishments; who grew impatient if her daughter would bring up a problem that could not be resolved with a minute's worth of conventional advice, and who became enraged—instantly slamming the phone down on the receiver—at the slightest hint that there was something less than perfect about the quality of her mother's love.

Like many other young artists, this woman supported herself by working part-time as a telemarketer, a job that was supposed to provide the free time she would need to go on auditions. What my patient had not counted on was just how demanding her job would prove to be. As a telemarketer, which is a euphemism for a high-pressure sales person, she was expected to call up people out of the blue, who did not want to be called, and by rigidly adhering to a prepared script, to rapidly sell them any of an arbitrary number of household products. She was to remain on the phone, going from customer to customer, for most of the sixty minutes of each hour of the five-hour shift she happened to be working on, taking only minimal breaks in order to go to the bathroom or refresh herself with a drink of water.

To insure that the necessary self-control was being exercised, monitors would regularly patrol the telemarketers' glass-partitioned booths and check on the quantity of calls that had been made and, especially, the number of sales recorded. And on special occasions, the owner herself, a proud, independent woman reputed to be a self-made millionaire, would personally make the rounds: carefully examining the productivity sheet of every telemarketer, watching the room like a hawk for infractions of company protocol, while periodically stopping to engage in self-conscious, contrived pleasantries calculated to lessen the palpable tension engendered by her visits.

When I asked my patient how she felt about these heavy-handed surveillance tactics—fully expecting she would be at least inwardly chafing at such corporate one-upmanship and hardly prepared for her instantaneous, heartfelt, and somewhat awestruck retort, "She takes control right away"— I immediately realized that unconsciously she had internalized salient traits of her supposedly noxious, take-charge mother. (It is perhaps one ironic measure of the power of the controlling personality that it can foster its incorporation in the other.)

What follows, in order to make this clearer, is a common profile, drawn from a number of patients I have worked with, of what is often taken to be a controlling personality.

Typically, the person seems intensely focused on what she wants and everything, including the needs of the other, are regarded as either means to an end or an obstacle to be overcome. Such tunnel-visioned single-mindedness can easily seem ruthless and inhuman in its disregard for everything outside of its ken, which in itself can be frightening and over time disempowering. That the person is in headlong pursuit of the fulfillment of her aims cannot help but put the other on the defensive (the intuitive understanding that nothing you could want that is independent of the person's needs could possibly interest her inhibits any budding desire to initiate contact). In its stead is a realization that there is no interpersonal space in which to pursue any personal satisfaction; the only thing left being to defend one's territory, try not to get pushed around, and not lose anything one already has. The experience is akin to attempting to interrupt someone who is plainly busy and working intently to finish something that is obviously important—in order to ask him something that has nothing to do with him.

The controlling personality, therefore, characteristically seems more clear-headed, goal-oriented, and no-nonsense than most people, as though he has a head start on you, as though all issues of ambivalence, uncertainty, self-doubt, and identity confusion have been at least temporarily surmounted or suspended. Since the majority of us rarely feel this way and less so in the company of another—where, although we may know what we want, we can never be sure of the other's intention—this can be daunting.

We are intimidated by someone who takes it for granted that he is more serious than we are and appears to be challenging us to say quickly whatever is on our minds.

It immediately becomes apparent that abruptness is a salient characteristic of the controlling personality. The message being unconsciously sent is that—in an analogous psychic sense—he is hurrying to catch a train and you are in his way.

If this is so, the question becomes, what is the effect on the other to be controlled in this fashion?

1. Typically, there is an almost instantaneous narcissistic injury accompanying the realization that someone would want to do this to you, would have so little appreciation of your attributes, that the very best use of you they can think of is to only and thoroughly exploit you.

2. There is a simultaneous sense of being profoundly misunderstood. It is startling to perceive that someone could actually believe she could get away with such treatment, that you might possibly find it acceptable, or, worse, that she was basically indifferent to your opinion of the matter. If that were the case, it could be only because she had no idea of who you were as a person.

3. There is the creation of an immediately adversarial relationship. From that point on—even if the person superficially complies due to perception of the other's greater force of personality or power (e.g., being your boss)—the interaction will be characterized by attempts to control, followed by efforts to countercontrol, which trigger renewed attempts to control, and so on. In such a transaction where each is struggling to win power over the other, it is instructive to note everything that is left out and that now seems to both parties to be utterly beside the point: empathy and the need to relate, to be intimate, spontaneous, playful, expressive, and to be understood. Every impulse to be decent goes out the window. It is as though all possibilities or memories of the pleasure that one person can take in the company and presence of another have dried up or been forgotten.

   It is obvious the creation of an adversarial relationship can have immediate consequences. If one can expect only a kind of psychic warfare vis-à-vis the other, it makes sense to raise one's guard, tune up one's defenses, trot out one's strategies and gamesmanship. This is a description, of course, of a competitive relationship, but a competition without the saving graces of mutual respect and appreciation of your opponent's prowess (as in professional sports at its best).

Inasmuch as the controlling personality usually vehemently denies that she or he is being controlling, the person cannot help but come across as profoundly *dishonest* in the ways he is relating. Not only does the other, therefore, feel devalued by the manner in which she is being treated, but, as a violent counterreaction, almost instantly she loses respect for the controlling personality. It is a short step from this to feeling hated by the person—who is not only horribly mistreating you but also lying about it— to vigorously hating the person back, however secretly, and to thereby being subject to paranoid fears of being exposed for one's covert psychic malevolence.

For all of these reasons, someone who has characterologically learned to depend upon the secondary gains that derive from being a controlling personality will find reinforcements both in the other's compliance and in society's glorification of the successful uses of behavioral power—and will have scant motivation to give it up.

EVERLASTING SHAME

Andy is a tall, lanky, absent-minded graduate student who enjoys day-dreaming while he rides the subway train, which may be the reason he is oblivious to the young man, dressed like a manual laborer, his arms wrapped around a large, upright board balanced against his knees, who is seated at right angles to him. It is only when the train rather abruptly lurches to a stop—causing the man and his board, reeling forward, to bang into Andy— that he is recalled from his reverie. Now he cannot help but notice the round, youthful face, with the startled, contrite look about eight inches from his own, and he certainly feels the board colliding with his right arm.

"I'm sorry," whispers the man, pulling the board to his chest and gently easing himself back into his seat. Whether emboldened by the crooning apologetic tone of voice, or simply irritated at being physically rousted from the privacy of his thoughts, Andy—glancing briefly but sharply at his intrusive neighbor—does not bother to hide his annoyance.

"You look scary."

Although apparently the same voice from the same young man of just a moment ago, the subtle change of intonation, now not even faintly solicitous, and the change of expression, now devoid of emotion and utterly still, are enough to be menacing.

Unwilling to accept his feeling of vague but inexplicable threat, Andy, turning to his right, but making sure to be safely civil, decides to check on what he just heard, "Excuse me?"

And bending slightly forward, as though to make sure his words and message were accurately delivered the second time, the young man repeats, "You look scary." For a few seconds, Andy studies the expressionless face, searching for clues, and waiting, hoping, for an explanation that does not come. He feels his heart begin to beat more rapidly. Quickly he averts his eyes from the young man seated to his right and tries to act as though whatever did happen is over with. But clearly something is wrong. Although he does not dare to look, he can sense that he is being stonily stared at.

For the next ten minutes, as they ride together—mute, motionless, and in tandem—on the subway train, Andy agonizes over the meaning of those three little words. Could they have been intended literally? Could the man—perhaps overreacting to his initial flash of annoyance—have been trying to convey that he had been really somewhat intimidated? If so, then why grimly repeat himself, why stonily stare, why sit motionlessly in a kind of statuesque rage? No, reasoned Andy unhappily, those were fighting words, taunting words. What had begun in an effort to conciliate ("I'm sorry") had ended in sadism: "You look scary" plainly being meant as the mocking threat, "I am supposed to be afraid of you?"

In the session that followed the incident, Andy spoke about the seemingly bottomless depths of his subsequent humiliation. He had been bumped fairly hard by a board while innocently minding his own business. He had not protested the jarring impact and slight injury except perhaps for a tiny display of understandable irritation. He had been forthwith challenged to a physical fight. He had been gracious enough to let this pass and allow the offender to regain his composure and act civilly. He had been once again challenged to fight. Now he had had no choice—short of engaging in mayhem in a public place—but to keep his head down, his face burning with shame, to swallow his pride and hope that no one else was witness to his degradation.

Although Andy's account of what happened had seemed quite plausible, as his therapist, I could not be sure of the underlying motives of the man who accosted him on the subway. In spite of that, it is fairly certain that probably millions of times daily in our country one person will intend not only to degrade another but to rub his nose in it. This, of course, is simply an instance of what has been discussed as the desire to humiliate the other, but so extreme that, in most cases, the perpetrator is both aware of and vindictively proud of his intention.

Typically, as it did with Andy, it will precipitate a full-blown crisis of self-esteem in the victim. On the one hand, to not respond and meet the challenge head on—instead taking flight into oneself and letting fear of the person's shocking aggression win the day—is to pave the way for unending self-recrimination and flagellations. On the other hand, to resist or refuse to be intimidated is to enter a dangerous no-man's land, to go one on one with someone who has willfully chosen to defy one of the strongest social taboos—never try to take away every vestige of the other's dignity. Only someone in an extraordinarily aggressive mood would dare to be that provocative. Since such aggression therefore seems almost unnatural, to realistically contest it would seemingly require a comparable amount of abnormally intense aggression.

But it is just this—because intentional humiliation is almost always experienced traumatically as a shock to the psyche, no matter how much it has occurred in the past or how anxiously anticipated—that the victim cannot do. Much more likely is that he will embrace an involuntary, although markedly defensive, posture. Reinforcing his retreat will be the dread that—inasmuch as he cannot now imagine that he could have possibly provoked or deserved the inhuman abuse he is receiving—should he change his mind and decide to go on the attack, the other may very well go berserk.

He is thus caught between a rock and a hard place: between the prospect of being annihilated and the prospect of everlasting shame. Although he does not use these words, the victim typically thinks that only someone possessed of psychotic hatred would want to thrust him in such an agonizing existential dilemma. While, by contrast, it seems clear the aggressor—regardless of how pathologically sadistic he may be—could not live with his debasement of his victim unless on some level there were a projective identification of the other as one who is obviously and consummately despicable.

What makes this so painful for both parties is that two people who experience each other as almost alien beings—a transactional rupture of empathy so profound that it borders on a temporary psychosis—are nevertheless locked together in an intensely passionate, if adversarial, interaction. (It is no small part of the seductive pull of the sadomasochistic contract—which itself can be looked upon as a defense against fears of engulfment and symbiosis—that it seems to offer a way to be fiercely bonded with another, while still being totally uncommitted.)

Finally, adding to the pain of the one who has been humiliated is what might be called the *memorial power of shame*: to be unable to defend oneself or at least try to against a brazen attempt to deliberately degrade one is to incur a sense of shame that few people are likely to forget. It is this ability to instill a psychic trauma with just a single act that lends it such a mesmerizing aura of power in the eyes of both the victim and sadist.

THE POWER STRUGGLE

The antithesis, of course, to passively swallowing the other's sadism is to combat it. Invariably, this leads to a fight that—if the participants are sufficiently aggressive—can become physical. It is clarifying, however, to contrast this kind of an everyday, unstructured fight with a professionally regulated one, the clearest example of which is a prize fight:

Two supposedly evenly matched opponents who are both well prepared *choose* to enter the ring. This in itself is frightening: That someone who has had a lot of time to think it over, who is not being provoked in any way by his opponent to fight, who can pursue other activities, nevertheless wants to go into the ring. It must mean he has an extraordinary capacity to cope with the anxiety associated with doing something that is truly dangerous. This is why, regardless of what one may think of the brutality and inhumanity of two men trying to literally knock one another unconscious, the physical courage required to enter and survive in the ring is widely admired.

Not surprisingly, in light of the great risk entailed in consenting to engage in a prolonged encounter with a presumably equally skilled, professionally trained prizefighter, numerous precautions—prefight physical, cut-men, ringside doctor, and so on—are taken. Perhaps the greatest precaution, however, is that it is decreed that it is a contest that has to be fought according to rules, rules that will govern every aspect of the encounter: the size and construction of the gloves, weight of the fighters, length of the round, rest period, number of rounds, how they are to be scored, what type of blows are to be considered fair or foul, what parts of the opponent's body are to be considered legitimate targets for attack, what parts of one's own body can be used for striking the other (for example, the shoulders, forearm, elbows, knees, feet, back of the hand, head, and teeth are all disallowed).

How important these regulations are can be seen by how even seemingly the most savagely aggressive fighter will welcome the bell signaling the end of a given round and the beginning of a mandatory rest period—at which point they will often touch gloves—and, especially, the bell signaling the end of the fight where it is customary, even after the most brutal of ring wars, for the warriors to embrace one another, openly proclaiming admiration and affection for the prowess and courage of their opponent, regardless of the outcome.

If one now compares this with a fight with a stranger in the street, it immediately becomes apparent there are no rules governing the fray—as rules, in order to exist and be adhered to, need to be recognized and agreed upon in advance. Although two strangers who get into a fight in the street will, of course, each have a particular style of fighting reflecting the level of aggression with which they are comfortable, what matters is that that style will not be known to their opponent. One of the things, therefore, that makes a street fight so very dangerous is that, other than an intuitive first impression of the kind of adversary his antagonist is likely to be, a person really has no reliable idea of what he is getting into. Is one merely standing up to someone who is only upset but has no honest intention of seriously hurting the other? Or is the person an experienced, expert, and (unfortunately) vicious street fighter, someone who looks forward to and savors beating an opponent to a pulp? An altercation with a stranger is dangerous, therefore, because it transcends the known rules of civilized agreement and disagreement where—although allowance is made for numerous unpleasantries to occur—there is an implicit guarantee that, assuming the person plays by the rules, not only will he get through trying situations, but also he will emerge in good shape.

By contrast, in a street fight, rules as such—which do not exist beforehand—will have to be improvised on the spot. The difficulty in doing this will depend in no small part on the difficulty in determining who is to be the aggressor and who is to be the defender. (From this standpoint, a sadist can be defined as someone who has mastered a certain technique for managing the potential trauma of a power struggle over who is to be humiliated and a victim as someone who has not. In such a contest, the humiliator truly will typically have considerable experience upon which to fall back, while the designated victim, more likely than not, will have only fantasy—such as one's picture of what it might be like to be arrested for the first time. This may be why the sadomasochistic contract—in order to sufficiently manage the potential for traumatic humiliation so as to enjoy the sexual arousal that is at least one aim—relies on ritualization [e.g., see Masud Khan's 1979 technique of perversions]. Another way to say this is that, although there may be unwritten rules that govern the encounter, the victim is much less likely to know them than the sadist.)

It is instructive to compare fighting between human beings with that of other animals. As Konrad Lorenz (1970) has noted, when an animal, such as a wolf or lion, is heavily armed so that it is easily capable of killing a vanquished rival, natural selection provides an instinctive inhibition against so doing. Thus, the killing bite of the lion is almost never released while fighting with another lion, and the wolf that is being thoroughly beaten by another has only to bare the most vulnerable part of its throat to insure—no matter how enraged its opponent may be—that it will not be killed. In that case, the message seems to be: "See how helpless I am, how easily you could kill me. You have nothing to fear; there is no danger coming from me." By contrast, with animals such as human beings, who are not biologically armed (e.g., no fangs or weapons to be selected against), there has been no evolutionary need, again according to Lorenz, to provide an innate inhibition when it comes to killing conspecifics. What this means is that there is no comparable instinctual check against killing one another in human beings as there is in lions and wolves.

One other difference concerns time. Fights among animals tend to be concrete, nonpsychological, and biologically driven. Everything else being equal, the stronger party usually wins, and, when they are over, they tend to be over. By contrast, in humans—since you cannot control the psyche as easily as you can the body—fights tend to last longer, or rather their aftermath is longer.

In spite of this, power operations characteristically are transacted quickly and are as opportunistically abrupt as possible. There is therefore a sense in which *no one fights fair*: that is, each party, even if contending within the parameters of the rules, is unconsciously looking for a power advantage. It follows, in the case of altercations that are markedly antisocial, such as a street fight, they will be manifestly unfair, and this will apply to even the most decent person who, entirely against his will, has been forced into a position of justifiable self-defense. Fairness goes out the window as soon as a power struggle begins to escalate in the direction of a frank physical confrontation. By being unfair, I am not referring to someone who resorts to so-called dirty or foul tactics; I am using the term *fair* not as it is customarily employed in professional sports—where the concepts of fair and foul play exist as a primitive polarity primarily defined by arbitrary but enforceable rules that, in practice, mean one does everything one can to manipulate and bend the rules so long as one does not get caught (e.g., if you're not caught, you're not cheating)—but in the therapeutic sense of displaying a decent regard and empathic consideration for the rights, feelings, and needs of another person with whom one happens to be in genuine conflict.

Inasmuch as parents' modus operandi is often to bully and practice tough love with their children upon the first whiff of discord, it is unrealistic to expect the abstract concept of fairness to counterbalance the dynamics of actual power operations other than to provide a reassuring sense that agreed-upon boundary points exist, beyond which unrestrained bullying by someone who holds the upper hand cannot proceed without incurring definite peer pressure and social censure. Another way to say this is that there is no viable role model at present to be culled from our familial upbringing, general education, or society at large vis-à-vis the concept of fairness when it comes to power operations.

If the concept of fairness is a social palliative, we may be more at the mercy of power operations than we would like to think. If so, it may be clarifying to look at how rules regulate behavior:

1. Perhaps foremost is that they set limits. They do not directly affect the dynamics, quality, or flavor of the interaction. To return to our

boxing analogy, they determine which actions are to be considered fair or foul.

2. Rules are the antithesis of role models. They are indifferent to anything that happens short of the "no trespassing" sign. Up until that point, you can do anything you like. In other words, rules are not interested in and do not relate to anything and everything that exists *within the rules*. It is only behavior that threatens to go beyond the borders of permissible actions that draws their attention. It follows rules have a negative, policing function and are therefore strictly about power—the maintenance and enforcement of power and the punishment of those who violate it.

   This is particularly evident in the realm of professional sports in which contact is allowed. The most brutal punishment can then be meted out by one contestant to another, so long as the game is being played by the rules, and, ironically, when this is the case and there results the occasional tragic death in the ring or the spinal cord injury on the football field, the predictable public outcry is not for the game to be played less savagely but for the *rules to be changed*.

3. A policeman is an excellent example of the principle of a rule made incarnate. So long as a law has not been broken or is not about to be broken, he does not care how or even whether people live or die. It is as though his interest in a given interpersonal field can become animated only around the predetermined boundaries of a regulation, the taboo place where there is perhaps the greatest opportunity and temptation to violate a law. The flip side of this, of course, and an important unconscious secondary gain, is that rules also exist in order to show where lawlessness—the freedom to be as wanton, unrestrained, narcissistically empowered, greedily ambitious, and controlling as one dares and, on the positive side, to be as expressive of the true self as one wants—can be practiced with impunity.

4. In spite of which, it is obvious that, typically, rules, in their near-total self-absorption, function narcissistically, but it is a particularly potent form of narcissism because it is backed by real power.

Now to return to how fairness is used in a power struggle. Not, as mentioned, in the sense of an empathic and decent regard for the rights and needs of the other with whom one is locked in conflict but in the form of rules as used in sports. A fair fight, then, would be one in which both parties showed a healthy knowledge of and obedience to mutually agreed-upon rules designed to guarantee a level playing field. Again, as stated, one of the greatest dangers presented by the prospect of a street fight breaking out is the impossibility of trusting with any reasonable degree of confidence that the rules for fighting fairly between strangers are going to meaningfully coincide.

It becomes immediately apparent that a primary reason rules exist is to indicate the kinds of behavior that—because they, too, are deemed too dangerous to the self or harmful and vicious to others—are to be prohibited. Rules are therefore reassuring in that they tell you what *cannot* happen. They also tell you what will happen in terms of the things you must do in order to comply with them (thereby helping to structure your life). By telling you what cannot happen, and what must happen, rules imply that the persons or authorities that instituted them have the power to enforce them. However, in order for this to be in fact true, the force authorizing the rule must prove greater than the force resisting it.

In Bion's terms (1970), it could be said that part of the seductive appeal of rules is that they promise a container that will not crack under pressure. Much as one may loathe being restrained when one does not want it, there is comfort, especially during times of emotional turbulence, to know that limits exist (giving hope that turbulence will come to an end). In the unconscious may be this equation: rules = limits = termination = discharge/closure/resting.

Finally, for all of these reasons, the fear of getting into a fight that one would much rather avoid, or of losing a fight, can be traumatizing. It follows the power one has is most effective when it is feared. This is the secret the bully knows well—and from that perspective, it could be said that the power that is not feared is not power. Which is why it is such an efficient regulator of the other's behavior. Once feared, it does not have to be used, thereby saving enormous energy: for example, the average policeman who almost never uses his gun because he doesn't have to. The consolidation of power, therefore, will characteristically be the product of only a few traumatic encounters in which the superiority of one's forces was indelibly impressed upon one's adversary. This may be why childhood memories of one's worst bullies typically tend to be quite meager, in spite of the fact that the narcissistic injuries incurred can be quite pervasive.

It is yet another reason why power struggles, especially intense ones, almost invariably aim for the knockout blow. The message being clear: If you choose to challenge me, you will not only lose, but lose traumatically.

"YOU'RE BLUFFING!"

The analogue in humans for the variety of physiological mechanisms and adaptations—the lion's mane, markings around the eyes, baring of fangs—that exist in the animal kingdom for the express purpose of tricking their enemies or rivals into thinking they are bigger or fiercer than they really are, is the interpersonal strategy of bluffing: the art of making the other believe, in short, that one has more power than one does. Not surprisingly, the dynamics can be quite complex.

1. Perhaps the key underlying assumption is that one cannot trust that one has sufficient resources to realistically confront a perceived threat. By simple projection, there is the fear that the would-be opponent can not only see this but also be emboldened by it, thereby becoming even more of a threat. The most logical alternative, then, is to engage in what Erving Goffman (1959) has called impression management—trying to disguise and compensate for inner defects by the presentation of an attractively cohesive, imposing, and, if necessary, threatening front.

2. Bluffing implies there is no honest backup, no intention to stand behind what one appears to be saying and doing. It follows that bluffing compensates not only for its hidden defects but also for its undeniable lack of sincerity and commitment. Since the bluff by definition is in what Sartre has called bad faith, it runs the risk of being exposed at any moment (by being called), and it therefore unconsciously strives to achieve its counterfeit aim as quickly as it can. Another way to say this is that the bluffer is typically in a hurry to win his bluff because he generally feels time is not his ally. The bluff, therefore, tends to be larger than life—not in the physical sense of the lion's mane—but rather in the gestural sense of being (what they call in acting) too big a gesture. Because of this, the bluff is not just an exaggeration, enhancement, and advertisement of

one's strength. It is also, to the extent that it impersonates another presumably more powerful persona, an abandonment of the true self. The result is something even less authentic than a false self: an impersonation.

3. When successful, bluffs—like instilling the fear of power—are psychic energy savers. They can influence the behavior of the other without having to invest much of themselves. It is obvious, however, that for someone to have a successful career as a bluffer, it is important to be able to back up the bluff when it is called. Bluffs, in other words, work best when they are not perceived as bluffs. Which is why bullies, when challenged, if they can, like to administer a serious beating to their critics: the message being, "Don't ever make the mistake of thinking that I am bluffing."

There is a myth that bullies are often bluffing, that they are afraid to pick on someone of equal strength and cannot stand the pressure of a fair contest. The kernel of truth in this perception is not that bullies are afraid of a good fight—real bullies love to fight—but that they find losing unbearable (because of a defect in their self, which they are anxiously trying to compensate for by an orchestrated show of strength in something at which they are quite good). And since bullies unconsciously know they cannot tolerate a loss, they look for an edge, such as a weaker opponent or someone who appears to be afraid of them. The fact they sometimes collapse spectacularly upon losing is a reflection of their fear of the humiliation of losing and not their fear of the pain of combat.

I think this is amply borne out, for anyone who follows violent contact sports such as boxing and football, by the biographies of contemporary star players: wherein some of the most physically fearless and brutally tough athletes in the history of the game will often confess how, as youngsters—driven by broken, abusive homes or feelings of deprivation and inferiority, yet also sensing an awesome physical power—they would take it out on other youngsters, perceived as more socially advantaged, by savagely bullying them. From this perspective, it could be said that one possibly socially redeeming value of dangerous professional contact sports is that they channel the destructive energies of incorrigible bullies into safe conduits, providing undreamed-of substitutive rewards and recognitions, and thereby displacing the need to discharge their hostility directly upon innocent people. In other words, a secondary gain of violent contact sports—from the standpoint of society—is that it stops some of its more efficient and talented physical predators from running loose in the streets. Although one could not prove it, it is hard to imagine—if one looks at the incredible aggression that is released and more or less dissipated in the arena of big-time professional contact sports—how such animalistic emotions could be similarly curbed in the everyday world without comparable, socially sanctioned rechannelling, accompanied by unprecedented rewards. (As a simple thought experiment, think of the most mythically tough, fiercely combative sports icon you admire and then picture the probable course of his life if he had failed to be drafted into professional sports.)

4. Depending on the underlying motivation, there are two kinds of bluffs: (1) the one born of panic, when the person is usually on the brink of being exposed, humiliated, or harmed, and (2) the one born of manic confidence—the bluff, that is, of the seasoned poker player, corporate or street bully who knows how to and enjoys instilling feelings of inferiority and insecurity in the other.

Interpersonal examples of everyday bluffing:

Q. (*from a policeman*) What are you doing?
A. (*from a startled pedestrian*) Is there a problem, officer?

The person pretends to be someone who is utterly unperturbed, with nothing to fear, and not someone who, regardless of his innocence, is typically terrified of the policeman's power.

Q. (*from an insecure, suspicious wife*) Do you ever think of having an affair?
A. (*from a guilty husband*) Of course not.

Here, a married man who—while perhaps not seriously entertaining the idea, but who has fantasized countless times about what it would be like to once again share in the swinging, hedonistic pleasures of his bachelor friends—is caught off guard. Feeling unable to or uneasy about responding truthfully (which may or may not upset or threaten his wife), he concocts an answer and a persona that he wants to believe cannot fail to impress and satisfy her.

It follows that, at the unconscious moment of the decision to pretend, the anticipated compromise of his authentic self will tend to seem acceptably expedient. When the discrepancy, therefore, between the power the person thinks he has and the power he imagines is necessary to handle the other is substantial enough, a bluffing transaction will occur. Put another way, a bluffing transaction is one in which the person makes no attempt whatever to express, in even an attenuated way, his true self but, instead, forsaking it, opts to present a makeshift persona that is designed strictly according to perceived power needs.

This is especially confusing in everyday life, where one is not ordinarily subject to role regulations and where, therefore, it is usually unclear as to how much expression of the self, opposed to a show of power, is expected or required. The person can then be susceptible to guilt that he may be shortchanging himself by investing too much in conveying a favorable impression. By contrast, there is considerably less existential guilt over this issue when the person is enacting a role that is transparently based on power: that is, being a boss, policeman, or soldier. When that is the case, the bluff as such is incorporated into the structure of the role, often typically manifested in the uniform where the intent is plainly to enhance the natural image. In itself this can be intimidating—delivering the message that "most of my resources are going into the maximization of my power, which, if necessary, can be focused on constraining you." Although conflicts over the usage of power that come up in the enactment of a rule—because they have been well defined and sanctioned beforehand—tend to be expedited rather quickly, tensions concerning the thwarted needs of the self are more likely to be denied, suppressed, or ignored.

Perhaps the most common bluff in today's power-oriented society is to deny being either emotionally or intellectually vulnerable.

Thus (to someone visibly upset):

Q. Were you frightened? [or] Were your feelings hurt?
A. Not at all.

And (to someone plainly confused):

Q. Do you understand?

A. Yes.

In our information-infatuated age, people almost universally feel over-whelming pressure—in order to be accepted and respected—to pretend to have access to far more data than they in fact have or is really possible for any one person to have. In turn, this gives rise to some of the dynamics of interpersonal bluffing: where (as noted by Goffman) unconsciously people understand that one of the primary collusive aims of social interaction is to allow all participants in good standing to bathe themselves in a better light than they deserve, providing, of course, they do not abuse it by asking for too much or by really expecting the other to literally take them at their word and treat them accordingly. Goffman (1957) gives the example of the host who customarily acts as though she is willing to extend every conceivable hospitality to her guest on the condition, of course, that she is not taken up on it and asked to do more than the required minimum. Another way to put this is that a large part of being social entails politely looking the other way whenever one realizes the other is bluffing vis-à-vis his or her self-image (providing one's own self-interests are not thereby adversely affected). This may be due to the almost universal social habit of endeavoring to wear an appropriate mask whenever we are interpersonally perceived. And from the standpoint of our theme we can add that when it is issues of the self and not of the social persona, it is nearly inevitable, and second nature, to try to assume a mask of power whenever we feel misunderstood, mistreated, or in any way threatened.

Finally, there is the sense in which all defense mechanisms—intrapsychic and interpersonal—can be thought of as bluffs, not only to the other, but to the self as well. Defenses, after all, characteristically operate as though they are working in concert without a hitch and are up to handling any contingency. Ironically, defenses—which by definition are the result of defensiveness—tend to deny that they themselves may be the product of or affected by the very same conflict that they have been constructed to attenuate or resolve. From an object relational point of view, it could be said that defenses are born of mistrust: sought out when there is little hope of the self being satisfied or nurtured by relating to the other. Defense means defense against real or imagined threat and attack. They can be thought of as psychic armor. To arm oneself means to mobilize one's resources of power, such as a facility for instilling fear in the other through the art of bluffing.

It is therefore part of the definition of power operations that it will try to *appear more powerful than it really is*. Accordingly, power has no use for the true self, much preferring to believe in the efficacy of facade and impression, specifically as it impacts on the other. Which is why someone who is being nonintimate—except perhaps when making a point of being aggressively hostile—will typically try to bluff the other into thinking he feels more intimate than he does, if only because it is so painful for both parties to admit otherwise.

POWER PLAYS

1. *Being Withholding*

A simple power play that is disarmingly effective derives from the almost inexhaustible availability of opportunity for one person to tellingly withhold approval from another.

The preconditions for withholding approval are a perception that the other will not be satisfied to just do whatever he is doing but requires a degree of validation from the person, which, in turn, implies that the person presumably knows how to discriminate and can be counted on to render a reasonably objective appraisal if he or she elects to do so. The other then completes what he set out to do and, after a certain amount of time has elapsed, along with some standard cues to the person for approbation, waits for a positive response. When approval is withheld in this common scenario for any of a number of reasons, a compelling dynamic can get played out.

Typically, the performer wonders whether the person is critical of the performance but rather than say so, says nothing, hoping that the person perhaps may be lulled out of his or her judgmental frame of mind. Or he may conclude that his performance was so unremarkable that it actually passed by completely unnoticed. In either case, the performer is likely to feel rejected. Whatever self-esteem issues were meant to be ameliorated by the performance of the act have only been aggravated, except now there does not appear to be any immediate relief in sight. Whatever hope there was for affirmation has more or less collapsed. More painfully self-conscious than before, he can only bide his time, go through the motions until he can get away and try to figure out what went wrong.

Each person knows on some level, both consciously and unconsciously, that every other person she encounters will require minimal affirmation: that she exists; that she is a human being; that she has a true self, a social self, and a repertoire of specific attributes, qualities, skills, and a history of experiences; and finally, that she is thereby a person entitled to certain rights to be validated by acts of deference (Goffman). And there is no one who will not be affected in some way if he perceives or imagines that he perceives any other person who seems to be withholding any of these fundamental affirmations. Each of us therefore realizes that we have the power to disturb the psychic equilibrium of anyone we meet—if we care—simply by failing to register the appropriate validation required by that person, which, of course, will vary considerably from individual to individual.

It is worth noting that a good part of the necessary affirmation that is sought is not so much because one needs to hear he possesses minimal worth, but because he needs to be reassured he is not going to suffer the trauma of encountering someone who will manifestly find his presence unbearably offensive. Although most people who are not grossly handicapped physically, socially, mentally, or psychologically will be able to count on the majority of those whom they meet (out of a sense of a certain existential solidarity as well as the rules of civil social interaction) to accord them a modicum of credit for being fellow members of the human species, they will never be sure that a given individual may not be the exception who will despise them at first sight. It is just this interpersonal catastrophe, neither probable nor that uncommon, that people devoutly wish to avoid.

And the greatest reassurance—far more than any perfunctory run-through of the social amenities, which are designed to cover up rather than reveal honest feelings—will be an indication that the other has sensed and appropriately responded in some way or another to a real dimension of her true self. But this, of course, is what is so rarely seen, at least in any unambiguous fashion. In its stead, people are left to ponder how what has been said and done secretly reflects what each of them thinks and feels, doesn't think or feel, values or devalues, and likes or dislikes about the other. Ironically, as mentioned, not only can validation of what could be called the social self be an obstacle to the search for such meaningful interpersonal signs, but if misused (and it often is), it can become a source of active invalidation of the true self. This is because there is a hunger for intimacy and recognition of the significance of the true self that, when enough time has lapsed, will no longer be satisfied with the simple stroking of the social self—the unconscious attempt to restrict the relationship to the level of only a banal exchange of meaningless pleasantries.

But there's the rub: Affirmation of the true self—unlike that of the social self, where one can rightfully protest infractions of interpersonal protocol (acting in an insensitive, indifferent, or insulting fashion; showing insufficient deference; and so on)—cannot be solicited. It is instead to be freely given, and it is considered beneath a person's dignity to point out that he or she requires to be more genuinely liked, loved, or esteemed. (By contrast, as shown by Goffman [1967], there is a well-established repertory of social protocol allowing the person to vigorously contest instances of unjust social degradation and violations of the so-called civil rights of the self). It follows that the person who is in the position of withholding approval may feel that he has an ace up his sleeve, with all attention being focused on the mini, psychic soap opera of whether he is going to come through and reward the performance that is tacitly being played out (all of which allows deeper issues of the self pertaining to intimacy to be safely ignored or sensibly postponed).

For all of these reasons, each of us has the potential—simply by withholding approval, especially of the self—to thereby almost endlessly tantalize the other. And when the one who is withholding validation is someone who is intent upon playing a power game, the message often becomes: only when my transaction is satisfactorily completed will approval be given. Put another way, approval is meted out according to how well the other facilitates the person's wish for empowerment. Approval in this instance is for the act, the performance, the result, the denouément, and the aftermath. It is never prior, never for the process alone, and never on behalf of the self.

2. Psychical Relativity

There is a huge difference between acknowledging that—while viewpoints are subjectively informed—there may be common grounds for integrating differences and the idea that relativity subverts the authority of any one perspective and that even the deepest perspective based on the widest array of digested life experience is just an opinion! This, of course, is the ethos of egalitarianism applied litigiously to the interpersonal realm. To assert dogmatically that every idea is equal is to politicize both thinking and the psyche. Someone insisting on psychical relativity, therefore, is really making a political rather than a substantive, veridical statement: that is, what essentially matters is not truth as such, but the right of the psyche to vote.

By saying, "that's your opinion"—in other words, I have as much a right to express myself as you do—one unconsciously subverts what is often a potentially meaningful incongruity or misalliance of selves into a pseudopolitical issue that, in turn, typically becomes an interpersonal blind alley.

3. When It Comes to Pain, Everyone Has His Price

The great psychoanalyst W. R. Bion (1992) considered the capacity to bear the pain of development, which, in his view, entailed the bringing together of the primitive and the sophisticated parts of the psyche to be an intrinsic feature of healthy growth and a milestone of maturity. By contrast, the power player has a different use for psychic pain: He may wonder how much of it the other can endure and to that end calibrate the amount of pressure to be applied. The unconscious assumption, then, is that if the inequity of power is sufficient, it cannot be withstood. (In other words, when it comes to pain, everyone has her price.) From such a perspective it follows if the other is being uncommonly resistant that either the imbalance in leverage has been inadequately demonstrated or inadequately applied.

It is a characteristic of the power player, therefore, that he cannot believe that a substantial differential in psychic force can be surmounted or safely absorbed. For him the only possible answer—since he believes winning is everything and no one can be satisfied with losing—is the marshalling of more power. For the power player, pain arises either when one has too little leverage or as an immediate response to the direct impact of someone else's greater power. From this vantage point, pain is regarded as a reaction to a loss of power and *not* to the loss of love, of intimacy, or of a relationship. It is the stunned reaction to a forceful blow rather than the symptom of impoverishment, lack of nurturance or nourishment, or the sign of a void in the self.

There is a sense, therefore, in which power can be perceived as an antidote to pain, and the more one is in pain, the greater will be the need for power. But to acknowledge that one is in pain—analogous to the loss of face experienced by the depressive upon recognition that he or she feels unloved—is to acknowledge a weakness, and not surprisingly this is often displaced by the less shameful awareness that one is merely thirsting for power.

The relationships that each person has to his or her pain can therefore be conceived of as a distinctive object relation. Pain, for example, can unconsciously be regarded as the psychic equivalent of illness, something that symptomatically points to a concealed, unhealthy locus. It can be experienced as a mysterious inner rallying force that polarizes all those parts of the self not in pain versus those that, unfortunately, are. To the degree that it can thereby quickly organize self-experience, it can make sense of what might otherwise seem ambivalent and chaotic. By creating the immediate goal of intrapsychically uniting against a common enemy, pain provides instant meaning. Someone in real pain, for example, does not doubt what he wants to do—primarily to relieve the pain—although he may be quite discouraged as to how and where to begin.

The endurance of pain is often taken as a red badge of courage. To the extent that one is suffering but has not submitted to one's suffering, there is evidence of courage. Pain can then be interpreted to the self as proof that one is alive—not numb and deadened. Indeed, since no feeling is more vivid than pain—so long as one can feel that—one cannot be dead. In addition, pain can also be proof that one cares. Since most psychic pain concerns loss of some kind, pain shows one is not indifferent, cynical, or unconnected to what happens.

Finally, pain can be confirmation that one is interesting, a romantic who perhaps has a touch of the suffering poet in him, with depths or a soul, if you will. It can thereby be a sign that one's life is after all dramatic and not humdrum and boring; that one is not insensate, not something finished but a person in flux. It can be a reminder that one has an inside, is not a machine, and can serve as an evocative warning to anyone within earshot, "Be careful. I can be fragile, too."

More importantly, it can be a signal that someone is not okay and may be in need of attention, of being helped or loved. It can even be an ironic symbol of hope—inasmuch as really severe pain can seem unbearable—

that change (and the motivation to make change happen) must be in the offing, and, to that extent, it can unconsciously indicate that something dreadful is coming to an end or to a head.

Above all, perhaps, pain is a plea that a person should be judged by her vulnerability and not just her strength. But it is obvious that the power player disregards most of these meanings of pain. Instead, she is content basically to gauge how well the other can withstand pain by trying to appraise how he will respond to pressure, manipulation, intimidation, and so on. Even more tellingly, she does not see it as relevant to assess the amount of frustration and subsequent resistance that the concomitant suppression of the other's true self will engender.

4. The Betrayal

One of the things a therapist is privy to are the acts of betrayal, to which we are all vulnerable. Someone confesses to his lover that he has never really loved her, tells his friend that he no longer respects her; confronts his parents with the bitter recrimination that he believes that he has been given very little in life. To say or do something profoundly wounding such as this is to immediately put into disarray an other who now can do little but mobilize her defenses. Savagely going on the offensive, therefore, is to ensure that basic trust is impossible. By creating an interpersonal drama based on deeply hurt feelings, a scenario is established in which two people can no longer come together, but which seems poignant and meaningful enough to perpetuate. Because they are so vivid, the pain and sense of betrayal make it easy to overlook the fact that the new inner, usually secret relationship that has been fashioned is comparatively lifeless and static.

One of the remarkable aspects about such grudgelike object relations is how much they seem to give the self while not giving at all. By continually reenacting the original scenario of abandonment, they simultaneously stimulate and elicit lively revenge fantasies. But they go nowhere. Unconsciously, the sense that reparation is impossible because irreparable harm has been done—that therefore appropriate retaliation, in order to be commensurate to the enormous unjust deprivation incurred, would have to be frighteningly and perhaps uncontrollably global in its destructiveness—make it seem necessary to seal off and internalize any honest expression of feeling. It is thereby repetitive and even obsessive without seeming so.

The violation of what Erik Erikson (1950) has famously called a basic sense of trust—the inculcated childhood belief that one is entitled to expect to be dealt with fairly—adds the weight of family tradition to the injured party's indignation. It follows that the matter is further compounded when the act of betrayal is perceived as a direct consequence of an advantage in power enjoyed by the perpetrator (e.g., such as a boss). Unconsciously, the complaint that is lodged is that anything short of the empathic use of one's authority is unfair. The instances of unempathic hierarchical power that permeate our social landscape—in spite of their insistence that they are built on meritorious achievement and not a thirst to lord it over subordinates—in this way run deeply counter to our familial expectation of fair treatment and to that extent seem a betrayal of basic trust.

Thus, an underling, an employee, or anyone who feels abused in a relationship in which the other is perceived, for any reason whatsoever, as holding the reins almost insidiously gets hooked on the power inequities, unfairness, and the drama of injustice, in short, on everything that is depriving about being subjected in reality or imagination to a transaction based on power. Imperceptibly, the complexity of the relationship becomes overshadowed by the internal lamentation over the hurt one has received, while simultaneously the often theatrical quality of betrayal of basic trust—creating a kind of soap opera of the self—can provide a pseudoreparation for the sense of underlying, obsessive deprivation of the one who feels betrayed.

5. The Power of the Grudge

Closely linked to the sense of betrayal is the feeling of entitlement, the investment in holding onto and being mad at someone who is perceived to have wronged you. The person who is being mad may then variously experience himself as appearing dynamic, proud, impressively well defended, independent minded, dangerous to be around, showing heart, and not only taking himself and any injustice done to him quite seriously but capable of reacting with courage—all of which contribute to a sense that something is building toward a possibly interesting change (the aggressive counterpart to the uses and meanings of pain).

Typically, being mad is abetted by the unconscious wish to keep on feeling that way, as opposed to impulsive anger where the drive is for immediate discharge. Being mad can therefore be conceived as a kind of coy, withholding, or exhibitionistic anger. Such a person may want to punish the other with rejecting feelings rather than with a concrete action or deliver what is intended as emotional blackmail: a plain threat of what might happen but hasn't happened yet, unless some appropriate reparation is made (in contrast to the expression of punitive anger, which is analogous to a sentence being passed and is meant to be a deterrence against a repetition of the original offense).

It follows there can be something unpleasantly mesmerizing about witnessing and experiencing another person who is mad at you. The other may then seem to have her finger figuratively on the trigger, to be poised on the edge of a psychical diving board, to be in a state of precarious knife-point balance, her emotion like a pulsating, coiled spring: as though she is about to reach the end of her tether, is nearing her threshold of volatile discharge, where the slightest adverse pressure might push her past the point of no return.

Although obvious, it is worth noting that being mad creates an atmosphere of interpersonal suspense. Sooner or later the emotion, unless it abates, will become too intense to be sustained, and this will be true even for someone who can hold onto her grudgelike anger for years. Characteristically, the times when it is actively displayed or revived are comparatively rare—because anger by its nature is a self-immolating emotion that, once it has sufficiently primed itself and reached its peak, will instinctively seek discharge or downtime.

The other, who unconsciously knows this, therefore waits and wonders not only when it will be over but what is going to happen thereafter. There is an intuitive understanding that someone who stops being mad thereby creates an emotional and interpersonal discontinuity—with no real transition existing from being visibly angry to becoming more safely civil—that typically will inaugurate a moratorium of sorts. This is the time when the other may try to muddle his way back and retrieve what can be retrieved of the prior, preanger relationship, while simultaneously recognizing that the relationship as such—even if the show of anger has been comparatively minor—has perhaps been permanently changed. All of which means that added interpersonal investment may be required in the future.

So long, however, as the person continues to be demonstrably mad, the other must brace himself or herself, putting the true self on hold. And therein lies its power. Someone who is actively being mad is tantamount to being in fifth gear when it comes to her normal level of aggression. Unconsciously she knows—due to her adrenalin rush—that she probably has access to more combative energy than at almost any other time and, because of this, she is likely to be feared.

6. The Payback

In those famously chilling words—"You have to answer for Santino"—which occur toward the end of *The Godfather*, Michael Corleone tells his instantly terrified brother-in-law that he is about to be held accountable for having fingered Santino to be assassinated.

When it is the psychopathic version of holding someone to account that is being depicted—as portrayed in gangster movies such as *The Godfather*—closure usually does not arrive until sometime after the guilty party has been murdered. This example, just because it is so extreme, shows clearly what can be so intimidating about the enactment of accountability.

Perhaps foremost is that issues of relating do not enter into it. Whatever happens to the culprit—his fate—will depend instead on the application of a comparatively abstract principle or rule of behavior. When the criterion that matters is a pragmatic one of consequences and not the quality of one's actions, the other who is being put on the carpet, in effect, is being accused of a kind of behavioral negligence (or malpractice if it is professional ineptitude that is being singled out).

Now this, of course, is in contrast to ordinary interrelating, where there is an unconscious and reciprocal sense that at any moment either party may have just engendered a narcissistic injury in the other and, if necessary, a concomitant evaluation of a range of options for making reparation (before it may ever reach consciousness in the form of a wish to make the other responsible). It is worth noting, however, when accountability is the issue, it is only one person who is being held accountable and only one person who is exacting it.

It becomes immediately apparent that what making the other accountable for his actions does is to thereby stop the forward thrust of the relationship—like calling a moratorium until the alleged injurious past behavior has been dealt with. Analogous to the reaction to a perceived criminal act, all bets are off; the regular perks and privileges that go along with everyday interrelating are rescinded until the pattern of offensive behavior has been satisfactorily rectified.

The point is that this is scary. What normally is either not dealt with or relegated to unconscious communication is now being held up to a potentially ongoing public scrutiny. It follows that almost automatically the opportunities for spontaneous and playful interacting are annulled as behavior is now looked at from an essentially moralistic framework. From the standpoint of intimacy, therefore, trying to make the other interpersonally accountable is a nonreciprocal, hierarchical transaction of often punitive intent.

The typical response of the person being held accountable is initial shock at how seriously the other is taking behavior that just moments ago seemed to have been acceptable, often followed by an attempt to defuse whatever accusations are being made with a show of propitiating behavior —perhaps a gently scolding or disclaiming smile as though to say, "Oh come on." If the attribution of misconduct is not forthwith recanted, various defenses will come into play: an exaggerated display of how surprised one is, meant to thereby disown agency (even if the objectionable behavior in question did happen, it was purely unintentional); angry indignation; outright denial; counterattack; and projective identification ("No, it is *you* who are being offensive to me").

The most general defense strategy will be to attenuate the new tone of moral gravity by reminding the aggrieved party of all those past aspects of the relationship currently under fire that speak against the allegations of misconduct and to thereby suggest a more benign interpretation of the objectionable behavior in question. In the sense that here the intent plainly is to recontextualize an experience that has been injuriously received by the other, we can speak of the unfolding of a psychic, interpersonal equivalent of a criminal trial: a process wherein for every accusatory statement that is presented, a defense of some sort will be thrown up.

Such relatively simple resistance can be surprisingly effective. It is often overlooked that even a defensive posture that is ineffectual from the standpoint of raising cogent counterarguments is still powerful to the extent that it delivers the message that the person has abandoned all hope of collaborating and is instead intent on channeling all available energies toward an oppositional stance. (To make this point even clearer, think of how much of the rules and etiquette of social interaction are there to prevent one or the other from abruptly giving up on the tacit goal of inter-personal compatibility in order to retreat into a manifestly defensive mode.) It is obvious this kind of armored presentation of the self will be unsettling to the other if only because it indicates that added work will now be necessary to deal with it. (Perhaps this is most classically illustrated in the characteristically tortured and protracted nature of the criminal trial where so much is riding on the outcome—literally life, liberty, and the pursuit of happiness—of the adversarial relationship of the parties.)

It is worth noting that intimacy, by contrast, will often try to construc-tively confront whatever psychic truth there may be in the reprimand of one's partner and even to collaboratively revisit it in the service of working on the relationship.

It follows someone who is being held accountable will have no such luxury. Mistrust, coupled with active defensiveness, will govern the trans-action as each party will tend to seek an advantage and leverage over the other. Sooner or later there will be a near-exclusive reliance on strategy, game playing, one-upmanship, winning and losing, attacking and defending. This is the stuff, of course, of power games, which, therefore, will go hand in hand with the need to hold someone accountable, the per-formance-based perspective of the power-imbued state of mind lending itself irresistibly to such transactions. And the gross lack of relating will be rationalized by such standbys as hierarchical nurturance: for example, "This is for your own good" or "You'll thank me for this one day" or "I am entitled to do this."

Not surprisingly, the dynamics of adult accountability will, in large measure, be a derivative of parent-child interactions as internalized in ego-superego relations. If, as shown, parental transactions aimed at eliciting accountability from their children are so rarely empathically enacted, and if the pervasive social sanctions designed to enforce proper respect for such standard authority figures as an employer, a teacher, a police officer, a professional, or anyone else in good social standing are even more strik-ingly devoid of empathy for the putative offender—it is easy to see, in such instances, how an almost knee-jerk, transferential sense of being unfairly deprived will develop.

And perhaps nowhere will this be more clearly in evidence than in the relationship of our own ego to our own superego. Again, if we assume that the parental prohibitions and admonitions from which the nucleus of the infantile conscience was formed were characteristically harshly adminis-tered (bullying the child being the modus operandi) and that the parental role model for behavior considered praiseworthy from which the nucleus of the ego ideal was formed was typically enacted in a pressuring way—it is no wonder we are so vulnerable to interpersonal reprimanding. To find the root of this susceptibility, we have only to look at the ordinary dynamics of a commonplace conflict between ego and superego.

It is characteristic of such an inner conflict whenever we think we are letting ourselves or others down that, on the one hand, we believe we are behaving badly and inexcusably in our own eyes, while, on the other hand, we are certain we can and should do better. Typically, we then imagine what we should have done and wished we had done. Walter Mitty fantasies of heroic self-vindication, however, tend to provide scant comfort as sooner or later we return to a sober consideration of what others who wit-nessed or will hear about our distinctly less-than-worthy presentation of ourselves are likely to now think of us. Perhaps then in an effort to recover we may console ourselves with all the possible extenuating circumstances of our imagined recent disgrace, dredge up all the countering favorable aspects of our past performance—psychic character witnesses called to our defense—and map plausible, reassuring strategies for damage control in the future.

Note that in all of this the conscience stays disapprovingly silent, and the ego ideal, meant to inspire us, seems even more inaccessible than before. It is significant to me, therefore, not only how remarkably little nurturance is afforded in such everyday crises of self-esteem by our con-science and ego ideal—that, rather than dynamically interacting with our self, impose themselves as more or less structurally frozen, indifferent, and forbidding presences—but how ready we are to accept such intrapsychic deprivation. For how rare it is when we feel that our conscience, instead of judging us, likes us and that our ego ideal, instead of frustrating us with its aloofness, actively encourages and even cares about us. Ironically, the parts of the psyche that nurture the self (what Bollas 1987 has called subject relations) do not seem to come from the conscience and ego ideal. This is another way of saying, of course, that in general ego-superego relations tend to be profoundly nonreciprocal and hierarchical. In one important sense, they thereby are an intrapsychic guarantor of our vulnerability to worldly, interpersonal power plays. (As Freud 1923 noted, it is as though the oedipal laying down of the superego simultaneously creates a permanent weakness in the ego in its relations to the new internalized structure.)

It follows that power operations, more often than not, will dominate the relations between the ego and superego. And here is a primary intrapsychic root cause of why it can seem so natural and irresistibly right-minded to fall into, buy into, invest in, resist, or pursue what we have been describing as power plays and games. (It is obvious the relations of our ego to our unconscious, as illustrated in the paradigmatic defense mechanism of repression—conceptualized by Freud along lines of domination, patriarchy, and banishment, as Christopher Bollas has ingeniously pointed out—entail power operations on an even grander scale, but this is not the place to go into that.)

THE INTIMACY THERMOSTAT

Today, to a significant extent, the story of relationships is the story of disappointment, burnout, and estrangement, and the office of the modern psychotherapist is often sought as a kind of psychic recovery room following the traumatic amputation of a prized portion of the self.

Although such loss is most commonly presented from the perspective of the person who feels abandoned, it was Samuel, an unemployed, embittered thirty-five-year-old actor, who made the case most memorably in therapy for the necessity of, and often the intense pleasure to be derived from, deserting a relationship gone sour. No small part of this pleasure was the palpable consternation of someone who—habituated to smugly taking Samuel's friendship for granted—was now clueless as to how to account for the sudden and radical withdrawal of his former interest.

In therapy, Samuel would solemnly detail the method by which he would exorcise from his life the presence of a friend who had hurt him too many times to ever be forgiven again. The first and most important step was involuntary and internal but would pave the way for his strategy of deadly withdrawal. He would wake up one morning and begin brooding about a particular friend who had disappointed him, or he would be walking in the street and experience (as he described it) an epiphany of "nothingness." Where before there had been a complicated network of feelings, both tender and hateful, now there was a void, a numbness.

It was a numbness that was liberating. Shorn of his feelings, especially the feeling of guilt, he was free to express the hostility he had up until now kept hidden. Samuel could at last do what he had really wanted to do for a long time. Should he encounter the friend in question in public, he would most likely nod curtly, continue to walk, and make a point of not stopping to converse. Out of the corner of his eye, he would steal a glance at his friend's face, hoping to catch signs of unmistakable dismay. If thereafter the puzzled friend would telephone (perhaps hoping to clarify what seemed a mystifying rejection), Samuel would screen the message with perverse pleasure and, of course, refuse to return the call.

And that would be just the beginning. What had seemed a troubling, although isolated, incident would soon be repeated. Samuel would make sure of that. He would bide his time, waiting for the secretly blacklisted friend to make a predictable overture for getting together: to suggest perhaps meeting for a drink, attending an interesting party that was being planned, taking advantage of some complimentary tickets to an off-Broadway show, or arranging for an extended, catch-up conversation. Now there could be no doubt—when once again Samuel would inexplicably fail to respond in his customary way—that something was wrong. But what?

Phase two, the "guessing game," was the part that Samuel most enjoyed, when he would feel like an unseen puppeteer pulling the strings that made the relationship go. From his own periodic bouts of paranoia, he well knew just how tantalizing and unsettling the sudden disappearance of a presumed friend could be. He knew how doubts that could not be answered and would not end concerning the motives for abandonment would over time prove unbearable. He knew that few things are as imposing, as unbreakable, as bottomless as silence. To Samuel, silence, deftly timed, could therefore be both eloquent and passionate. The more he would withdraw, the stronger he felt. The less he spoke, the more he was understood. The more absent he became, the more present, unavoidable, and terrible his anger would appear. He had only to keep the mystery alive, to lurk in the background, to record the whispers and innuendos surrounding his orchestrated disappearance reported back to him by mutual acquaintances, and to note the confusion, the hurt feelings, the loss of face that was being fended off, and the revenge that he thirsted after would surely be his.

Although few would care to go to the Iago lengths of a Samuel, the cooling off of the intensity of any given relationship is a natural and probably universal occurrence. Providing that the loss of interest is roughly reciprocal and that there is some mutual acceptance of what is happening, this usually does not pose an unsurmountable problem. By contrast, few things are as unsettling as the realization that a supposed friend is gradually or suddenly withdrawing a customary level of warmth, interest, and friendliness without an appropriate explanation (and who, when challenged, will typically deny what he or she is doing).

The disappearing other will then immediately become more mysterious and, to a certain extent, more desirable. Automatically the person who is feeling rebuffed will take note of the other's growing absence and begin to pay more attention: either silently observing the signs of withdrawal in order to determine their hidden significance or actively courting the former friend in the hope of rekindling the old warmth. Sooner or later, however, it will become apparent that the other not only is acting mysteriously, but, much more to the point, is being mysteriously angry.

The power of mysterious anger to manipulate and control its target is considerable. There is, for example, its aura of the wounded victim, the sufferer too proud to speak who is silently licking his wounds. There is the intrigue engendered by a sense of danger: doubt about the source of the anger can subtly change into doubt over what would be a safe defense—in turn giving rise to an anxiety that an attack could come at any time and that anything could provoke it. The fact that the other is being strangely secretive about his anger can suggest not only that it may be too extreme to be voiced but that the other has lost, or really has so little trust in, the person's capacity to understand his point of view or to make reasonable changes, that it is pointless to bring it up. Furthermore, there is the distinct possibility that the anger was so toxic that it completely nullified the store of positive nurturance gathered in the course of the relationship and sufficiently numbed the other so that what is now being manifested is "genuine" indifference rather than sullen withdrawal.

Whatever the cause may be, the other clearly has undergone a fairly dramatic transformation in his perspective on the value of being in contact with the person. The new relationship is a nonreciprocal and secret one, and this cannot fail to tantalize someone who may alternately feel excluded, abandoned, punished, banished, devalued, and discarded. It is also tantalizing to withhold any realistic promise of closure to whatever the problem may be. After all, until the individual who is acting so unlike himself says otherwise, there is always a chance that the former relationship may somehow be restored, and thus there is a small ray of hope. Typically, of course, this is not the case: The one who is withdrawing intends to do so even more, but rather than invest in the relationship to the extent of being open about it, he would prefer to be mysterious concerning the true status of what is going on (thus being able to strongly influence the person, but with only a minimum of input and interaction). Not surprisingly, in the worst-case scenario, the erstwhile friend, yielding to paranoid suspicion, may conclude that a trial of the past relationship has already been secretly conducted by the other and that a sentence has been rendered without the person ever having had the chance to be present.

To terminate in a clandestine fashion and radically withdraw from an ongoing relationship with some history to it is only one extreme measure of being mysterious in a manipulative way. There are other methods. Indeed, it might be said, from the broadest possible interpersonal perspective, that each and every relationship—from the standpoint of warmth, friendliness, openness, depth of feeling, spontaneity, and degree of intimacy—has a certain set point, a homeostatic *temperature* to which it strives to return. (Of course, if the relationship truly grows the set point will correspondingly expand, but until a new plateau has been established it will characteristically tend to be stable.)

Now although each dynamic moment is different and will fluctuate upward or downward from the particular set point, the person—unconsciously responding to his own predetermined, interactive temperature as though to a relational thermostat—will typically make efforts to counter the vicissitudes of random mood deviations. Thus, for example, if he is feeling unduly cranky, depressed, or withdrawn, he may attempt to balance this by an added show of empathy or thoughtfulness toward the other or, at the very least, an admission of being sub par (e.g., "I guess I'm having a bad day"). Contrarily, if he is acting uncharacteristically joyful and celebratory because of some expected good fortune, sooner or later—when the elation wears off—he may unconsciously compensate for this by, perhaps, a retrospective show of bemusement over his recent somewhat manic mood (thereby indicating to the other that he or she can once again expect him to be his old, more reserved self).

It immediately becomes apparent that if someone wishes, for any of a number of narcissistic reasons, to arbitrarily *change the temperature of the relationship* without bothering to let the other know why—the working on and sharing of meaningful, dynamic relational fluctuations being, of course, a hallmark of intimacy—it is quite easy to do so. One has merely to follow the path of least resistance, accept the inevitable drop in the mood of the relationship without endeavoring to correct it, as is usually the case, and thereby will be able to secretly savor the predictable jolt that such provocatively mysterious cooling off is bound to deliver to the other's peace of mind.

Another method, besides following the path of least resistance, is to actively lower the temperature of the relationship (typically occurring after someone has suffered an unacceptable and real or imagined narcissistic injury). A popular way to do this is to start subtracting what Eric Berne once ingeniously called *strokes* (the classic stroke being the all-American "Hi," accompanied with a smile). First, it is determined how many strokes one has been customarily dispensing and how many are expected, then—depending on the magnitude of the offense and the need for distance—the subtraction follows accordingly.

It is worth noting that Berne's strokes were meant to describe the attempt to maintain a kind of social homeostasis and were primarily used after an absence of contact as a means of displaying the appropriate enthusiasm upon reestablishing contact with someone whose presence was supposedly missed. By contrast, what we are talking about here refers to what might be termed the basic level of interpersonal intimacy that has been attained. From that perspective, the subtraction of mandatory strokes of social deference is only one way of dampening the relational intensity and complexity of the interaction (the unconscious aim in this case being to disengage or divorce the self and not just to sabotage the continuity of convenient social rapport).

For all of these reasons, to secretly cool off one's investment in the other is an especially potent and easily accessible power operation—in light of the fact that at almost every interpersonal moment an unconscious decision may be made by either or both parties as to whether the relational set point needs priming, and if so, whether or not it is worth the effort.

BEING COURAGEOUS

As a young psychotherapist, I was sufficiently taken with Alfred Adler's powerful observation that it required courage to overcome the crippling effects of neurosis (1956) that I attempted to incorporate it into my so-called nascent technique. Whenever a patient, therefore, would show uncommon fortitude in facing up to an objectively harrowing emotional ordeal—especially someone who had a history of backing down and giving up in the face of psychic adversity—I would say, "That took courage." To my surprise, it proved a simple but surprisingly effective intervention. With few exceptions, the patient was genuinely heartened, sometimes telling me afterward he had never before been validated in that fashion in his life. As a therapist, I could not help but be impressed by the meaning that the attribution of courage held for my patients and from that point on began to study it in its own right.

Being courageous, I realized, implies that there is a part of oneself that one trusts will speak up for and, if necessary, fight to preserve certain elements of the self. This, in turn, implies that these elements are considered worthy enough to do battle over. Someone in touch, therefore, with her courageous self is likely to feel that excitement and the burst of energy that comes from the exercise of her healthy narcissism. There may be no more convincing sign of self-valuation than a display of bona fide courage on behalf of the true self. (As Christopher Bollas 1987 has noted, each of us has internalized a particular style of parental care that we then transfer onto the way we handle our own self as an object.)

One of the fondest memories of childhood and one of the safest times perhaps is when our parents were fighting, in a healthy sense, to protect us. It may, therefore, be that being courageous is, in some measure, a defense and denial that one is unloved, uncared for, and not respected. This may partly explain why character disorders, sociopaths, and borderline types—those who seem especially isolated, abandoned, and impoverished in their object relations—so often prove to be fierce fighters on their own behalf, as though they would rather die (and they sometimes do) than let the shadow of dishonor fall on the self. In other words, by fighting so ferociously to protect their public reputation, they may be unconsciously striving to enact a primitive family romance of what it would be like to be jealously and parentally safeguarded; that is, only a bloody, life-threatening struggle in which they are battling someone who is intent on seriously harming them can convince them that at least someone would be deeply upset if they perished. In this way, one can come to look upon one's courage, especially if it has been publicly demonstrated, as one's psychic bodyguard.

By contrast, if one has never really shown unquestionable courage, ambivalence concerning one's self-worth can only be reinforced. One may then wait for a test in which one can at last prove one's fortitude as a necessary definition and validation of one's identity. One may feel that only certain courageous acts can lend a stamp of authenticity to other cherished values and attributes of the self. After all, it is almost universally believed a parent will risk himself for the child he loves. Contrarily, a lover who will take no chances to protect his or her love object from clear danger will not be considered much of a lover, while a solider who professes to love his country but who goes AWOL upon being called to battle will not be considered much of a patriot. (Adam Phillips 1996 has noted that one of the reasons mourning is so important is because it seems to prove to us that we really do need objects, and Ludwig Wittgenstein 1969 has remarked that no one seems to doubt the authenticity of someone who screams in pain.) Analogously, showing courage may be significant in that it proves to us, by the risks we are willing to take, that certain values are indispensable.

Although we may sometimes call upon it, courage does not seem to be something under the auspices of the ego or will, a skill that one develops. Rather, it is something that reveals itself, that one discovers or fails to discover—an unconscious reservoir of untapped resolve that rarely gets summoned into play except at moments of crisis. One waits for one's courage as one waits for another. (Of course, in contrast to the ordinary person, there is the Man of Courage—for example, a professional daredevil—whose life is based on and fueled by the dangers and risks to which his seemingly insatiable fund of courage expose him.)

Shakespeare's famous boastful hero, Julius Caesar, because he is imbued with courage, cannot be killed *psychically* by adversity. That is, if the hero, no matter how beleaguered and seemingly doomed, can always manage to find sanctuary in his courage—his seemingly endless resolve to fight on no matter what the odds against him—then literally he cannot be killed in spirit, but only in body. Instead, he dies only once—biologically. By contrast, the coward dies every time his courage fails him.

In this sense, courage is a shield, a manic shield, against the fears of our own mortality. Paradoxically, if we have this fierce, self-protective love called courage, it can seem we cannot die, which, unconsciously, is what the excessively courageous person believes. On the other hand, if there is a manic element informing acts of courage, eventually there should be some kind of crashing and deflation. And this is what we see: Even the bravest, seemingly invincible prizefighter, once beaten, can appear to be a different man. You might say, therefore, that the courageous individual can tolerate any adversity so long as he or she remains courageous: that is to say, does not feel fear, especially what is perceived as cowardly fear. Perhaps courage, because it is an expression of an extreme emotional state, has to psyche itself up and polarize itself—no halfway measures will do.

THE DYNAMICS

Patients naturally report a variety of experiences associated with acts of courage. Here, however, are some common denominators that come into play when a person is acting and feeling courageous.

1. Typically, the ordinary, nonheroic person tends to take a deep breath before undertaking something that is viewed as patently dangerous. Being courageous, then, can feel like letting go of a customary lifeline and instead embarking on a kind of radical jumping off—psychically analogous to leaping off a diving board higher than one has ever encountered—into an uncharted territory of great risk. It can feel like a quantum leap from a familiar place equipped with a normal support system and a basic safety net to an area that has no safety net. That the passage from being ordinary to courageous is so often discontinuous, with no transition whatsoever, can make it seem heady and exciting, and, although it may appear obvious, it is worth noting that one important reason for being courageous is that one is intolerably bored or feeling deadened.

2. To be courageous is also to have one's thoughts and emotions organized into a goal—as though one is fighting a common enemy of the different parts of the self. So long as one is engaged in courageous deeds, therefore, one does not need to struggle with an identity crisis. It feels good to be courageous because all of one's defenses will then be in play, due to the state of high arousal caused by the perceived danger, with the result that one feels well defended, and therefore, paradoxically, very safe while, of course, simultaneously being uncommonly threatened. Such dynamic ten-

sion and dialectic—"Am I secure, powerful, and about to be triumphant?" or "Am I recklessly imperiling myself and on the brink
of being seriously hurt?"—lend it its experiential soap operaish
quality. There is probably no other time in our life when we feel we
are living out a real-life soap opera than when we act daringly.

3. A person then feels uniquely honest, authentic (you are putting
your money where your mouth is), self-revelatory, open, and
expressive. By showing what you most care about, put most stake in,
need most to preserve and protect, you are showing a core part of
one's true self values. There is therefore a sense of making contact,
genuinely communicating, and, in spite of the fact the other is often
viewed as an opponent, being somehow intimate.

4. There is a feeling of rushing to a closure of some kind. Unless one
is merely being stoical, such as bearing up to continuous depriva-
tions (e.g., at a job one hates or in prison), an act of courage typically conveys a sense of imminence. And the end that is in sight,
being primordial—will one survive and conquer or go down and be
humiliated?—more often than not comes quickly (at the conclusion
of the combat or tribulation). It follows that characteristically there
is the belief that something of immense importance to the individual is about to be determined.

For all of these reasons, being courageous can feel as though one is
being idealistic. By risking a good part of what it has taken a lifetime to
consolidate—a person's basic sense of security in the world—one shows
dramatically that one is living by a code of conduct, an ethical sense of the
terms on which life should be lived, that transcends the law of self-preser-
vation. Herein lies the dignity of being courageous.

On another level, of course, being courageous, to the degree that it is
a response to an extreme situation, can defer ongoing intimacy issues of
the true self with the rationalization that one is dealing with a self-evidently meaningful situation (which renders everything else irrelevant).
And, finally, being courageous, involving as it does great risk, involves
great choice. If ever one doubted it, one is at last a true existentialist par-
taking in the Sartrian great no. For doesn't one say no to everything in oneself, to the other, or to the world that tries to persuade the person that it is
wiser not to risk so much and to be far less courageous?

POWER AND COURAGE

By definition, courage is the capacity not to lose heart in the face of being an underdog, overmatched, or unequipped to deal with a formidable opponent or obstacle. Put another way, it is the essence of courage that it strives not to submit to a transaction based on power, regardless of how superior that power may be. From the standpoint of the one in power, therefore, the courage of the other is a rebel or dissident that needs to be nipped in the bud. Thus it is that the bully, as mentioned, looks to punish as severely as possible any incipient show of bravado from a disgruntled victim, while the corporate higher-up will do everything to define it as an irrelevant, although disruptive personalization of a situation characterized by an admittedly inequitable distribution of power, but, nevertheless, one presumably based on merit.

For someone, therefore, who is intent on gaining his or her ends essentially by means of power, the courageous protest of the other is viewed primarily negatively—as *resistance*. As such, it is a stumbling block, a thorn in one's side. The clearest example of this, perhaps, is the policeman's attitude—bolstered by the fact that the law provides stiff penalties for anyone resisting arrest—to a show of defiance by someone who is in the process of being interrogated. From such a perspective, oppositional courage is no more than resistance to be overcome. What makes suicidal, kamikaze courage—the courage of a terrorist, hijacker, or mad bomber who is willing to die—so terrifying is its ability to temporarily turn the tables and thwart overwhelming superior forces. (Which it does by revealing the weakness of entrenched power—that it depends on the other's submission, due to fear, and is not prepared for complete refusal to rationally acknowledge the likelihood of defeat. Because of this, it doesn't know what to do and is not prepared to handle the solitary fanatic or lunatic who does not happen to have any sane respect for its evident superiority of power.)

On the other hand, there is a curious relationship between the one who has power and his own courage. The person who wants to show power tends to move slowly, calmly, at his own pace, as though certain of the outcome of his actions, with as much fearless confidence in the rightness of what he is doing as can be mustered, independently of the responses or especially the needs of the other. From that standpoint, an act of courage, inasmuch as it is typically a manifestation of a fierce oppositionalism to a real or imagined adversary and to that extent is basically *reactive*, is incongruous with the autocratic, isolationist stance of the power broker. Furthermore, since courage, by definition, is a passionate acknowledgment of and attempt to surmount a plainly disadvantaged if not weakened position, it is incompatible with the one-upmanship overview of the power player. This is borne out in the respective differences in their styles of fighting: Unlike the man or woman of courage who valiantly strives to overcome a frightening adversary, the person of power endeavors to merely smother, immobilize, crush, or teach his opponent a much-needed lesson.

POWER AND RELATING

It is a characteristic of a transaction based on power that it endeavors to take as much and give as little as possible, to appropriate, and, when necessary, to demand tribute. One way to accomplish this is to use the power of the structure that is conferred by the role definition to impress upon the subordinate other that she is indeed getting something, being a beneficiary just by brushing up against the person in charge, and that it may not be necessary to give anything else. The classic example of this in our society is the American boss: where there is often the implicit expectation that you are grateful for the nearness, the availability, and the security attached to the presence of the one on top (an attitude ridiculed in the old joke, "I'm going to give you something greater than a raise—my handshake!").

It follows from this that the person who has authority will hold in his hands a disproportionate share of the primary resources for getting the job done, that decisive action will not be reciprocal, does not depend on feedback, but flows in one direction only, from him at the hub outward to a field of group tension or concern. This carries with it a corollary assumption— that the subordinate other's contribution is secondary, if not often useless. Which sets up a third assumption, that for the boss merely to interact with, include in any way in his actions, or take time out to answer a question of one of his underlings, is to give something of genuine value.

From the standpoint of giving and true nurturance, therefore, the transaction based on power, even when seriously pretending to be serving the other's needs, acting functionally or cooperatively, really believes it has only to be itself, to discharge and exercise its own power, in order to convince most outsiders that it is relating in an acceptable fashion (explaining why there is almost a universal, maddening sense of frustration by the recipients that their needs count hardly at all when in contact, especially, with officially entrenched, hierarchical power structures).

It is worth noting that when giving is from the hands of power it is almost always top-down, hierarchical, presumably originating from the highest point of either a psychical, familial, societal, business, or social structure and then trickling down to a designated subordinate person, interaction, or situation, less developed or advantaged, that is meant to be the beneficiary of its largesse. Thus, nurturance delivered from a position of authority is also essentially nonreciprocal, an aftermath that follows so seamlessly and insidiously from the fact that power operations are typically unilateral that it is overlooked.

If this is so, what, then, is *hierarchical nurturance*? It means, among other things, that the giver gives not because he wants to or happens to be nurturing but because he is empowered with and under an obligation to distribute a substantial supply of services and goods. Whenever a seeming intent to nurture, therefore, travels along traditional hierarchical lines of power—a boss, for example, offering a generous group health insurance plan or a liberal allotment of paid vacation days to employees—it is usually almost impossible to disentangle and properly evaluate the two motives: the wish to show off and exercise power from the wish to authentically nurture the needs of the other.

The paradigm, of course, for confusion generated by hierarchical, nonreciprocal nurturance goes back to the family of origin. For how does the infant/child determine and sort out whether the parents who protect and provide do so basically because they are powerful or because they truly love him or her? The same basic ambiguity applies in even greater measure the further up one moves in one's development on the ladder of social services and support systems: Can one ever tell if the educator, the physician, priest, or policemen educates, treats, sermonizes, or safeguards because he wants to or has to? Parents, of course, like most people who are empowered, are not as perplexed on this issue as their children: The clear prestige and social sanction accorded to traditional enactments of hierarchical nurturance make it unnecessary to doubt the authenticity of the giving.

As opposed to this, as I am sure the reader is by now aware, I believe that true intimacy and nurturance, at least among adults, is fundamentally a bottom-up affair. It is conceived in the singularity of the moment, a reciprocal interaction spontaneously arising between two subjectivities having little or no need to borrow from or depend on the secondary benefits of hierarchical power.

On the other hand, hierarchical nurturance is not to be confused with genuine nonreciprocal nurturance: for example, the parent who is in tune with her child's true self needs, loves her child for himself, and gives for the sheer joy of nurturing a growing self, which, although and because it occurs so rarely, is what I consider the highest form of intimacy. By contrast, hierarchical nurturance is basically about power, which it officially denies with occasional gestures of pro forma recompense.

It follows that one way to escape from the ongoing constraints and complexities of reciprocal intimacy is to shift the focus from nurturance, which can be a long-term affair, to power, which at least in principle can be short and sweet—that is to say, by politicizing the relationship. What does it mean to politicize a relationship? It means to put the experiential enactment of the interaction in brackets and to step back and concentrate on the various inequities in power, privileges, and civil rights presumed to exist as a result of familial, societal, cultural, and sexist stereotyping. The implicit assumption being that it is far more important to right what is politically wrong than it is to actually continue engaging in the relationship in its present depriving and unegalitarian form.

Thus, the relationship is diagnosed as politically sick and is quarantined, so to speak, until it can be, if not cured, at least put on the road to convalescence. From the standpoint of our theme, what is important is the underlying assumption that by aggressively focusing on the politics of the relationship—the vicissitudes of the dynamics generated by the inequities of power between the players—somehow one is being more nurturing to the other (supposedly by working to facilitate at some distant point in the future a more politically correct climate for interrelating) than if one were being honestly, empathically, and personally giving in the here and now. In short, to politicize a relationship is not to have and not to be in one but to compensate for this lack with the narcissistic empowerment that comes from dabbling in the politics of the self.

To politicize a relationship, therefore, means to endeavor to raise to consciousness certain interpersonal inequities assumed to be sexist in origin and the by-product of large and devious social forces that, dangerously, are being taken for granted. In this sense, to politicize means to introduce issues for political consideration, and hopefully revision, that hitherto were not considered grist for the political mill. (I discuss this in detail in my book *The Singles Scene*, 1994.)

On the other hand, it is obvious, if we are talking not about the consciousness raising vis-à-vis sexism that still flourishes on the singles scene—but about the interpersonal dynamics deriving from enactments of firmly established roles, that it is *typical of the politics of power to deny that politics is involved.* (Even in a presidential election, where the politics of power is most nakedly in view, it is customary for the candidates to repeatedly and categorically deny that the acquisition of political power, for the sake of power, is a motive for their feverish pursuit of the highest office in the land.) Put another way, a power operation is one that tends to assume that any issues of active politicking over alleged inequities and abuses of rights have long ago been resolved (justly) in favor of the status quo, and all that remains is to properly function according to the modus operandi. It is obvious this is particularly easy to do when one is operating under the umbrella of an institutionalized, societal, professional, or business role, and it is considerably harder to do when the field of action is the interpersonal one in which democratic values supposedly prevail (to then subtly or overtly control, influence, or coerce the behavior of the other in such a presumably egalitarian context will require enough psychic force to merit the appellation "power").

For all of these reasons, hierarchical nurturance is a handy avoidance of the challenge and demand of real giving. Once again the analogy to parent-child nonreciprocal giving is useful. It is so difficult for ordinary parents to satisfactorily discharge their obligations to their children in conformity to basic social and legal standards, to clothe, feed, house, educate, send to school, while keeping them on the approved developmental track without having to resort to visible abuse, that, having done so, it is natural to believe that they have performed rather admirably. Parents whose children are perceived as normal by those who are supposed to be able to judge them understandably tend to take pride in their accomplishments. It is worth noting that no one really asks them, or seems to care, whether they have functioned as good parents because they have wanted to or felt they had to. And it follows that most parents who have suffered the ordeal of raising and disciplining children, who more or less have suitably adapted to the complexities of modern life, will not question themselves too carefully on this crucial point either. That they have not buckled under the weight of the extraordinary parental demands placed upon them is more than enough.

By contrast, children instinctively will have almost no empathy for the rigors of being a parent unless, of course, they are in the hands of dysfunctional, abusive parents (e.g., alcoholics) who *insist* that they do. They will, however, be exquisitely sensitive to all those occasions when there is a plain conflict of interests and an ensuing power struggle, those times when their parents will retreat behind bullying, self-serving tactics. And they will resentfully note, especially at those instances when disciplinary punishment is being administered, how little empathy is really manifested for the suffering they are undergoing, the pain they are experiencing, and the deprivation they are being forced to endure.

Now to analogize this unique, nonreciprocal, parent-child relationship to the world of adult power operations. One immediate difference is that parents, in spite of or because of the nonreciprocity, are expected to be empathic, whereas consenting adults (unless in the so-called helping professions) who are engaged in inequitable power transactions are not realistically expected to be empathic. The availability and exercise of their power in a functional way—for example, dispensing necessary information or services in howsoever a lordly manner—is considered nurturance enough. Typically, analogous to the parents' overview of how much is required just to minimally discharge their responsibilities, the person who thinks he or she is in charge, in fact or fantasy—and who is aware of what it takes to acquire, maintain, and wield power—tends to be quite satisfied with doing that and only that. Hence, the flourishing of hierarchical nurturance. And finally, analogous to parent-child interactions, the person perceiving himself on the short end of the stick will be attuned, despite any and all secondary benefits accruing from the exercise of superior authority (it is, of course, the essence of intimacy that the nurturance is *never* derivative of power operations) that the transaction is profoundly self-serving.

LOVE, WITH AND WITHOUT THE STRINGS

In the ideal parent-child relationship, the child is valued for his or her self and does not have to pay back the parents for all their nonreciprocal sacrificing by performing. The child is not required to earn love but receives it just by being.

But, even so, taking this ideal to the extreme, when is the point when a parent's nonreciprocal acceptance of a delinquent child's seemingly complete lack of interest in autonomously investing in the worth of the attachment by working to enhance it—not by performing for parental approval or to gratify narcissistic parental needs, but in a child's way (enriching the bond as he or she sees fit)—become instead outright abuse at the hands of their children? To put it another way, if it is to be a viable, nondestructive relationship, the child needs to reciprocate, not equally, but in some phase-appropriate, meaningful fashion. It is probably true, therefore, that so-called unconditional love does not exist (at least not after the period of primary maternal identification and resulting infantile omnipotence as described by D. W. Winnicott 1965).

When we come to consenting adults, however, where intimacy is supposed to be an achievement and project of two people, the same question becomes considerably more complicated, but no less pressing. At what point, when simply allowing the one who is loved to be—where such being manifestly does not seem to reflect in any way an awareness of the existence of the self of the other—does it become abusive indifference at the hands of the beloved? And at what point does our request or demand in the face of narcissistic withdrawal that the loved one pay attention and relate to us begin to become—not an overture for closeness—but coercion? What is important here is not that there can be no clear answers to such questions, but the implicit understanding informing them that in mature love the ability to work on the inevitable conflict of interests and resulting interpersonal tensions is an indispensable indication of the underlying psychic investment. In other words, in the unconscious work can be a proof of love.

It is worth noting that working on behalf of the best interests of both partners in the service of mutuality is a far cry from performing in order to gain approval and affection as a reward for gratification of the other's narcissism. A healthy adult relationship, therefore, whether personal or professional, always involves some reciprocity. The average employee, for example, does not have a reciprocal say with his boss regarding what, when, and how he is to work. But this obvious inequity in autonomy is at least partially balanced by another inequity—the nonreciprocal economic arrangement in which the exchange of monies travels only one way, from the employer to the employee. Thus, the oft-noted nonreciprocal nature of the therapeutic situation is somewhat compensated for by the fact that the therapist works primarily in the service of facilitating the patient's difficulties in living but makes no such request in return. Of course, two inequities do not make an equal, whole relationship.

It is important that in a power transaction, by contrast, the work that is done is not considered a sign of underlying intent to nurture and to relate, but a measure instead of the skill, resources, and determination of the person. What counts is the result, the bottom line, who gets to use what and whom. In a power transaction, the prestige one has and how one can influence or, if necessary, perform for the other become meaningful, superseding how one relates.

"I DID IT MY WAY"

Today it is fashionable to talk about pseudointimacy, as though we know what intimacy is. But what about pseudo-autonomy, which we rarely hear about? This may be defined as a sense of independence that is based—not on the ability to express and actualize the deepest needs of the true self— but on the instrumentality, efficacy, and capacity of the false self to impact, manipulate, and control the other.

Pseudo-autonomy, therefore, is a feeling of power, bolstered by the illusion that psychic force is tantamount to freedom. This, of course, is not to deny that having power thereby grants one a certain freedom not to be intruded upon, easily discounted, or restrained in the familiar way that others are and to be able to say, pretty much whenever one wants, with impunity, "Don't tell me what to do." It is a freedom to be able to gratify, rather than actualize or express oneself, to acquire and appropriate, rather than to relate.

So it is no accident that some of our most obnoxious and abrasive talk-show hosts are also some of our noisiest libertarians. In other words, pseudo-autonomy unconsciously goes hand in hand with political power, political autonomy, what might be called the civil rights and libertarianism of the self. At its root is the angry, obsessive, and sometimes paranoid assertion that almost no one has the right to tell him what to do, in spite of the fact that he often blatantly lords it over everyone he considers less politically enlightened.

Pseudo-autonomy, therefore, tends to be based on visible displays and outer versus inner power. It is more dependent on an other from whom it can pretend to act conspicuously independent. It gravitates toward the social. It obsessively seeks and needs validation of its identity from others, unlike genuine autonomy, which works privately and unconsciously within the domain of the self. Not surprisingly, pseudo-autonomy is fond of recharging and reinventing itself with a kind of pop existentialism, the favorite motto of which is, "Life is about choices."

It is obvious there is something heady about feeling empowered, to believe that people cannot push you around because they fear you. The illusion is to believe that because they fear you, they respect you. What is then overlooked is that there is a difference between political freedom and what Christopher Bollas (1995) has termed unconscious freedom: that is, as history has repeatedly shown, someone can be desperately driven, and psychically constricted, yet have awesome political power. The difference coming down, perhaps, to that between action-mobility (Goffman 1967) and psychic fluidity.

The flip side of pseudo-autonomy is that it tends to be all or nothing and cannot admit, because it cannot integrate, its own dependence and vulnerability. In therapy, the classic example is the patient who can feel free only if he leaves a relationship and is no longer in contact with his need for another. He must feel self-contained and self-sufficient in order to feel independent. To feel truly differentiated, he needs to be unrelated to the other.

Finally, pseudo-autonomy is an excellent defense against the fragile, dependent psychic elements underlying the stance of power. From the standpoint of intimacy, if I had only one word to characterize an interpersonal transaction essentially based on power, it would be "hollow." At its core, it is constituted not so much by its antihuman or malignant intention but rather by its profound absence of any redeeming, vital humanism. It is as though the person who has really committed himself or herself to a power play, whether situationally or characterologically, has entered a kind of dead zone in which values of empathy, compassion, spontaneity, playfulness, and intersubjectivity simply do not exist, having been displaced by the absorbing, animating, and earnest pursuit of pseudo-autonomous self-aggrandizement.

By underscoring the hollowness when it comes to human relatedness, it is not meant to imply that such a person is anything less than formidable when locked in a power struggle. Quite the contrary. Like the professional prize-fighter who, no matter how psychologically and emotionally abandoned, abused, impoverished, and demoralized in his childhood, fights fiercely and unforgivingly once he steps into the ring, the inveterate power broker, to the discouragement of his adversaries or victims, generally proves to be a tougher and better competitor than they are.

By contrast, it is in the area of kindness, empathy, and responsiveness to human needs that the person bent on the acquisition and enactment of power seems so bereft. And this is exactly what the recipient of a power transaction often intuitively senses: a chilling awareness of imposed isolation born of the recognition that the other with whom one is unhappily entangled seems to be operating from a psychical space in which the desire for intimate rapport simply does not matter.

POWER AND EMPATHY

Since we are considering everyday, nonsociopathic interpersonal situations that are practically universal, empathy, to a greater or lesser extent, must be present. With this difference: In a power transaction, empathy is directed toward the anxiety that the other is perceived to experience concerning issues over acquiring, maintaining, or possibly losing power. Thus, someone in power (for example, a boss) may be genuinely empathic to how a subordinate is reacting to being instructed, criticized, dominated, or, especially, ordered about. She may conduct corporate interpersonal seminars in order to discover a better strategy for dealing with what Goffman terms loss of face, but this loss of face will be vis-à-vis the imagined social perception of one's lack of deference. What such empathy will characteristically not reach to is that part of the true self that does not care about and is not caught up in conflicts over and resistances to power operations.

There is probably no more classic example of this than the stereotypical reaction of the boss who finds himself in the unpleasant position of having to fire a person who has been a loyal employee for a period of several years. There is then, usually, among other things, an unavoidable and fairly acute awareness of the mortification of the individual who is being discharged; a wish to offer partial, immediate reparation by guiltily enumerating all the presumed accomplishments of the one who is being summarily terminated; and the offer of the standard compensation in the form of severance pay and the willingness to provide a laudatory recommendation to prospective employers.

On the one hand, empathy is shown by the attempt to temper the disappointment and cushion the shock of the other with patent blandishments, such as, "I don't really think we're right for you and that you'd be happy if you stayed." On the other hand, such empathy, if not pseudo, can often simultaneously be self-serving inasmuch as the boss generally has the ulterior motive of tranquilizing the terminated employee in order to forestall a public display of retaliative anger or protracted, ostentatious sulking that would disrupt the customary work flow, while proving distinctly embarrassing to the company and potentially damaging to morale.

For all of these reasons, almost never does the person let go feel any true nurturance was received. Instead, the empathy in evidence is geared to the other's sensitivity and responsiveness to a painful loss of face and deference. The person qua person, other than as a reactor to a disturbing shift in power, does not figure in the equation. There seems little discernible interest in what significance the event—outside of the immediate dire consequences of loss of prestige, income, and so on—will hold in the mind of the person and in what way, for better or worse, her life course will now be altered. And, curiously, almost never is the event considered by the boss in the context of his present relationship with his ersatz employee. How does the manner, style, warmth or lack of it, and undeniable fact of the decision to terminate reflect on the history of the pair and what does it bode for the future?

It is in the nature of a blatant power operation, of course, for such interpersonal niceties to seem self-evidently irrelevant. And therein lies one of the sources of its ability to influence the other: by compelling him to think, primarily in terms of push and pull, levers and leverage, advantage and disadvantage, winner and loser, having face and losing face, so that when he does think of the relationship, he typically thinks of it resentfully, that is, in terms of the politics of power, which is a far cry from envisioning it in all of its multidimensions (only one of which is power). It follows it is also in the nature of power, and part of the power of power, that once it has reared its ugly head and the subordinate other has been officially disempowered, the underlying relationship as such is therefore tarnished and almost never can it go back—especially in regard to the possibilities of intimacy—to what it was before.

One of the great difficulties, as already mentioned, in parent-child relations when it comes to instructing, educating, disciplining, punishing, and ordering is to be able to put the obvious and enormous power differential in brackets so as to infuse the necessary doses of reparative empathy, and, accordingly, one of the reasons that so-called golden moments—when parent and child spontaneously, creatively, playfully take pleasure in one another's company—tend to be rare is that unresolved issues of power often tend to dominate.

As heir to this early familial difficulty, adult displays of empathy vis-à-vis power operations—especially those involving manifest inequities that are the product of discrepant role functioning—are too often limited to the understanding of the vicissitudes of power as they affect the self only in an immediate, worldly, and pragmatic fashion (and not to the needs of the true self, which are actually far more important at precisely this juncture).

With some justice, the preferred mode of interpersonal relating of someone who is engaged in a power play could be called using. Unconsciously, the interaction as such is reified as a commodity to be purchased at the lowest psychic cost. Competition, self-interest, and the desire to encroach upon the other's territory are seen as merely by-products of an underlying entrepreneurial agenda. So it is worth noting what the desire to use the other as product leaves out: a reciprocal urge to be used in turn, a curiosity in whatever can be obtained from the other regardless of whether it has any immediate practical benefits, a belief that something tangible can be learned from the other, that the future of the transaction may be much more important than the prospects of the present. In other words, use of the other may be something sufficiently complex that it has to be deferred, approached on its own terms, and allowed to evolve—that is, when it comes to interrelating as opposed to grasping and acquiring an object, one begins by building a foundation.

It follows that, sooner or later, there will be a dawning awareness that power plays are games no one can win. And it is a short step from that, as mentioned, to the realization that we live in a culture that is prone to the paranoid dread of being powerless.

chapter 4

paranoid secrecy

E very paranoid has a secret. Although obvious, it is surprising how much follows from that simple fact. We see at once that paranoid communication, by its nature, can be only elliptical if not radically asymmetrical. Almost always will the person who is relating in a guarded, paranoid fashion seem to be on a different wavelength. Statements or exchanges that generally connote mutuality, in their case, will prove to be counterfeit. Typically, once the conversation or interaction begins, there is a covert rush to attain premature closure. Analogous to Bion's schizophrenics who attack the links to thoughts, it could be said *the paranoid attacks interpersonal links.*

A variety of unconscious maneuvers are used to achieve this. By imparting, for example, a haughty tone of finality to the transaction, by bizarrely exaggerating or being grandiose about whatever one has done—as though to say, "Look what I did and pay attention to what I have accomplished"—the message is sent that it would be nothing less than an insult to pursue the matter further. (Of course, to the paranoid, it is a different story: Nothing seems more real and less grandiose, given the stress and effort that each minute part of a transaction seems to cost them, than the fact that whatever they do interpersonally is worthy of notice.)

In short, paranoid communication suggests there is a secret of sorts that needs to be maintained. Furthermore, the secret is what really matters and far outweighs whatever else is actually going on. This aura of ongoing hidden significance is what lends a spurious drama to even the blandest enactments of the characterologically paranoid person.

It follows paranoid secrecy can be intimidating and controlling. Secretive relating can be seen as a sign of the underlying rejection of the worth of the other. It not only implies there is nothing to be gained from frank disclosure but also suggests through its stubborn guardedness that any influence the other is likely to have is to be regarded as possibly toxic. Having a secret breaks up any simple flow or circuit of immediate contact. Instead, the relationship becomes that which exists between the holder of the secret and the secret and the observer of the secret and the secret rather than between self and other.

It is easy for someone who is strangely withholding to come across as being self-reliant in an intriguing way. A countersuspicion can grow that he may know something worthwhile—and, besides, it is practically impossible not to be suspicious of a secret. The other then begins to wonder: Why is the secret a secret? Is it because the person does not like, trust, or respect me enough to share it? Is it because the secret represents hostile intentions and there is fear of retaliation should this be discovered? Or does the secret refer only to its keeper?

In the typical scenario involving the perception of paranoid secrecy, there are three stages. The most benign is the first stage, when the other happens to notice a certain unexpected faltering or hesitancy betokening an inner conflict over how much to express. Often he or she may innocently inquire, "Is something wrong?" Very quickly then a point of no return is reached for the holder of the secret: If he reveals what is hidden, he can in one fell swoop diminish much of its power. If instead he elects, refuses, or is unable to disclose the hostile feelings, whether toward himself or the other, that he is harboring—what is at first perceived as perhaps an isolated train of thought—is immediately elevated into an attitudinal cast of mind. It follows the perception of intentional secretiveness is frightening because it always implies an indictment of the trustworthiness of the other. What it unconsciously suggests is that the *secret that is being withheld is the true nature of the relationship of the person with the other.*

Understandably, it is rare at such moments to comment, "You seem secretive." Much more common is it to begin to observe, silently and carefully, instances of its expression and to search for plausible explanations. Ironically, the observer of a secret over time becomes secretive, too.

Not surprisingly, one of the things the incipiently paranoid patient who enters therapy is most paranoid about is whether their prospective therapist will think she is paranoid. A central question, regardless of how professional or ethical her therapist appears to be, is whether he is someone to be trusted. And since, sooner or later, the patient who is feeling paranoid is going to project at least some of her paranoid ideations upon her therapist, there will be times when she strongly suspects her therapist of being secretly paranoid (a key symptom of which, of course, will be to wonder whether his patient is paranoid).

One of the first objects of the paranoid patient's search for significant clues will be the technique that is being used by the therapist. What, for example, is the real meaning of therapeutic silence: Is it the justifiable withholding required by the stance of neutrality? Is it contempt? Or is it indifference? Does the therapist, perhaps, *need* to project a blank screen in order to hide a disgusting self? Is the reason the therapist's comments, other than clarifying questions, are restricted to interpretation because the therapist believes he is better able to interpret psychic reality than the patient? What is the underlying point of the therapist's fixed policy concerning the time, fee, and cancellation and for whose benefit do the rules of the frame exist? Why did the therapist choose this profession and how is it possible in such a nonreciprocal setting to ever figure out if he or she has any genuine interest in the patient? Do therapists perhaps act in rule-bound ways because they are in reality pathetic social creatures, utterly lacking in spontaneity, who can function only under the protective façade of a precisely defined role?

The danger with such a paranoid patient is that her characteristic obsessive distancing, lack of contact, and covert hostility over time can engender self-doubt in the therapist: He may then begin to wonder, Does the patient mistrust me because she is paranoid or is it because I am unable to competently help her? In other words, the therapist becomes somewhat paranoid, which points to an essential feature of control games such as the power of paranoid secrecy to manipulate the other.

BECKY'S SECRET

She was one of the most intriguing patients I had ever met, her mystery all the more enhanced by the great secret she was carrying for the past fifteen years. Yet she was happy to speak, to touch someone with her palpable pain, to unpack it, to demystify it, and perhaps to find respite from what had been shadowing her since she was seventeen years old.

"From the dawn of my consciousness," exclaimed Becky, ever fond of waxing poetic, in response to my question as to when she first felt alienated from her family. One by one, she would link all of her troubles to lingering childhood memories of inexcusable family abuse. To her sadistic older brother, Jack, who freely tormented her as a little girl, and recklessly, incestuously pursued her as a young woman. To her pathetically self-absorbed, profoundly absent mother. To the father, who adored her but who, inexplicably and traumatically, died far too young. By twelve, in reaction to her losses, Becky had developed into a precociously aloof, self-reliant, athletically gifted, tomboyish girl: "a wild, forest child" (as she would put it) who loved to embark on protracted adventures in the outlying heavily wooded Californian suburbs in which she grew up, peddling her bicycle fearlessly into any territory she felt compelled to explore, perversely comforted by the thought that should something happen, no one would care.

Although increasingly mindful of the long, slow buildup of her homicidal rage, she continues to define herself by the explosive events of her seventeenth year, which, undeniably, had a life-changing effect. I could see that—fifteen years later—if only by the startling, mesmerizing immediacy with which she could effortlessly re-create her tormented adolescence. In yet one more flight from her true self, Becky had impulsively cut herself off from her California roots and migrated to New York. She hoped, like so many others before her, to find a new life as an artist. What she found, at first and for a long time afterward, like so many others before her, were odd jobs that she detested as a waitress, a telemarketer, a receptionist.

Becky's traumatic teenage eruption, the product of an intensely abusive, violent, incestuous family life, had resonated with me on a number of levels. For one thing, in the nearly two thousand patient intake interviews I had personally conducted, as just part of my training in an analytic institute, I had been privy to the sad stories of countless survivors of incest. And in the years I had spent as a volunteer counselor for the Home Advisory and Service Council—created as a last bastion for battered women from their sometimes criminally assaultive spouses—I had been therapeutically indoctrinated in the kind of savage beatings, hospitalization, even potential homicide that could readily ensue from a history of unresolved, unbridled, family abuse.

But there was more. Becky's arrival in my office had coincided with some increasingly disturbing social phenomena: the growing link, for example, between sports and violence, typified by the rape trial and conviction of Mike Tyson; immortalized by the nationally televised car chase of O. J. Simpson with a gun pointed to his head, the epochal trial, and yearlong media circus that followed; and currently kept alive (as I write this) by the indictment on rape charges of mega basketball star, Kobe Bryant. Coupled with this, there was pop culture's greedy cinematic exploitation of violence for violence's sake, of the most grossed-out, depraved human relationships conceivable, in the shameless race for the imperious, bottom line, corporate dollar.

The catalyst for me was the Columbine shootings and the media furor it provoked. It seemed the whole country in a collective panic had gone into crisis-intervention mode, demanding impossible answers and instant results. As a therapist, I could only note how all of the countless solutions that were endlessly proposed, in one form or another, were of a political nature. Massive national forces—military, educational, social, religious—were to be mobilized and coordinated into a proselytizing war against teenage violence. If ever there were to be a top-down preemptive strike, this was it. Overlooked was that the political solution, admittedly the single most potent factor, is but the last link in a very long and convoluted chain of events. If years of intensive psychotherapeutic work with patients teaches anything, it teaches that the manifold antecedents, the roots of any profoundly meaningful behavior—including even the seemingly senseless, homicidal assault on innocent bystanders—goes back a very long way to the beginnings, the origins of the human personality.

More than any other patient I had seen, Becky seemed to epitomize these themes. She represented for me the crucial missing link between a disturbed, abusive family background and the inevitable toxic transmission of ungovernable violent impulses. Her remarkable recovery, however, from a near-total breakdown as a teenager had shed a powerful light on the intricate dynamics and interplay between psychical collapse and the forces of inner rebirth. Especially important to me was the astonishing breadth of her radical mistrust, how her ever-vigilant paranoid suspiciousness, her unconscious conviction, and her knee-jerk reaction that she was forever cut off from the comfort and nurturance of genuine human contact, seemed to shadow her thoughts and feelings, everything she did and did not do. In short, Becky seemed memorably to particularize all the themes of this book. I saw her not as a clinical aberration, as a freak of sorts, but as a painfully graphic prototype and near casualty of the paranoia of everyday life. The acts of fury she was driven to as a hopelessly bereft teenager seemed but the tragic outcome of an unbearable alienation from her family, her friends, her therapist, and most of all herself.

Needless to say, the subsequent events of September 11—how our understandable national rage at an unprecedented public massacre had obliterated any possible interest in the ordinary paranoia that can so readily fan the flames of our global fantasies of imminent terrorist destruction—had only reinforced my sense of the relevance of these themes. Almost from the first moment I set eyes on her some years ago, I had an intuition I might one day want to write about Becky. Now, it seemed, a golden opportunity had arrived. But how exactly to do it?

THE PLAY'S THE THING

First, I was mindful that a quiet revolution has been taking place in the mental health profession regarding the presentation of clinical cases. No longer is the dry-as-dust, literal, chronological narrative de rigeur. More and more psychiatrists, psychotherapists, and especially psychoanalysts are making use of the postmodern plurality of forms available for personal expression. Underlying this is the increasingly accepted idea that there are multiple aspects, many perspectives, numerous avenues of approach—in short, more roads than one leading to the hallowed *truth*.

If anything, here was an emerging narrative philosophy that I had already long subscribed to. My first book, *Portrait of the Artist as a Young Patient* (1992), had been devoted to understanding the importance of creative processes not only in artists but in all aspects of the therapeutic situation. In *The Singles Scene* (1994), I had adopted an ethnographic approach. In *The Dark Side of the Analytic Moon* (1996), I had presented my nearly ten-year odyssey in analytic training institutes in the shape of an autobiographical memoir. In *The Puppeteers* (1999), I had presented my very long study of a manic depressive cult leader in the guise of a novella. And in my most recent book, *Like a Movie: Contemporary Relationships without the Popcorn* (2004), I had taken the iconic cultural image of the silver screen as a profound unconscious metaphor for the breakdown of intimacy in our time.

It was, in fact, this very last book that led me to what I would regard as an inspiring idea for Becky. Why not, I thought, present the typically intense visual immediacy, the distortion of the banal small details and coincidences of daily living into cinematic hyperdramatic scenarios—so characteristic of the paranoia of everyday life—into a more appropriately matching form, that is, an authentically *visual* medium? In short, why not present Becky's story, to both convey how she actually lived and experienced it, in the form of a screenplay?

After all, I reminded myself, I had spent many years treating actors, screenwriters, composers, and directors. I had been forced to acquaint myself with the peculiar dynamics and formal requirements of superintending the birth and successful delivery of a film project. My twin roles as creative writer and psychotherapist of artists had, I thought, uniquely prepared me for such an innovative venture.

Thus inspired, my first draft of Becky's story was in the form of a screenplay, intended as a very small independent film for an audience who conceivably might be interested in a thoughtful, in-depth study of the roots of violence. Also, I very much wanted to portray the subtleties of the psychotherapeutic situation with an authenticity and respect that I personally had yet to see in the ever-popular cinematic incarnations of the therapeutic persona.

Cast as a screenplay, therefore, Becky's story was sent out in the cold world. Over time, to my surprise, agents, managers, production companies, and publishers expressed interest. There was talk of indeed turning it into a small independent film, of trying to dress it up and sensationalize it for a more mainstream commercial audience, or of just publishing it instead as an original, literary screenplay.

In the end, I would decide against all these ideas. The right place I realized was here, in a clinical book. I would of course first have to fictionalize the names of the characters (e.g., Becky Jamison), and I would have to carefully disguise the pivotal homicidal violence—because it is so very revealing of the identity of the real person involved—that drives the action.

So here, then, in the original form that I wrote it, is the story of Becky Jamison. While the names and certain plot incidentals have been necessarily fictionalized, the presentation of themes and underlying dynamics are as true to life, I think, as anything I have written. With hindsight, I now see it was no coincidence that I chose to end my book the same way I began it—by calling upon the iconic medium of film to evoke the most interior, most hidden, and deepest of feelings.

SOMEONE TO PROTECT ME

FADE IN ON

At first the entire screen is white, then...

We see half of a man, standing in pressed gray slacks and seen only from about the waist down at a sideways angle with upper body and feet entirely cut off from view. About six inches away a solid wooden structure, a foot or so in diameter, rises in tandem to the legs of the man and is similarly without an identifiable top and bottom. The two partial images are each framed like a picture, although they are real and set almost in the middle of the still largely white screen. As such, they are as they have been described and do not acquire any specific meaning until...

A second image, similarly framed, appears to the right of this first image. It is a woman's face, strong and alive, looking at and studying this first image with an almost predatory intensity. It should be said that the effect here is intended to be odd, perhaps obsessional and definitely not comical, as the significance of her strange staring will increasingly become clear as the plot unfolds. Now...

At the bottom of the still largely white screen, a row of black circles appears. At this point, the magic of the CAMERA takes over and:

The black circles DISSOLVE into the backs of human heads, which belong to the audience members of the front row who are looking up at the speaker at the lectern, Dan Rainer. The CAMERA

PULLS BACK TO REVEAL

INT. SILVER OAKS GYMNASIUM. DAY.

Dan Rainer is at the lectern. Just under six feet, about thirty-five, he is handsome in a very relaxed sort of way, trim without having to work at it, unassuming, sincere, and strikingly thoughtful looking. The kind of person who would pause for a moment before giving the answer to someone who had just requested the time of day. A man who, quite simply, loves to think and will find any pretext to do so. It is apparent he is speaking in earnest, with an occasional expressive gesture of his hands, but his voice, although faintly heard, is still inaudible.

Now behind Dan, the CAMERA PANS the audience, allowing us to see what he is looking at. In the first row, among others, are Det. Ray Burns, Det. Joe Giminoni, Principal Lester Watkins, and, occupying the end seat—in a power pants suit, around thirty, with an alert, dynamic, bold face—is Pat McDougal, the woman who has been looking at the front of Dan's pants. In the middle rows are teachers, counselors, and parents who have assembled to hear his talk on "The Roots of Violence," with here and there a random pair of giggly teenage girls who have come to see whether the speaker is the heartthrob they say he is. While in the corner seats of the back row are two senior students at Silver Oaks: Bobby Rodgers, fidgeting in his chair and looking at his friend Becky Jamison, who, tall, slim, with blondish hair, is perched in her chair with her knees drawn up almost to her chin as she stares straight ahead.

The CAMERA pauses to look at Becky, who is looking at the speaker. Her face is plain, but quite pretty, open, and intense. Her thoughts here, as always, seem elsewhere. Her expression is a captivating mixture of puzzlement, pain, and determination, as though there is some deep childhood hurt, some inner mystery she is trying to get to, but which keeps eluding her. To her immediate left is Bobby Rodgers. His shortness, unfortunately, is his outstanding physical characteristic, which he tries to compensate for with a nimble intelligence that can find something of interest in almost anything in his surroundings, and especially in whatever his friend Becky Jamison does or does not do. Not surprisingly, although nearly inseparable, they are so physically disparate that they are often referred to as the odd couple.

The CAMERA returns to the speaker, whose voice finally can be heard.

DAN
(stealing a glance at the clock on the wall)

Time for one more question.

Like a shot, Pat McDougal's arm shoots up.

DAN
(seeing her and pointing in her direction)

Yes?

PAT

You seem against armed guards and metal detectors. But, in light of the national nightmare following Columbine, don't you think we can use them, if only as a public relations ploy?

DAN
(nodding in appreciation of her question)

I suppose if you look at it as someone's finger poised on the trigger, it's natural to think that way. After all, as counselors and teachers, you and I usually arrive very late in the story. But if you look at it as just the final link in a long and complicated chain whose roots go back at least as far as early childhood, then you get a different picture. What you get is....

Dan's voice momentarily trails off here, as the CAMERA briefly returns to Pat's face, where there is the same hunter's look as her eyes flick down and she stares, as before, at the front of Dan's pants. And we see again, but only for a second, the identical image with which the movie began. The CAMERA then quickly travels up to Pat's face as she lifts her eyes in the direction of the speaker, who is now in the homestretch of his talk.

DAN (CONT'D)

A peculiar inner world, populated with tortured images of predators and prey, persecutors and victims, devils and angels, good and evil, each violent universe very different from the others. To understand the lone event, or series of events, among thousands of competing events, that acts as a catalyst, that serves to transform a turbulent inner world into a nightmarish outer one, as in Columbine, takes patience. To enter that world takes time. You can't do that with armed guards and metal detectors. So, as I see it, the real problem is not the trigger on the gun, but the trigger in the mind.... Thank you.

Brief but enthusiastic applause as Dan, who hates public appearances but feels ethically obligated to do them, makes a beeline for the exit to his immediate right. And almost makes it before he is intercepted by...

PRINCIPAL WATKINS

Fine talk, Dan, but I want to continue this debate with you in person.

DAN
(managing to be polite without breaking stride)

I would like to very much. I promise I will.

Dan almost makes it when Pat McDougal, having caught up with him, stops him in his tracks. She grasps him firmly by the arm from behind and does not let go until he has turned around—not knowing whether or not he should be miffed at the bold way in which she has arrested his flight—to face her.

At the far end of the gymnasium, about to exit herself, Becky, who has been observing Dan over her shoulder, is also arrested by this forceful act.

PAT
(sensing Dan's confusion, with an immediately charming smile)

I'm sorry to have captured you that way. But I have something terribly urgent that I need to talk to you about.

DAN

I don't seem to recognize you.

PAT

I'm Pat McDougal, probation officer. We never actually met, although we passed each other a number of times in the corridor. A month or so ago, we spoke twice on the telephone regarding Richie Deevers, the felon who boosted a car from the Silver Oaks parking lot.

DAN
(remembering)

Oh, yes. You're with the division of juvenile offenders at
Silver Oaks.

PAT

I head up that division. And when I'm not doing that, I
teach self-defense at the police academy.

DAN

Oh? For women?

PAT

Men, too.

DAN
(relaxing a bit and offering his first smile)

That explains your grip. What's the urgent matter you
want to discuss?

PAT

A case I have to present that is giving me an awful lot of
trouble. I really need some help.

DAN

Give me a call and we'll set something up.

PAT

Unfortunately, time is not on my side. I have to present
tomorrow morning.

DAN

You want to speak on the telephone tonight?

PAT
(smiling)

At the risk of sounding incredibly pushy, I'd like, I'm begging you, if at all possible, for a personal consultation tonight.

DAN

Tonight?

PAT

I'll pay you. Name your fee. Double your fee, triple it, and I'll pay you.

DAN
(persuaded in spite of himself)

Okay. I'm free at eight o'clock. The address is...

PAT
825 Corona Drive
(then, sensing his dismay)

We got a department memo listing everyone's address so that Christmas cards could be exchanged. Remember?

DAN

Yes. Okay, I'll see you then.

As they shake on it, there is a CLOSE UP of Pat's hand as it slowly, confidently, and purposefully takes hold of Dan's fingers. At last, he makes his exit as Pat, who has accomplished what she set out to do, watches him leave.

PAT
(to herself)

I'd like to find out what your trigger is.

And at the other end of the gymnasium floor, Becky watches Dan leave.

BOBBY
(petulantly)

I thought you were in a big hurry to get out of here.

BECKY

Sorry, Bobby. Let's go.

The CAMERA returns to Becky's face for a lingering look at the face that almost immediately will reappear at the extreme bottom left-hand edge of the screen as . .
THE CREDITS ROLL.

They are accompanied by a connected series of frames—which start at the bottom left and travel clockwise, up the side of the screen, across the top, down the right-hand side, and to the bottom—each of which depicts a fairly typical scene from a day in the life of Becky Jamison. Thus, in the first frame, we see Becky, like a lonely long-distance runner, jogging through the early morning streets of the sleepy California suburb in which she lives. Then she is walking through the corridor of Silver Oaks, turning heads as she goes. Then sitting in the library, enraptured by the book she is reading. Then dreamily lounging in the back row of a classroom, lost in the private world of her own thoughts. Then driving by herself. Then standing upright on the bare back of her favorite horse, her arms extended on either side of her for balance, as they canter in a field. Then, in a gym, with Martin, a black belt, steadying the heavy bag as she delivers one after another a series of very hard and beautifully executed roundhouse and high front karate kicks. And, finally, pausing on the front porch of her house to look back at her mother, who has just called her from the door. These are moving frames, and as the credits roll, they roll. So that if the viewer were to fix on any one of them—say, Becky performing her trick of balancing herself in an upright position on the bare back of a moving horse—he or she would see a continuation of the action for as long as the credits are being shown.

As the CREDITS end, the CAMERA selects the final frame—Becky leaving her house—moves it to the center of the screen, inflates it to normal size, and the movie proper begins.

EXT. HOUSE DAY.

MRS. JAMISON (O.S.)

Oh, Becky!

She stops and turns toward her mother, who has hurriedly appeared in the doorway with a last-minute thought. Mrs. Jamison is a small, mousy-looking, scrunched-over woman. She seems frozen in a posture of extreme helplessness that she adopted shortly after her husband unexpectedly died of a massive heart attack five years ago and ever since has stubbornly refused to relinquish.

BECKY

What is it?

MRS. JAMISON

You didn't tell me where you were going.

BECKY

Out.

MRS. JAMISON

To the gym?

BECKY

No.

MRS. JAMISON

Are you going to ride your horse?

BECKY

The stable is closed, Mom, after 7 p.m.

MRS. JAMISON

For a drive, then?

BECKY

Just out.

MRS. JAMISON

Be careful, then.

Becky does not answer but continues down the porch steps, when she is stopped again.

MRS. JAMISON

I almost forgot the most important thing.

BECKY

Yes?

MRS. JAMISON

Your brother Jack is coming here.

BECKY

When?

MRS. JAMISON

Day after tomorrow.

BECKY
(irritated)

But I thought he was supposed to be at Berkeley.

MRS. JAMISON

He is. He's coming here to help straighten out Jane Foley's brother, Sam, who's in a lot of trouble.

BECKY

Is he going to stay over at Jane's house?

MRS. JAMISON

He's going to stay here.

BECKY

Great.

Free at last, Becky gets in her car, briefly acknowledges Mrs. Morris, the neighbor, who is taking out the garbage in the house across the street, while vigorously waving at her, and drives off. We see her as she travels through beautiful, tree-lined streets. But this is no idle pleasure drive. Instead, the mood here and the atmosphere are one of obsession, and the music should reflect this. Becky, after all, is in the grip of dark inner forces that she barely understands. Forces that are repudiated by a kind of beatific smile playing on her lips, as she reminds herself that she is headed toward a destination at the end of which is a satisfaction that at least partially has never failed to calm her down.

Now she looks out the window to her right. She sees a twelve-year-old girl riding a bicycle that, remarkably, is keeping pace with her car and even more remarkably looks almost exactly the way she did when she was twelve. Same blondish hair pulled back in a ponytail, same sweater and jeans she used to wear. And the same obsession. For this twelve-year-old, who is furiously pedaling her bike, seems no less eager to get to where she is going than Becky now is. So not surprisingly, they exchange glances and silently acknowledge one another. At this point, it is not clear how this little girl managed to materialize by the side of her car, and how, when Becky again looks, she has managed to disappear. That is, although she does not seem to be troubled by or to question the girl's amazing appearance, the viewer has no way of knowing whether Becky is imagining, remembering, or hallucinating what she apparently sees.

She arrives at last at her destination. An isolated, treeless, and darkened dead-end street. She parks her car and faces the other way. And so does the twelve-year-old, who pulls up and parks her bicycle by the car and pointing in the same direction. Feeling relaxed for perhaps the first time, Becky leans back, lounging in her car seat the way someone does who is luxuriously curling up with popcorn at a drive-in theater. And the girl does the same... before disappearing. We now see what Becky is looking at with such anticipation and excitement.

EXT. RANCH HOUSE.

This is a low, one-story structure, with a large living room window, brightly lit and quite visible from the vantage point that Becky now occupies. Just in time she seems to notice the man entering the room, a man whom, although she cannot distinguish his features from a distance, she knows by heart. It is the person she has come to look at from afar. What she is not prepared for, and did not want to see, is the woman who closely follows the man into the room. Becky cannot see, but feels she must, what this woman looks like, who she is, and whether or not she knows her.

So as her hand drifts uncertainly to her pocketbook, finds and retrieves (CLOSE UP ON) a pair of binoculars, she is faced with a moral dilemma. She is well aware that to spy on two unsuspecting people in this manner is a despicable violation of a person's right to privacy. She is also aware that if she refuses to satisfy her morbid curiosity, her mind will be tortured with thoughts for weeks, perhaps months on end. To help her, therefore, to resolve this dilemma and to make a decision, or perhaps to avoid making a decision, she conjures up from the past a very vivid and telling memory.

INT. OFFICE DAY, FIVE YEARS AGO.

Dan Rainer and Becky Jamison, age twelve, whom we now know was the girl on the bike, are seated in facing chairs.

DAN
(looking around)

Becky, I looked outside my window last night, and I saw
you hanging around my house again.

BECKY
(defiantly)

It wasn't me.

DAN

Yes, it was you.

BECKY

You couldn't see because there wasn't enough light to see.

DAN

A car came by and threw all the light that was necessary.

BECKY

It still wasn't me.

DAN

Do you know what someone who keeps hanging around
someone else's house and spies on them is called?

BECKY

What?

DAN

A stalker!

BECKY

(unable to suppress a laugh)

Dan, a twelve-year-old kid can't be a stalker!

DAN

(trying hard to remain stern)

All right, then, do you know what a Peeping Tom is?

BECKY

Someone like a character in a comic book.

DAN

A Peeping Tom is someone who secretly looks in the windows of other people's private homes. If you're eighteen and do it, it's considered a crime.

BECKY

(getting the point)

Alright, Mr. Rainer, it still wasn't me, but, since I see it offends you, if it was me, I promise I won't do it anymore.

DAN

(still parental)

It does offend me, Miss Jamison, and I would appreciate that very much.

But Becky, no longer able to resist her impulses, cannot keep a promise she has kept for five years. Slowly, she lifts the binoculars to her eyes.

INT. LIVING ROOM, FIRST FRAMED IN THE BINOCULARS' JOINED OVALS. Then, we move inside, where Dan Rainer and Pat McDougal are facing one another.

DAN

Okay, have a seat.

PAT

If you don't mind, I think better on my feet.

DAN
(a bit unnerved)

Suit yourself.

A series of QUICK CUTS follow from Dan and Pat, who seemingly are discussing Pat's problem in earnest, although we cannot hear them, to Becky, who, with the help of her binoculars, has immediately recognized Pat McDougal as the woman who was talking to Dan earlier today, and back again. Then, the professional part of their conversation apparently over, we can now hear Dan's voice.

DAN

Well, I think you have a good handle on the case.

PAT

Thank you. You were very helpful. Now, name your fee.

DAN
(waving it off)

Oh, no fee. Chalk it up to professional courtesy. We're on the same team, after all.

Dan gets up from his chair, thinking the visit is now over, and offers his hand. Pat does not take it, instead looks at him in a fascinated sort of way. Dan is puzzled. Her case in no way merited a personal consultation, and now he wonders what this odd woman is really up to.

DAN
(nervously)

Anything else?

For a moment Pat hesitates. She has not received the telltale sign or clue that Dan is attracted to her that she has been waiting for. But, she is a woman who is used to getting whatever she wants, and she is not afraid to take matters into her own hands.

PAT
(suddenly moving closer to Dan)

Well, there's this.

Firmly, boldly, she places her hands on the sides of Dan's face and kisses him, her tongue, meeting with only minimal resistance as it slides almost immediately into his mouth. It is a long, sexual, erotic, very intense kiss, and Dan, in spite of himself and against his better judgment, finds himself quickly responding. Her hand now wanders down to the front of his pants, locates his penis, the object of her obsession, which it deftly begins to pat and massage.

PAT
(in a strangely husky voice)

I've wanted to do that for the longest time.

But it is too much and too fast for Dan. Gently he tries to dissuade her, then push her back, but to his surprise finds he cannot budge her. So he steps back himself to escape her advances.

DAN

Don't you think we should talk first?

PAT

We just had a conversation.

And she does what to Dan is an utterly astonishing thing. Slipping her foot behind his legs, she quickly takes him down, pushes him to the floor, and straddles him with both her legs.

DAN
(angrily blushing and feeling it is imperative that he protest)

Is that what you do in self-defense class?

PAT

Shut up, Dan. You're already captured, remember? I'm not going to let you get away now.

She kisses him a second time, but longer and more sexually than before. Although Dan fleetingly wonders if she may not be disturbed or possibly dangerous, he again succumbs to the spell of the most liberated, boldly erotic woman he has ever encountered. He sinks back, deciding to go with the flow. And instantly sensing this, her nimble fingers begin to unbuckle and unbutton his pants. As though there is no time to waste, her head moves down, disappearing from view. Instead the CAMERA focuses on the face of Dan, who is caught up in both the thrill and the male fantasy of wild oral sex. But very shortly, the face of Pat McDougal, blazing with desire, rises into view.

PAT

Well, so much for your resistance.

She removes her panties with one hand, and inserts Dan's member with the other. She mounts him and rhythmically, in complete control as Dan leans back and surrenders to her irresistible dominance, she begins to gyrate above him.

Briefly, the CAMERA returns to Becky, who, stunned and sickened by what she has seen clearly, begins to lower her binoculars. But she, too, as much as Pat and Dan, in her own way is caught in the grip of lust and cannot resist again raising her binoculars.

The CAMERA returns to Dan and Pat, who almost in unison, reach a climax together.

PAT
(tilting her head back and screaming triumphantly)

Yes!

As quickly as she began, she finishes. She dismounts, gives Dan a last, businesslike kiss; puts her panties back on; collects her purse; and walks to the door. Dan slowly redresses, begins to sit up, and stares after her. At the door, Pat smiles and looks down at him with benign amusement, the closest she has come, or can come, to affection and tenderness. She opens the door and pauses.

PAT

Well, I hate to fuck and run. But I really do have a lot of
paperwork to do tonight. Dan, please get up off the floor,
and stop looking so ashamed of yourself. You just met your
first dominatrix, that's all. Trust me, you're going to like it.
I'll call, I promise. Until then, sweet dreams, pretty boy.

But Dan, still sitting on the floor, just looks at her and does not know what to say to this bizarre woman who has overpowered him emotionally and managed to seduce him with brutal efficiency. He watches her go with relief. His sense of humiliation grows and grows. Upset and angry, he gets up from the floor, walks across the room, and sits down at his desk. He clenches his fist as though in a gesture of protest, then buries his face in both hands as he tries to make sense of what has just happened to him.

The CAMERA returns to Becky, who, dumbfounded and repulsed by what she has seen, relinquishes her binoculars.

BECKY
(very upset, to herself)

You cunt...you skanky, unbelievable cunt!

She watches in a stunned way as Pat McDougal, who is leaving Dan Rainer's house, hurries with a brisk, marchlike stride to her car, which is parked directly in front. Without thinking, Becky, driven by a new impulse, starts up her own car and as Pat's car moves forward, so does hers. For several blocks, they travel in this fashion, with Becky carefully matching the pace of the car ahead of her. She tells herself she is only embarking on an adventure, doing something she has never done. Tailing another car. She is aware that her heart is beating rapidly. Aware that she must learn more about who this frightening woman is.

Now we see Pat, listening to and enjoying some jazz on the radio and seemingly savoring her latest conquest. She rubs and pats her lips together, then glances in the rearview mirror to check her makeup. But she sees something unexpected that freezes her. Another car suspiciously maintaining a steady distance behind her. To make sure, she executes as casually as she can a series of left- and right-hand turns that is repeated by the car behind her, the car that she now has no doubt is following her. Her mood darkens, her face grows hard as she almost instantly becomes combat ready. With her right hand, she fishes in her pocketbook, finds her handgun, and places it on the seat beside her. When she finds what she is looking for—a sprawling, two-story house, half hidden by a number of large trees with overhanging branches— she draws to a stop, calmly gets out, and disappears in the driveway.

Behind her, Becky stops, too. She crouches down and peers through the windshield. She tries anxiously to pick out the shape of Pat McDougal between the gaps in the trees, to make sure this is the house she lives in or is going to and that she has gone safely inside. But she cannot make out the doorway. So, with her heart beating faster and faster, she crouches even lower behind the wheel of her car and waits to see if she is returning. Five, ten, fifteen minutes pass this way, and Becky can wait no longer. Slowly she gets out of her car. Softly she closes her door. Cautiously, clutching her purse, perhaps for security, she crosses the one-hundred-and-fifty-foot span that separates the two vehicles. She does not know what she is looking for. Some sign, perhaps some clue that can give her just a little bit more information as to who the mysterious woman is. Finally, after what seems an eternity, she reaches Pat McDougal's car. She studies the license plate. It tells her nothing. She examines the vehicle. It tells her nothing. She looks in the backseat, the driver's seat, and the passenger seat, none of which tell her anything. Her investigation over, she decides to return to her own car.

But she does not see and does not hear the woman who slips from the shadows and comes up behind her.

PAT

What are you looking for?

BECKY
(jumping about a foot)

I wasn't looking for anything. I was just taking a stroll.

PAT
(stepping closer)

I watched you in the rearview mirror. You were following me for about six blocks.

BECKY
(panicking because she knows she is caught and beginning to stutter)

I-I know I was b-behind you. B-but I was just going in the same direction. I wasn't following you.

Impatient, Pat suddenly slaps Becky across the face. Very hard. Instinctively, Becky's right hand flies up to retaliate, but Pat easily parries it. She then grabs Becky by the front of her sweater and starts to pull her toward her. But Becky, enraged by the contact and no longer afraid, voluntarily moves closer.

PAT

I'm going to ask you again. Why were you following me?

BECKY

I saw you. I watched what you did.

PAT

You watched me?

BECKY

I saw you with Dan Rainer just now.

PAT

You were outside the window, watching?

BECKY

I saw you make him have sex with you. You seduced him!

PAT
(laughing)

Is that what they call it these days?

PAT
(noticing for the first time Becky's blue-and-gold school button) [CLOSE UP]

And who are you? Some lovesick high school pussy that he's been banging between patients?

BECKY
(indignant)

I don't even know him.

PAT

Oh, no? Well, then we'll have to tell him he has a secret admirer who likes to stand outside his window and watch him fuck.

BECKY
(beginning to panic)

Leave me alone, lady. I didn't do anything to you.

PAT

Tell me, when you were watching us fuck, did your little heart go pitty patter, wishing it had been you?

BECKY
(now enraged)

Fuck you!

PAT

All right. Enough of this. Let's see some ID, young woman.

Pat McDougal arrogantly and mistakenly assumes that Becky, because she knows who Dan Rainer is, also knows that she is an officer of the court. She reaches for her purse and tries to begin opening it up, expecting little if any physical resistance from Becky. But Becky jerks back, trying to extricate her purse in earnest from Pat's grasp. A furious tug of war ensues, during which Pat's handgun falls from her jacket pocket to the ground, but neither of them notices this. Finally, Becky breaks free and turns to run toward her car. But Pat, for the first time beginning to take Becky seriously as a physical adversary, catches her by her ponytail and violently yanks her head back.

PAT

I'm not through with you, bitch.

Becky relaxes, as though compliantly, enough to make Pat relax her grip, whereupon Becky suddenly kicks her in the stomach. It is a kick that surprises and hurts Pat's feelings more than it does her stomach. And it is now that Becky, for the first time, notices the handgun lying in the street and wonders if her life may be in danger. An untimely distraction that allows

Pat, having gathered herself, to deliver a terrific short right, executed like a boxer. It lands flush in Becky's face, drives her head back, and almost breaks her nose. For a moment, Becky sees some stars. Blood begins to trickle from her nose; she starts to go down. But she is much stronger than she looks and more resilient, and she knows she cannot afford to fall. So she steadies herself and resolves to stand her ground and protect herself. And an eerie calm, as it does whenever she makes this kind of a decision, takes hold of her.

PAT

Come over here, you little bitch. You just kicked the wrong woman in the stomach. I'm busting you.

Becky, who continues to not understand this woman is an officer of the court, as though in obedience, steps toward her. While Pat, certain the fight is over, removes from a pocket of her jacket a pair of handcuffs and prepares to arrest her. It is a second untimely distraction that Becky exploits to deliver a high front karate kick, perfectly executed, that Pat never sees coming. Which lands smack on her jaw, snapping her head back with the force of a powerful uppercut. Almost instantaneously it renders Pat motionless, statuesque, her eyes glazed over. Becky turns and madly runs toward her car. But after about fifteen feet, while glancing back to make sure that Pat is not in pursuit, she sees something that stops her dead in her tracks. It is Pat, still frozen, her jaw oddly moving, as she begins to tremble in grotesque, stutter-like steps, the way a prize fighter does who is reacting in a delayed fashion to a knockout punch that has just been delivered. For a terrible moment, Becky wonders if she should rush to her aid, if she should dare to take the risk that she may somehow recover and try to shoot her. But then Pat crashes sideways, like a tree being felled, in the direction of her car and her right temple sickeningly smashes into the front fender and bounces off. She rolls over on her back with her arms by her side and lies perfectly still.

Becky runs toward her. She feels her pulse but realizes she does not know how to take one. Her hands flutter up and down as she wonders whether CPR, which she has never done anyway, is the thing to do here. But she tries it, digging both palms rhythmically for several minutes into Pat's motionless chest. Then, she gently pries open her now-swollen jaw, places her mouth on hers, and begins to blow. Suddenly, blood, welling up from Pat's mouth, spurts into Becky's mouth. Horrified, she jerks backward, nearly throwing up. But she sees for the first time the handcuffs lying on the ground—which together with the handgun begin to suggest a nightmarish thought. Quickly, Becky searches through the pockets of Pat's jacket until she finds the wallet she is looking for. She opens it and sees that what she dreaded is indeed true.

CLOSE UP POLICE BADGE WITH PHOTO OF PAT McDOUGAL.

BECKY
(to herself)

What have I gotten myself into?

Stunned, she returns to her car, gets in, and drives off.

EXT. PAYPHONE/STREET. FIFTEEN MINUTES LATER.

BECKY
(shaking)

Hello, I want to report an accident. A woman is lying in the street in a pool of blood...near the corner of Corona and Glover Street.... She looks badly hurt...so please hurry.

Becky hangs up, gets back in her car, and drives off.
EXT. STREET. CRIME SCENE. ONE HOUR LATER.

There are yellow police lines. Two policemen, Det. Burns and Det. Giminoni. An ambulance, paramedics, a doctor, all milling about. Two hundred feet away, furtively hiding behind a tree in complete darkness, by the side of her car, now and then using her binoculars, is Becky Jamison. And these are the images culled from hundreds that will long haunt her: A doctor applying a stethoscope to the chest of Pat McDougal and shaking his head. A body bag being zipped up. But most of all, a policeman, squatting in the street, and calling attention to the blue-and-gold Silver Oaks button that he has found. Touching her sweater, she now realizes she has lost her button. A terrifying realization that propels her to get back in her car and, as stealthily as she possibly can, drive off. But Detective Burns, in the still night air, hears the engine start up and quickly turns in its direction. He stares as hard as he can at the back of the retreating car. He wonders for a moment if it is worth it to order a pursuit, but then he returns to the crime scene.

EXT. NIGHT. BECKY DRIVING. TWENTY MINUTES LATER.

She is crying as she drives.

BECKY
(to herself)

What am I going to do now?

As though to find solace in the lonely night, Becky looks out the window and sees herself as a twelve-year-old, wildly pedaling her bicycle. Once again they exchange glances, and she suddenly remembers as a child, after she had secretly and naughtily spied on Dan Rainer's house, how terrified she had been that she would be discovered, how desperate she had been to get home without being caught. However, there is to be no solace in this memory, she realizes, as she watches her twelve-year-old self accelerate, outdistance the car, and disappear into the darkness. And accepting that she is truly alone, that she has only herself to rely upon, she formulates a desperate plan and then feverishly drives home to execute it.

INT. JAMISON HOME. FORTY MINUTES LATER.

Tiptoeing like a cat burglar, Becky goes up the stairs and listens by her mother's bedroom door until she hears the familiar snoring. Then, she goes into her room, turns on the light, locks the door. Quickly she digs out the only battered suitcase she has from the bottom of her closet and packs it with whatever she thinks she needs for her imagined flight. As impulsively as she formulated her plan, she changes it. Sitting down on her bed, for the first time in this insane night, she considers, evaluates, and weighs her options.

BECKY
(to herself, softly)

It was self-defense....
(a beat) No one, of course, will ever believe me....
(a beat) And I can never tell anyone....
(a beat) But no one saw me....
(a beat) There's nothing to link me to Pat McDougal.
(a beat) Except a school button. Of which there are
thousands. (then, trying to pluck the best advice from the
countless crime novels she has read)
So do everything you always do and act normal.

What follows now are a series of QUICK CUTS as we see Becky: Montage: Unpacking her suitcase. Go to the refrigerator, make an icepack, which she applies to the puffy areas around her face. Gently pull on and examine her nose in the bathroom mirror to see if it is broken. Search for and find the bloodstains on her sweater and sneakers. Locate the closest approximations she can come up with in her skimpy wardrobe. Pack the discarded clothes in an extra book bag, which she hides on a top shelf corner in her closet. Steal into the bathroom, lock the door, leave the lights out. Shower hastily, feverishly scrubbing her body, as though to wash away the stains and memories of an evil night. And, finally, return to her room, lock the door, with the light still off, and sit on her bed in the dark, content for the moment she has done what she could. (THE QUICK CUTS stop here.)

On a bedside stand sits a treasured picture: herself as an eleven-year-old proudly straddling the shoulders of a joyful father. Becky picks up the framed photo, fondling it. She does not need to see it. And exhausted, but too terrified to sleep, to dream, her mind drifts back to a happier time.

INT. JAMISON HOME, DAY. SIX YEARS AGO.

Mr. Jamison, a splendidly built, tall man, filled with ebullient energy, is sitting at the breakfast table, wondering where Becky is. Jack, his fourteen-year-old son, already muscularly developed with a precociously powerful chest, dark, darting eyes, an angry, angular face, and a frame that seems always coiled and ready for action, is looking at his father and trying to get his attention. Mrs. Jamison, mousey as usual, is serving food.

> BECKY
> (O.S.)

Ahhhhh ... ahhhhh ... ahhhhh ... ahhhhh ...

> MR. JAMISON
> (turning in the direction of the noise)

Is that Becky?

Mr. Jamison gets up and walks to the foyer, where he discovers his daughter, who apparently has just negotiated the entire, single flight of stairs, walking on her hands, her legs straight up in the air, with the knees bent slightly backwards for balance.

> MR. JAMISON
> (obviously delighted)

Who taught you how to do that?

> BECKY
> (breathless)

I taught myself about a week ago.

Shaking his head in instant admiration, Mr. Jamison catches his daughter, lifts her to his shoulders, and, in a familiar ritual, begins marching her to the breakfast table. But Becky stops him with a plea.

> BECKY

Dad, please just one headstand.

> MR. JAMISON
> (unable to resist)

Just one.

Becky then, balancing her palms on her father's head, squats on his shoulders, steadies herself, then hoists herself in the air, executing a perfect handstand, with her hands positioned on the top of her father's head. A feat duly noted by both Mrs. Jamison and her son, who have gotten up from the breakfast table.

MRS. JAMISON

What wonderful athletic children I have!

JACK

She just can't show off enough in front of Dad, can she?

MRS. JAMISON
(to comfort her son, who is obviously upset)

I made the pancakes just the way you like, sweetheart.

Finally, they all sit together at the breakfast table.

MR. JAMISON
(who cannot get over his daughter's physical prowess)

You could be a gymnast!

BECKY
(beaming)

I want to be a runner like you, Dad.

JACK
(growing more and more jealous)

Dad, coach says I'm going to be first string on the wrestling team.

MR. JAMISON
(continuing to look at his daughter)

I didn't know you were still wrestling, Jack.

Slowly Becky returns the photo to its place on the bedstead, trying to savor the last drop of a golden time when she freely basked in the child's glory of being the apple of her father's eye.

BECKY
(sadly, emotionally, to herself)

I wish you were here, Dad....

(a beat)

Maybe you could tell me what to do.

The CAMERA looks at Becky, who, sitting dazed and numb on her bed, looks at the clock on her dresser, which in the early dawn light shows 6 a.m. (CLOSE UP), 7 a.m. (CLOSE UP), when she hears the familiar thump on her front porch she has been listening for. She steals downstairs, retrieves the morning newspaper, carries it to her room. Now her heart has begun to pound again as with trembling hands she opens the newspaper and reads on the front page POLICE WOMAN BEATEN TO DEATH.

Becky, after slowly reading the article and knowing that very soon she will have to leave for school and start facing the world, tries one more time to bolster her courage and firm up her resolve.

BECKY
(to herself)

It was self-defense....
(a beat) They're not going to find out....
(a beat) And, if they do, somehow I will convince them
that it was only an accident.

Around this time, between 7 and 7:30 a.m., on the CAMERA shows two successive CUTS:

EXT. DAN RAINER'S HOME. MORNING.

He opens his front door, picks up the newspaper, glances at the front page, and is stunned at what he sees. Now frightened that his reactions have been observed, he looks sheepishly around him and quickly withdraws into his house.

INT. OFFICE.

Detective Ray Burns, a large, overweight man, about fifty, with snow white hair, and an intelligent, inquisitive, calm, friendly face, looking much more like a professor than a homicide detective, is sitting at his desk. He looks up, when Detective Joe Giminoni—husky, athletic, and with a go-getter attitude—his new junior partner, appears at the door of his office.

DET. BURNS

You're here bright and early, Joe.

DET. GIMINONI
(holding up a leather appointment book)

I've got something.

DET. BURNS

Yes?

DET. GIMINONI

I got a hold of the super, who let me in Pat McDougal's office, and I found her appointment book. The last entry, at 8 p.m. last night, has the name Dan Rainer.

DET. BURNS

The guy who gave the talk yesterday?

DET. GIMINONI
(placing the open book in front of his chief)

The same.

DET. BURNS

That's good work, Joe. But it doesn't mean, of course, that Pat McDougal ever kept that appointment. Here's what I want you to do. Go back to her office. Talk to her supervisor, her colleagues, anybody who has anything interesting to say. Find out if there was anyone who threatened her, anyone she was worried about.... Get a list, if you can, of the students at Silver Oaks who were being seen by either Pat McDougal or Dan Rainer. And then check if any of them drove a Nissan Sentra.

DET. GIMINONI
(busily writing all this down)

What are you going to do?

DET. BURNS

I'm going to see Lester Watkins, the principal of Silver Oaks, who seems gung ho on law enforcement. I want to enlist his cooperation so we can discreetly investigate the student body for possible suspects, and then I'm going to pay a visit to Dan Rainer.

The CAMERA returns to Becky Jamison, still in her bedroom, who waits for the sound of her mother going downstairs to start breakfast. While she waits, she tries to convince herself she is capable of sticking to her normal routine by adhering to her daily and nightly ritual of performing exercises designed to enhance her breast size. Stripping to her waist, she examines her current development—from a frontal and side view—of her breasts, which, small and shapely, would give pleasure to many teenage girls, providing they were not as insecure as Becky is. Then—which the CAMERA shows in a series of quick CUTS—she rapidly, gracefully swings her arms forward, sideward, backward, upward, rhythmically twisting her torso as she does so for a period of about ten minutes. This done, she wipes the sweat from her brow and looks down before quickly covering herself.

BECKY
(to her breasts)

Grow, will you.

The noise of her mother's footsteps on the stairway propel her into a different direction.... She steals into her mother's bedroom to apply her rouge to some still discolored parts of her face. Never having done this, she takes her time to experiment, dabbing delicately and occasionally furtively looking around.

MRS. JAMISON (O.S.)
Are you using makeup now, sweetheart?

BECKY
(startled by her mother materializing in the doorway)

I thought I told you never to sneak up on me.

MRS. JAMISON

I was just on my way to the bathroom, dear.

BECKY

Then go to the bathroom.

MRS. JAMISON

You've decided to use makeup?

BECKY

I have a slight rash and I'm trying to add some color.

MRS. JAMISON

Want some help?

BECKY

No. Go to the bathroom.

Becky returns to her room, glances one more time at the clock, gathers her books and her purse, takes a deep breath, and hurries out of the house. Where, to her annoyance, Bobby Rodgers is waiting in the street for her.

BECKY

You here again?

BOBBY

I had car trouble.

BECKY

For the third time this week?

BOBBY

I know, but my car's on its last legs.

Together they get into Becky's car with Bobby, as soon as they are seated, observing as discreetly as he can the friend whom he worships and finds endlessly fascinating.

BOBBY
(studying her sweater)

Where's your button?

BECKY
(first startled, then incensed, then exploding)

Fuck you, Bobby. It's like you examine me with a microscope every time you see me and if you find one thing awry, you throw it up in my face.

BOBBY
(deeply hurt, but trying to cover it with sarcasm)

The waste of a mind is a terrible thing. You really ought to have someone look into your paranoia. (a beat, then because he cannot bear for Becky to be angry at him) Look, Becky, it didn't take a Sherlock Holmes to spot that one. Every day for the past three years, you've worn essentially the same outfit: existential black sweater with your pin on it, dark jeans, and sneakers. The absence of your school pin not only sticks out like a sore thumb, it practically represents a change of style.

BECKY
(glad to pretend this is only a laughing matter)

Actually, I am searching for a new look.

They start off for school in silence, Bobby well aware that their forced banter is a pretext for whatever is preying on the mind of his friend. Then, noticing the newspaper in her book bag—and correctly inferring, since she never brings a paper to school, it must be because of what happened to Pat McDougal—he tries to use it as an ice-breaker.

BOBBY

Did you read about Pat McDougal?

BECKY
(realizing he has spotted her paper)

I saw the headline and glanced at the article.

BOBBY

Did you know who she was?

BECKY

No.

BOBBY

Well, she was the woman who was talking to Dan Rainer yesterday, whom you were looking at.

BECKY
(pretending to be interested)

Really?

BOBBY

I already have a theory as to who's the murderer.

BECKY
(welcoming the diversion)

So who's the murderer?

BOBBY

Otto Frankel.

BECKY
(teasing)

Is there any possibility your theory is biased by the fact Otto likes to bully you at school?

BOBBY

I'm intending to be a police psychologist, remember? This is strictly business, not personal.

BECKY
(amused)

What is your theory based on, then?

BOBBY

Three things. First, Otto is already rumored to have killed someone once. Second, when his girlfriend, Rita Jenkins, was caught selling pot in the girl's lavatory last year, part of her probation was to see Pat McDougal, and she hated her guts.... And three, Otto is enough of a moron to think that killing Pat as a form of payback might impress Rita.

BECKY
(nervously)

But the article doesn't say anything about a Silver Oaks student being a suspect.

BOBBY

I thought you only glanced at the article.

BECKY

Well, I did. Well, did it say anything like that that I missed?

BOBBY

No, but they do mention Silver Oaks High twice. If you can read between the lines, if you understand the police mentality the way I do, you realize they are not going to show all their cards at once.

BECKY

Well, Bobby, just make sure Otto doesn't find out you suspect him, because if he does, he'll wring your little neck.

BOBBY

Becky, I may be a lot of things, but one thing I am not is
stupid.

Thus acting as though nothing has changed, though both sense something
is different in their relationship, they arrive at Silver Oaks, where they
quickly strike out in different directions.

INT. SILVER OAKS HIGH. SAME TIME.

Becky knows she is in an exhausted state, with images of last night flit-
ting in and out of her mind. Her one goal is to just get through this first,
posthomicide school day. So she walks even more quickly through the long
corridors than she normally does, as though she is trying to hurry up time.
She is even less aware of the heads that always turn whenever she passes
by, less responsive to the voices that occasionally call out her name. And
we see her dazed progress through this initial horrible school day in a
series of QUICK CUTS: Becky barely acknowledging Mr. Traister, her
English teacher, who tries to congratulate her on her Dostoyevsky paper.
Becky sitting trancelike at the back of a classroom. Unable to read the book
she has opened in the library. Unable to eat the food that sits on the tray in
front of her in the cafeteria. One event, however, does manage to snap her
out of her stupor, at least temporarily. An encounter with the two students
at Silver Oaks whom she regards as her nemeses.

CLOSE UP OTTO FRANKEL AND RITA JENKINS.

At twenty-one years of age, with his shaved head, massive arms, and
tattoo that brags "Born to Lose," Otto is both the oldest and most notorious
hoodlum in Silver Oaks. The one thing he likes better than drugs and sex
is violence, his favorite story being that he once killed a Mexican pimp in
a bar in Tijuana. No one, of course, including Otto, knows if this story is
true. All Otto is sure of is that when he walked out of that bar, the Mexican pimp whom he had just beaten to a pulp was lying in a pool of blood
on the floor and looking very lifeless. By his side is Rita Jenkins, his girlfriend, nineteen years of age, pretty but in a tough-looking, whorish way,

who, constantly changing her image, is dressed today all in leather in the manner of a biker's chick.

Becky, who usually gives them a wide berth, but hardly noticing them on this day, almost bumps into Rita coming from the opposite direction before seeing her. She tries to move around her, but Rita deliberately cuts her off and maliciously blocks her path.

                    BECKY
                 (very annoyed)
        Don't you ever step aside for anyone?

                    RITA
            (surprised and defensive)
             Why should I?

                    BECKY
        (now moving around her, while continuing to stare at
                     her)
           Because it's called good manners.

Rita and Otto share amused glances, as though to make light of this uncharacteristic display of defiance. Becky, however, has already forgotten this. She is concentrating instead on the clock on the wall, which tells her this horrible first school day is about to end. But now she remembers with a start that there is something important she has forgotten to do, some critical piece of evidence she has not yet disposed of.

EXT. DUMPSTER, HALF AN HOUR LATER

Becky, nervously looking to her left and right, is putting her bag of blood-stained clothes in the dumpster and closing the lid.

                    O.S.
                (from behind her)
        What are you doing?

Becky whirls around and sees Bobby Rodgers yet again.

                    BECKY
                  (suspicious)

Are you following me?

                    BOBBY

No, I was just driving by, I live only two blocks from here,
remember?...And I saw you.

                    BECKY

I thought your engine didn't start.

                    BOBBY

Well, it started up. What were you doing?

                    BECKY

I was throwing some of my mother's garbage away.

                    BOBBY

Why didn't you use the garbage pail in the front of your
house?

                    BECKY

Why do you want to know? Am I under investigation, too?

                    BOBBY

We'll get to your alibi later. Meanwhile, answer the question. Why didn't you use the garbage pail in front of your
house?

> BECKY

Because my mother didn't want me to, and Bobby, shut up and stop grilling me. Can't you see I'm in a bad mood?

> BOBBY

I do see. So what's bothering you?

> BECKY

If I had wanted to talk about it, I would have.

> BOBBY

But I'm your friend.

> BECKY

My nosy friend.

> BOBBY

All right. But will you help me with my college applications tonight?

> BECKY

No, Bobby. There's something I have to do.

And there is. Becky remembers that there is one more appointment in her day she has to keep if she wants to maintain a pretense of normalcy.

INT. DAN RAINER'S OFFICE. AFTERNOON.

DAN RAINER is sitting at his desk with a cup of coffee, reading and rereading the article on the murder of Pat McDougal. He is wracking his brain for a possible clue in their strange encounter that in retrospect might foretell the horrible fate lying in wait for Pat McDougal.

O.S.
(his secretary's voice on the intercom)

A Detective Burns is here to see you.

DAN
(visibly shaken, sucking in his breath, but determined to
see this through)

Send him in.

Quickly, he discards the coffee cup, folds the newspaper, and occupies his
therapist's armchair.

DET. BURNS
(respectfully opening the door but not coming in)

Dr. Rainer?

DAN

Mister. I'm a psychologist.

DET. BURNS
(pleasantly)

Mr. Rainer, may I come in?

DAN

Yes, sit down. Call me Dan.

Smiling, he seats himself, looks at Dan, says nothing at first, almost as
though he is waiting to see what he will say, then:

DET. BURNS

I was at your talk yesterday at Silver Oaks.

DAN
(surprised)

I didn't see you there (a beat), but then I never focus on
the faces in the crowd.

To which Detective Burns says nothing, continuing to look at Dan. And
now, suddenly, Dan thinks he sees the trap and understands what this initial cat-and-mouse game is all about.

DAN
(trying to sound matter-of-fact)

I take it you're here because you probably know that Pat
McDougal was at my house at eight o'clock in the
evening.

DET. BURNS

Well, I do now. When did you find out about what happened?

DAN

Actually, I was just reading about it just before you came
in. And I was thinking, if I didn't hear from the police, I
would give them a call.

DET. BURNS

Do you get your newspaper delivered?

DAN
(puzzled by the question)

Why, yes.

DET. BURNS
(turning his head in the direction of the
newspaper, lying on the desk)

Was that newspaper the one that was delivered to you this
morning?

DAN
(more puzzled)

Why, yes. Why do you ask?

DET. BURNS

Well, I should think that the murder of Pat McDougal,
being a front-page story, involving someone you had just
seen on the very night in question, would certainly have
caught your eye. But you just said you only learned about
it a few minutes before I arrived.

DAN
(seeing the trap too late and not knowing how to
respond)

Well, I (a beat) often barely glance at the paper in the
morning (a beat) and take this time between sessions to
relax and enjoy it with a cup of coffee.

DET. BURNS
(flatly, as he takes a notebook from his pocket)

I see. All right, could you tell me in detail everything that
happened between you and Pat McDougal last night.

Dan, knowing he has just been caught in a stupid lie, welcomes the question as a chance to demonstrate, and hopefully impress, Detective Burns
with his near photographic memory. He gives a practically verbatim
account of his conversation with Pat McDougal, stopping at the point
where she kissed him.

DET. BURNS
(busily writing)

I have to ask you the name of the case that was discussed,
as it could be an important clue.

DAN
(eager to give it)

I understand. Oliver Cairiston.

DET. BURNS

Okay, is there anything else?

DAN

No. Nothing I can think of.

DET. BURNS

What did you do after she left?

DAN

Nothing. I stayed at home and read.

DET. BURNS

Did you speak to anyone on the telephone, did anyone
call you, anyone come to your house who could verify that
you were home all last night, specifically between 9 and
10 o'clock?

DAN

No. But is that when she died?

DET. BURNS

Who said anything about her dying?

DAN

Well, the paper said...

DET. BURNS

The paper said she was beaten to death.... Would you call that dying?

DAN
(feeling he can be perfectly honest in this regard)

I see your point. Well, it may be that I wanted to distance myself from an act too close for comfort and too traumatic to be taken in. So perhaps I unconsciously converted it to something much less threatening, something natural and nonviolent.

DET. BURNS

Would that be an example of the defense mechanism— now what is it called—denial?

DAN
(feeling more and more one-upped)

I suppose so.

DET. BURNS

Here's my card. Keep in touch, and if you think of anything else, anything at all, give me a call.

DAN

I will.

Detective Burns starts to get up, then stops himself, as though remembering something he has been meaning to ask.

DET. BURNS

What was it that you read all night?

DAN

I read, actually reread, *Crime and Punishment* by Dostoyevsky.

DET. BURNS
(enthusiastically)

Raskolnikov murders the old woman pawnbroker and her
sister.... Of course, my favorite character was Porfiry
Petrovich, the genius detective....

(a beat)

How far did you get?

DAN

I'm up to the end, where Raskolnikov and Sonya head off
for Siberia.

DET. BURNS
(as though contemplating a matter of probability)

A curious coincidence, isn't it? On the night a woman
visits you who is shortly thereafter brutally murdered,
you spend the night reading a crime classic.

DAN
(beginning to feel like a harassed
Lieutenant Columbo murder suspect)

Not really. I have a patient who's very interested in that
book, and, you might say as part of the treatment, I'm
rereading it.

DET. BURNS
(reopening his notebook)

The patient's name?

DAN
(getting angry for the first time)

That's completely confidential, you know, and she had
absolutely nothing to do with this case anyway.

DET. BURNS

She?

DAN

She, he, it. It's confidential.

DET. BURNS
(as though sympathetic)

I know, Dan, my questions can seem irksome.... But it's
not personal. I'm just doing my job.

DAN

And so am I.

DET. BURNS

I understand. Call me if you think of anything.

Upon which Detective Burns really does get up, shakes Dan's hand in a
perfunctory way, and lets himself out.

CLOSE UP DAN'S FACE. DEEPLY UPSET.

DAN

(to himself)

Well, I blew that one all right.

He returns to his desk, reopens the newspaper, tries to read it yet again, finds he cannot concentrate, and throws it in the wastebasket. He looks at his clock, sees that his next patient is not due for ten minutes, and hits the intercom button.

DAN

(to secretary)

If my next patient comes early, buzz me.

Then, not knowing how to distract himself from his racing thoughts, he begins watching his own clock. CLOSE UP of the clock, three rapid CUTS of three separate readings, five minutes apart. And ten minutes later, precisely on time, the intercom rings.

SECRETARY (O.S.)

Your patient has arrived and is on the way in.

Dan quickly crosses over to his armchair, composes himself, and watches as his patient enters—whom we now see from Dan's perspective, but from the shoulders down—crossing the room to the facing armchair.

CLOSE UP BECKY JAMISON SEATING HERSELF.

And an immediate mutual silence, longer than usual, develops between them, as Dan wonders if he can forget his troubles enough to concentrate on his patient, and Becky ponders how she will get through a session in which there will not be one truthful thing she can possibly say to her therapist. But suddenly Becky gets an idea of how to both break the ice and kill some time.

BECKY

I was at your talk yesterday.

DAN
(after waiting in vain for Becky to offer a comment)

Did you think of coming over and saying hi?

BECKY

I was thinking of it, but I saw you talking to a woman and didn't want to interrupt you.

Another tense silence springs up between them, in which it is Becky this time who is waiting for a response. Then, receiving none, she decides to apply some more pressure....

BECKY

I was with Bobby Rodgers, who just told me today that that woman was Pat McDougal, the woman who was murdered last night.

DAN
(knowing he has to reply)

Yes, it's quite a tragedy.

BECKY

I was thinking today, it must be strange, it must be awful to be with someone who shortly thereafter is murdered.

DAN
(suspicious now of his patient's motives)

The focus today, Becky, seems to be on me. I'm wondering ...is there some reason you don't want to talk about yourself?...Are you mad at me about something?

BECKY

Should I be mad?

DAN

You're playing with me. There could be any of a thousand reasons why something I did, or something I did not do, was in some way offensive to you. But you have to tell me what it is.

BECKY

I'll use one of your lines, Dan.... Search within your-self.... The answer is within you.

DAN
(now absorbed in what she is saying)

Becky, what's wrong? You're not yourself today.

BECKY
(suddenly very tired)

I don't know, Dan. Lately I've been thinking it's been so long since I first came here and so much has happened to me.

DAN
(trying to grasp what she is really saying)

Yes, it has.

And now Becky, exhausted, on the brink of falling asleep, lets her mind drift back to the beginning, the beginning of therapy, as Dan quietly watches her....

INT. JAMISON HOUSE FIVE YEARS AGO. MORNING.

Jack is seated at the kitchen table, as his mother hovers over him, serving him breakfast. He is sipping on a morning beer, something he has started to do soon after his father died, as he waits anxiously for the arrival of his sister, who, typically, is the last to arrive. Now she comes and as she crosses behind Jack's chair, he surprises her by suddenly pulling her toward him and quickly kissing her on the lips.

JACK

No hello to your big brother?

BECKY
(angrily jerking herself free and wiping her mouth with her hand)

Oooohh! Kissing on the lips is disgusting!

JACK
(insulted by this)

I guess to you it is, dykey.

BECKY
(almost in tears)

Mom, he called me that name again!

MRS. JAMISON
(thoroughly confused)

What name?

BECKY

He called me dykey.

JACK
(enjoying himself now)

I called her Becky.

MRS. JAMISON

That's what I heard, too, dear. Now sit down and eat your
breakfast before it gets cold.

BECKY
(petulantly)

I don't want breakfast. Give my share to your pet, Jack.

Becky turns around and decides to continue her search for her cat, Bill,
who seems to have temporarily disappeared.

BECKY
(in a singsong voice to herself and to Bill)

Bill, Bill, you'd better not be where I think you are. You
better not be in Jack's room.

MRS. JAMISON (O.S.)

Jack, go get her. She has to eat breakfast.

BECKY
(fearfully walking up the stairs)

Bill, remember how mad Jack got when you urinated on
his bed last week?

Becky reaches the top of the landing and cautiously approaches the room
even she is forbidden to enter. She does not see or hear her brother, who
has silently come up the stairs and is beginning to follow her. Becky hesitates before the partially ajar bedroom door, frightened of what she will
find, but eases it open. To discover Bill placidly lying on the sheets in the
center of Jack's unmade bed.

JACK
(standing right behind Becky now)

I smell urine.

BECKY
(a jittery kid to begin with, jumps a foot)

No, Jack.

Terrified that Jack will punish Bill in the evil way she suspects he did the last time, which Jack vigorously denies, she rushes to protect her cat, pushes him aside, and points to the sheet.

BECKY
(desperately)

See, Jack. No stains, no urine.

JACK
(who has a hair-trigger temper, which he is
now on the brink of losing)

I don't care. I've seen that fucking cat roll around in his own shit. And I don't want him on my bed.

As Jack moves toward the cat, Becky tries to scoop him up first, but Jack roughly shoves her out of the way. As he reaches to grab the cat, Bill, normally docile, in a sudden frenzy of claws and teeth, horribly mangles the back of his hand. And Jack goes berserk. Disregarding the still furiously clawing animal, he takes it by the tail, swings it in the air, and tries to hurl it, like a missile, through the room, out the now opened door, and into the hallway. But Jack, now in the grip of his own frenzy, the back of his hand beginning to pour blood, does not see the bedpost to his right, which stops the whirling body of the cat—dead cold—in midair. Horrified, Jack realizes what has just happened, what he has in fact just done. Calmly, he sets the cat, with its head dangling grotesquely to one side, back on the bed. And there can be no doubt that Jack is truly and deeply sorry for what has occurred. It is not that he cannot feel guilt, it is that he cannot tolerate the emotion for more than an instant without converting it to something more gratifying. To make sure of what he thinks has happened, he runs his fingers over the limp-lying cat's neck, which clearly is broken. So Jack, sighing sadly, as more blood continues to flow from his hand, steps back so that

Becky, who has been standing very quietly, frozen and terrified, can see what has just happened to her cat.

> BECKY
> (now seeing Bill)

Why is he lying like that, Jack?

> JACK

He's dead, Becky.... It was an accident. His head hit the bedpost.

> BECKY
> (leaning over Bill)

He can't be dead, Jack. He's not even sick.

> JACK

His neck hit the bedpost. It's broken. Look, Becky.... It was an accident.

Jack runs his fingers over Bill's neck to demonstrate his point. He turns away to look at his own mangled, bleeding hand, and Becky does what Jack just did. She runs her own fingers along her cat's neck. She probes his body, trying to coax him back into life. She strokes, fondles, whispers to her cat, but mostly she feels him. And gradually Bill's deadness meets her touch and begins to seep into her spirit. For just a moment, she mourns her freshly killed cat and is heartbroken. But Becky then does what can only be called an act of temporary insanity. She sees a sharpened pencil lying on a notepad on a bedside stand, and it reminds her of a knife. She thinks she wants to, she must now kill Jack, who killed Bill. She picks up the pencil and, wielding it like a dagger, viciously stabs Jack in the side of his head. She does not aim for his left eye, but neither does she make any attempt to avoid it, the point embedding itself in Jack's flesh about a quarter of an inch from the left eye socket. Once again his feelings are deeply hurt, and once again he responds by becoming infuriated. With one hand he holds Becky at bay, who, windmill style, is flailing, kicking, and screaming vengeance upon her murderous brother. With the free hand, he explores the new wound and when he sees fresh blood, he grows more enraged. His fingers dig viciously into his sister's cheek, and for a moment or two he contemplates what a pleasure it would be to strangle her.

JACK

(still holding her at bay)

So the little dyke wants to stab her big brother in the eye?

He wraps her in a bear hug, savors for just a moment the sensation of her tiny body trapped and wiggling in his powerful arms, and then slams her as hard as he can to the mattress of his bed. But still she struggles, still she screams. So Jack pushes her face into the bed, clamps his fingers around her mouth, climbs on top of her, and completely pins her to the mattress, almost side by side with Bill.

JACK

(lying on top of her)

Shut up, you little bitch.... Don't be such a troublemaker. ... It was an accident. I didn't mean to kill Bill. He had distemper anyway, and we would probably have had to have him put to sleep.

MRS. JAMISON

(in the doorway)

What's going on here?

Almost simultaneously Jack and Becky jump from the bed to plead their respective cases.

JACK

(holding up his bleeding hand)

It was an accident, Mom. Bill's neck got broken.... He had distemper and we would have had to put him to sleep.

MRS. JAMISON

Jack! My God, your hand!

BECKY
(hyperventilating, barely able to talk)

He broke Bill's neck. Look, look....

Very confused, Mrs. Jamison follows Becky to the bed and stares at Bill. But she quickly turns away and hurries to examine the extent of the damage to her adored son's hand. And Becky, with no one in the world to console her now, hysterically throws herself back on Jack's bed, cradles her dead cat in her arms, and begins sobbing to herself.

INT. JAMISON HOUSE. THREE HOURS LATER.

We see Becky, sitting on the top of the stairway, her chin in her palms, quietly eavesdropping and looking very worried. We then see Jack, his hand and his temple bandaged, and his fraught mother—both of them believing that Becky has sobbed herself to sleep—talking freely.

JACK

Mom, we have to take Becky to the doctor.

MRS. JAMISON
(alarmed)

Doctor, Jack?

JACK
(pointing to his left eye)

Mom, she tried to stab me in the eye.... Another half an inch and I'd have only one eye.

MOTHER

My God. She didn't mean it, did she, Jack?

JACK

She's paranoid, Mom. She thinks I'm calling her a dyke when I'm only calling her Becky. She even accuses me of burning her cat with a lighted cigarette.

MRS. JAMISON
(wringing her hands anxiously)

Are they going to put her away in a hospital, Jack?

JACK

I don't know. The doctor will decide that.

INT. OFFICE DAY. TWO WEEKS LATER.

We see Becky, with her mother behind her, as she looks down a long corridor.

MRS. JAMISON

Go ahead, Becky. It's the door that's open at the end of the corridor.

BECKY

And he's not a doctor?

MRS. JAMISON

No. He's a psychologist.

BECKY

He's not going to send me to a hospital.

MRS. JAMISON

No.

BECKY

And if I don't like him, I don't have to come back?

MRS. JAMISON

I promise.

With that Becky, cautiously at first, and then defiantly, walks down the hall and into the designated office. Where we see Dan Rainer at a desk, who immediately gets up.

DAN
(warm and friendly, extending his hand)

I'm Dan Rainer, and you must be Becky Jamison.

Becky does not respond, does not accept the hand that is offered, but instead seats herself in the chair facing his desk. When Dan closes the door, to insure privacy, he is surprised to see Becky get up from her chair and reopen it.

DAN
(who accepts this)

You want the door open?

BECKY
(at her most provocative)

How do I know you're not a child molester?

DAN

Well, do you think a professional agency like this would allow a child molester to see children?

BECKY
(stubbornly)

How would I know?

DAN
(curious)

Where'd you hear about child molesters?

BECKY

Every time I go out to play when it's dark, my mother warns me about them.

DAN

You don't seem really afraid of them though.

BECKY

I'm not worried about what's outside of my house. It's the scumbag inside who concerns me.

DAN

Who would that be?

BECKY

My brother, Jack, of course. Who else?

DAN

You want to tell me why you think he's a scumbag?

BECKY
(pleased with her little joke)

How much time do we have?

DAN

(already captivated by his young patient)

All the time in the world.

BECKY

(now placing her elbows on the desk and leaning forward)

Okay. Listen up.

We are now back in real time, with Dan Rainer continuing to look at Becky
while she's remembering.

DAN

Becky, I don't know when I've seen you so lost in your own
thoughts.

BECKY

(suppressing a yawn)

I was thinking way back to when I started therapy. It seems
so long ago.

DAN

It was. You seem tired.

BECKY

I am. I didn't sleep much last night. . . . I think I have an
upset stomach.

DAN

(noting for the first time Becky's missing school button)

I see you're not wearing your button.

> BECKY
> (quickly)

Yes. I think it fell off.

She is so exhausted she closes her eyes and for a moment begins to drift off but wakes herself. She looks at Dan, who is beginning to speak but stops short as (CLOSE UP) his mouth begins to fill with blood, and (DIS-SOLVE) his face begins to change into Pat McDougal's face. She wakes with a violent start, realizes she had actually started to dream, and is deeply ashamed.

> DAN
> (concerned)

Becky, did you just see a dream image? Your eyes were closed, you know.

> BECKY
> (stubbornly)

No. I just started to drift off.

> DAN

You seemed so frightened.

> BECKY

Don't push me, Dan. You know I don't like that. (a beat) (then glancing at the clock) Our time is up.

> DAN
> (ironic smile)

That was convenient....

BECKY
(getting up)

Good-bye, Dan.

DAN

See you tomorrow.

BECKY

Sure.

She is glad to leave, relieved that this terrible session is at last over.

INT. DOJO. NIGHT.

Martin, a black belt, whose clean-cut Jimmy-Stewart-straight-shooter manner belies the very real intelligence and sensitivity he has, is holding the heavy bag for Becky, now in her karate uniform. She is delivering a drum beat of high front and roundhouse karate kicks, the same series depicted in the opening credits. They are talking between kicks.

MARTIN

You're really kicking the bag hard today.

BECKY

It's my way of sublimating my anger toward the world.

MARTIN

Is that what your shrink says?

BECKY

Actually, he was the one who first suggested I take up martial arts when I was twelve.

MARTIN

Well, by now you're good enough to go for a black belt.
You're as good as anyone in this school. (a beat) Even me.

BECKY

Was that so hard for you to say?

MARTIN
(smiling)

A little.

They stop. Martin then decides to demonstrate the flying side kick, made
famous by Bruce Lee, which he has just mastered. When he sees she is
delighted, he teaches it to her and urges her to try it. Reluctantly agreeing,
she runs at the heavy bag, takes off, but makes contact barely a foot off the
ground and falls unceremoniously on her side.

BECKY
(getting up)

Well, I guess that was my flying ankle kick.

MARTIN

Don't be discouraged. You just took off for your jump the
wrong way. Here.

Martin then demonstrates the correct takeoff position and tries to help her
assume the same stance by placing his hand on her shoulder and hip. But,
to his dismay, Becky very angrily pulls away.

BECKY

Don't touch me like that, Martin.

Martin, who has been a perfect gentleman for two years with Becky, knowing this is what she needs, could not be more hurt. He is too proud, however, to take being put in his place lying down.

MARTIN

For Christ's sake, Becky, I was only teaching you a karate move. I wasn't making a *move*. Maybe you ought to increase your sessions with your shrink.

And Becky, who hates it whenever her bluntness causes someone unnecessary pain, especially someone she loves, is immediately and genuinely remorseful.

BECKY

I'm sorry, Martin. I've got a lot on my mind.

MARTIN

You always have a lot on your mind.

BECKY

Can I ride Storm tomorrow?

MARTIN
(who has trouble saying no to Becky)

Sure.

INT. OFFICE NEXT MORNING.

Detective Giminoni, reading from his notes, is reporting to Detective Burns, who leans back in his chair and listens.

DET. GIMINONI

No one recalls any particular case Pat McDougal was worried about. The only assault cases she handled in the last year were Mickey Hunt, Carlos Martinez, and James Robinson. Mickey Hunt and Carlos Martinez are currently in reform school....James Robinson was out of the state on the night of the murder. And I've already verified that.

DET. BURNS

Well, that gets us back to square one, which means Dan Rainer. I met with him yesterday, and I'm almost certain there's something he's not telling me.

DET. GIMINONI

You think he might be the killer?

DET. BURNS

No, I'm not saying that....He may know something that he thinks is purely personal but might lead to the murderer.

DET. GIMINONI

What do you want me to do now?

DET. BURNS

Keep doing what you're doing. As I've already told you, make a list of all the cases Pat McDougal worked on for the past three years. Also, find out the names of all the students at Silver Oaks whom Dan Rainer was seeing. And find out, if you can, if any of them drove, owned, or had access to a Nissan Sentra.

DET. GIMINONI

That and the Silver Oaks school button I guess are the only real clues we have.

DET. BURNS

Unfortunately.

DET. GIMINONI

What are you going to do?

DET. BURNS

I'm going to try and find out what Dan Rainer is keeping from me.

INT. SILVER OAKS HIGH. AFTERNOON.

In one corner of the girls' locker room, Rita and her three cronies, Mary, Louise, and Daphne, are standing around in various stages of undress after their gym class. As far away as possible, and off to herself, Becky is hurriedly redressing, while Rita, the locker room leader, still in her bra, holds court.

MARY
(deferring to Rita)

Looks like your friend bought it last night.

RITA

The lesbo got what she deserved.

DAPHNE

Do you think Otto may have done it, as payback for you?

RITA
(laughing)

I wish.... But Otto was with me Monday night, all night. (a beat) But let's ask Becky who she thinks did it.... She always knows the answer in class.

LOUISE

Where is she anyway?

DAPHNE

Hiding in the corner, protecting her precious body, as usual.

Rita looks around, locates Becky, and begins to walk over. She waits for her audience to join her. Then...

RITA
(enjoying this)

Don't make fun of her. She's just shy. (seeing that Becky is still in her familiar leotards) Becky, when are we ever going to see you in a bra?

Instinctively Becky, who is standing with her back to Rita, puts her hand to her breasts. She knows she is on the verge of blushing. And this infuriates her. For three years, mainly because of Dan Rainer, she has refused to allow herself to be baited by Rita Jenkins. But since Monday night something has been happening to her. She does not see the point in holding back anymore. She does not see the point in forever monitoring her rage. She does not see the point in continuing to be loyal to Dan Rainer or to the principles of therapy. So she wonders how much more of this she can take, how much more of this she will take. And her sense that she has now drawn in her mind a line in the sand, so to speak, calms her down, as it always does. Her sense that she can now act when and if she chooses, on her own terms gives her the freedom to bide her time.

RITA
(growing increasingly bold)

Is that true, Becky.... Are you too ashamed to let us see your breasts?

DAPHNE

Maybe she doesn't have any.

(laughter)

RITA

Sure she does. She's just shy. What she needs is encouragement.

Rita undoes her bra strap and exposes her very full breasts. The excitement and anticipation in the locker room as to what she is going to do are almost palpable.

RITA

Look, Becky, here are my tits. This is what they look like after you've been fucked by the best.

(a beat)

Did you know, by the way, your brother Jack used to love to suck on them?

LOUISE

Maybe Becky wants to suck on them, too.

(more laughter)

RITA
(thinking she can now get away with saying
and doing just about whatever she pleases)

Come on, Becky, just take one little peek at my tits and then show me yours.

Rita moves to within a couple of inches of Becky's back, her bare breasts nearly brushing up against her. But Becky has at last reached her limit.

BECKY

(in a calm, menacing voice)

Rita, shut the fuck up.

An instant silence descends upon the locker room as if there is a sense something is about to happen. Mary, Louise, and Daphne glance anxiously at their leader—a bully who has just been called out—and who is obviously flustered. But Rita is also a fighter who does not like to back down. So she tries to save face.

RITA

(seductively)

Don't be so heavy, Becky. We're just playing, you know. It's only a sex game. I've shown you mine, now you show me yours...and it's over.

To coax Becky, who's back is still to her, to turn her around, Rita tentatively and gently lays her hand on her shoulders.

BECKY

Why don't I show you this instead?

Stepping back, spinning around in one deft motion, Becky fires a whistling punch, meant to be a warning shot, but which actually catches the tip of a startled Rita's nose and smacks into a partially opened locker door. But, although terrified, Rita is also thrilled—after all, this is the first time in three years she has gotten a rise out of Becky—and she quickly recovers.

RITA

(rubbing her nose)

Whoa! Maybe you really are butch, as they say.

But Rita, who quickly refastens her bra, is already retreating to her cronies for support.

DAPHNE
(putting an arm around her shoulder)

Come on, Rita. Leave that freak and her tits alone.

LOUISE
(after first maintaining a safe distance
and speaking in a low voice)

She's just a jealous, ugly dyke, and she knows it.

RITA
(feeling she must get in the last word)

Oh, Becky, I think there's something you should know.
Otto once killed a pimp in a Tijuana bar.

BECKY
(finally turning to face her and everyone else)

We all know that, Rita, and we're all as happy and as proud
as we can be for Otto. (a beat) But it looks as though the
best man lost.

The locker room then quickly empties, as though they cannot get away fast
enough from someone they do not and do not want to understand. A lonely
figure, still in her leotards, Becky examines her knuckles, which are beginning to bleed. She knows she has won only a stupid victory. She has out-
bullied a bully.

BECKY
(to herself, staring into the CAMERA)

I just made a fool of myself.

(a beat)

Dan, Dan, Dan.... Why do I act this way?

INT. OFFICE DAY.

Dan, trying not to look worried, is entering Detective Burns's office.

> DET. BURNS
> (looking up from his desk)

Thanks for coming down to headquarters so promptly, Dan.

> DAN
> (taking a chair)

Sure.

> DET. BURNS

You're a psychologist, you deal in honesty. So I'm going to get right to the point and be honest with you, too....

Detective Burns pauses for dramatic effect while Dan wonders if this is just a cheap ploy designed to impress academics and intellectuals.

> DET. BURNS (CONT'D)

I have a strong suspicion that you didn't tell me everything yesterday.... That's common, you know.... Witnesses, for example, who happen to be at a certain place just before it becomes a murder scene afterward tend to fixate on the crime itself. They often dissociate anything personal that does not seem directly relevant to them.... That way, they justify concealing any embarrassing, tangential fact that they may desperately not want to become public knowledge. But, not being professionals, they don't realize that very often those are the very things that contain the key to solving the case.

DAN
(interrupting)

How does any of this pertain to me? I wasn't within miles of the murder scene.

DET. BURNS (CONT'D)

Let's say, for argument's sake, you have some kind of history with Pat McDougal and you don't want it to be known. So you decide to forget to mention it. Maybe you are afraid it would lead to something that might cause you to lose your license. Maybe you think that whatever went on between you and Pat McDougal is your business. Well, that personal relationship might be the key to the case.

DAN

Why do you think I'm holding something back?

DET. BURNS

Several things. First, it's obvious to me you chose to cover up the fact that you were aware Pat McDougal had been murdered long before you said you were. That suggests that you were very reluctant to come forward and volunteer a very important piece of information. That you were the last known person to see the murder victim alive. Second, it seems you went out of your way to impress me with your apparently photographic memory about a conversation that from all I could tell had absolutely nothing to do with the murder. That suggests you wanted to divert my mind from whatever it is you don't want me to find out. And third, your whole manner... you seemed on pins and needles from the very first moment I laid eyes on you ...speaks of a man who's hiding something.

DAN
(curiously beginning to find this exchange stimulating)

I see your points. But you know, as Dostoyevsky once famously said, psychology is a two-edged sword. In other words, evidence that seems to point in one direction can just as easily, from another perspective, point in the opposite direction. So, look at it from my point of view. Let's say I am absolutely innocent of this murder and had no knowledge whatsoever it was about to be committed, which, of course, is the truth, then why would I want to step forth? And if I were contacted by the police, what could be more natural than that I would become rattled, fearful that I will be wrongfully suspected? And if I realize that I am being looked at very suspiciously, as I certainly saw was the case with you, why wouldn't I grow increasingly defensive and evasive?

DET. BURNS
(seemingly listening respectfully)

That's true. All I can say is that there is a difference between someone who is telling the whole truth so far as he knows it but is frightened he won't be believed, and someone who knows he is telling less than the whole truth and is frightened he'll be tripped up. And after twenty years in homicide, I think I can tell that difference. And there's one more thing....

Detective Burns pauses once again for dramatic effect and Dan Rainer senses that here is the payoff.

DET. BURNS (CONT'D)

California has rather harsh laws on accessories to a murder, that is, on people who are judged to have deliberately withheld a piece of information relating to a capital crime. Right now you've done nothing wrong. If you were to vol-

unteer an additional piece of information to me today that
you suddenly recollected, I would accept that as just an
innocent error. But if it was discovered later on that you
deliberately withheld the very same piece of information,
that could make you an accessory to the crime.

Quickly, Dan makes his decision. He decides, although uncertain whether
he is rising to meet a legitimate challenge or falling into a well-laid trap, to
match Detective Burns's apparent candor with his own.

DAN
(taking a deep breath)

Well, now that you put it that way, there is something I
neglected to tell you.

DET. BURNS
(taking out his notebook and hoping his
pounding heart does not betray him)

Good. What is it?

In exquisite and graphic detail, Dan, beginning with the kiss and ending
with the dramatic exit, completes his story. He leaves nothing out. The
shame. The humiliation. The sexual degradation ... is all included.

DAN

Those are all the gory details, every one of which is
deeply relevant to my personal feelings in this matter, and
I hope explain why I dreaded having this become part of
a police file.

A brief but profound silence ensues during which the two men exchange
searching glances.

DET. BURNS

Well, I think you'll agree, you've just told me a very odd story.

DAN
(no longer afraid of Detective Burns)

I think if you look at any piece of human behavior close enough, sooner or later you observe something that is truly odd. Something that does not seem to fit into any preexisting category of knowledge.

DET. BURNS

I suppose. But this seems quite a bit more odd than most things.

DAN

That's true.

DET. BURNS

Let's see if I understand this. If—oh, by the way, we collected some fresh prints off the victim's body—we were to fingerprint you and find that your prints matched those on the corpse.... Your explanation would be that that was not because you happened to be at the scene of the crime, but that, maybe only minutes before, for some bizarre reason, for the first time in your life, you happened to be engaged in sex wrestling with a secret dominatrix? Doesn't that sound unbelievable to you?

DAN
(for the first time, getting angry)

To an outside observer, to a police mind trained to rely solely on statistical profiles, stereotypes, and crude probabilities, someone who knows absolutely nothing about me, I guess it does sound farfetched. But to someone who does know me, who knows how I've devoted the last fifteen years of my life to exploring the roots of violence and trying to help others benefit from it... then the thought that because

I had been sexually humiliated...as I was...I would cold-bloodedly track down and butcher another human being... is utterly and fantastically improbable.

DET. BURNS

Calm down, Dan. You haven't been named as a suspect yet.

DAN

Am I supposed to be thankful for that?

DET. BURNS
(kindly and fatherly)

Dan, like you I live my life according to what I believe and trust, not what I can prove. But unlike you, trust is not one of the tools of the trade in the career that I've chosen for myself. No one cares what I believe. No one cares, for example...if I happen to believe what you just told me—which, by the way, I do—they only care if I can prove it. (a beat) So, Dan, if I were to ask you if you would voluntarily consent to let me have you fingerprinted, what would you say?

DAN
(after thinking this over)

All right, you can fingerprint me.

DET. BURNS

And if we asked you to take a lie detector test?

DAN
(exasperated now, feeling more and more like a
harassed Lieutenant Columbo murder suspect)

Look, Detective Burns. I could have asked for a lawyer—I didn't....I've just now agreed to be fingerprinted....I don't see the necessity for a lie detector test. . . . I know they can give false positives. . . . Why subject myself to any further humiliation? (a beat) What I will do, though, is this. If, after you've thoroughly investigated this case, gone through every conceivable suspect, and you think there would be some benefit in my taking the test . . . I will . . .

DET. BURNS
(genuinely grateful)

Thank you. Thank you very much for your cooperation. . . . Oh, Dan . . . Just one comment . . . Do you see how much what you've told me has helped us? I know in your mind, because you are certain you are innocent, there is no connection whatsoever between the fact you were sexually humiliated and the fact Pat McDougal was murdered shortly thereafter. But now think, Dan. Isn't it quite possible that the actual murderer was someone who was sexually humiliated like you were, but who, unlike you, is deeply unbalanced emotionally? So, in one fell swoop, you've given us a new fertile field to investigate. We check out all past personal and sexual relationships of Pat McDougal and search for the most unstable, likely suspect. Do you see why we pursue these things?

DAN
(smiling amiably)

When you put it that way, I do.

The two men get up, shake hands, aware that a genuine bond of mutual respect and admiration seems to have sprung up between them.

INT. JAMISON HOME. DAY.

Becky is sitting on her bed trying, without success, to read a book.

MRS. JAMISON (O.S.)

Becky, Jack's here.

We see Becky looking tense, serious, almost transfixed.

JACK (O.S.)

Becky!

We see Becky, puzzled, turn slowly in the direction of the voice, which is coming from the threshold of the doorway of her bedroom. She turns slowly to the figure standing in the doorway. It is Jack, but Jack as a fifteen-year-old, who, very angry and menacing, now enters the room.

JACK
(looking at his sister)

Becky...

But the Becky he sees is Becky as a twelve-year-old, who well knows the meaning of Jack's dark face.

JACK
(advancing on her)

You were in my room again, weren't you?

BECKY
(pacing like a cornered animal)

No, I wasn't.

JACK

My things were moved. Don't lie to me.

BECKY

It must have been Mom, then.

JACK
(advancing further)

Mom hasn't been in my room.

BECKY
(agitated)

Then it was you, Jack, you must have moved your own things without realizing it.

JACK

I told you I would punish you if you went in my room again. Remember?

The beatings, which are by now ritualistic, are always the same. Becky tries to escape, but Jack grabs her roughly by the nape of the neck, pulls her across his knees as he sits on her bed, and holds her head down. She screams, but both know there is no one in the house but Becky and Jack to hear them. Then, his face contorted and furious, Jack administers his spanking, striking her on the buttocks, his hard palm rising and falling like lashes from a whip. The beating does not stop until Becky relents and tells Jack what he must hear.

BECKY

Jack, please, I beg you to stop.

JACK

You admit you went into my room?

BECKY
(screaming)

Yes!

JACK

And that was bad?

BECKY

It was bad.

JACK

You promise never to do it again?

BECKY
(beginning to sob, knowing it is now finally over)

I promise.

JACK
(gently massaging her buttocks)

I hope I didn't hurt you.

BECKY
(through her sobs)

I promise... I promise... I promise. I promise.

JACK
(fondling her hair, stroking her cheek)

I love you.

Always the beatings end with Becky's spirit being broken, but this time, which is why Becky is vividly reliving it, something different happens. As soon as Jack leaves the bedroom, she sits up with determination.

BECKY
(to herself)

I'm going to tell Dan.

(a beat)

And ask him to stop the spankings.

INT. OFFICE. DAY. ONE WEEK LATER.

Becky, very frightened; Mrs. Jamison, very confused; and Jack, fuming with resentment, are sitting together in Dan's office on his couch.

DAN
(to Jack)

Becky tells me that you spank her so hard, sometimes she has black-and-blue marks on her buttocks for days.

JACK
(defiantly)

She's a tomboy. She must take half a dozen hard falls a day.

DAN

Becky calls them beatings.

JACK

I call it old-fashioned discipline.

DAN

And some people call it child abuse. (a beat) Look, Jack, I'm not here to arbitrate. These spankings have to stop, completely. Otherwise, I'm legally obligated to report you to the proper authorities.

JACK
(exploding and rising up from his chair)

All right! They'll stop!

(moving across the room and getting in Dan's face)

And look, bud, a word of warning, I'm up for a wrestling scholarship, so don't even think about fucking up my school record.

Jack storms out, slamming the door viciously behind him. Everybody is upset. Becky cringes, Mrs. Jamison looks mortified, and Dan wonders what he should do next.

MRS. JAMISON

Mr. Rainer, please don't think ill of my son. This is not the way he is at home.

BECKY
(putting her hand on her mother's arm)

Mom, don't be embarrassed. Dan's a therapist, he sees this kind of thing all the time.

DAN
(sighs)

I find it interesting how nobody seems to relate to anybody else in this family. Mrs. Jamison, you seem interested only in protecting your son. Becky, you seem interested only in comforting your mother. And Jack... well, Jack thinks only of himself.

The CAMERA returns to Becky as she sits on her bed, remembering all of this.

MRS. JAMISON (O.S.)

Are you coming down or not, Becky? Jack's here.

And Becky, fueled with fresh anger, goes downstairs to face her brother.

INT. JAMISON HOUSE. LIVING ROOM. SAME TIME.

Jack is sitting on the couch, chatting with his mother and sipping a beer, but as soon as he sees his sister, he jumps up in an excited manner.

JACK

Bee, how are you?

BECKY

I don't like that name, Jack.

JACK
(flustered)

Oh, sure. Becky, how about a kiss for your bro?

Becky ignores this, walks across the room, seating herself in the chair furthest from Jack. As she does so, Jack's eyes follow her, fascinated as always by everything she does.

JACK

Want a beer?

BECKY

You know I don't drink, Jack.

JACK

Bee, I mean Becky, I've been away two months. Can I have a hug at least?

Becky, ignoring this, looks at the floor.

MRS. JAMISON
(nervously looking at Jack)

Well, I'll leave you two to catch up.

As she goes in another room, Jack, exasperated, stares helplessly at his sister.

                              JACK

What's the deal, Becky? Are you going to be giving me the cold shoulder forever?

                             BECKY
                 (for a moment she begins to, but
               doesn't let herself, feel sorry for Jack)

All right. You want to make small talk? So how's Berkeley?

                              JACK
                      (grateful for this crumb)

Well, there's good news and there's bad news.

                             BECKY

What's the good news?

                              JACK

I'm winning all my wrestling matches, so my scholarship at least is intact.

                             BECKY

That's good. So what's the bad news?

                              JACK

Well, I just can't seem to wrap my mind around any of my studies (a beat...pauses, sheepishly looking for sympathy)...(then, getting none)...Is Rita Jenkins still at Silver Oaks?

                         BECKY
                        (coldly)

Yes.

                         JACK

How is she?

                         BECKY
                    (getting annoyed)

You know we never speak.

                         JACK

Becky, what's wrong with you? Why do you always break
my balls? I'm your big brother, remember?

                         BECKY

Is that what you call it?

                         JACK
        (unable to restrain himself, as he smiles sadistically)

Tell me, Becky, have you broken the ice yet? Have you
had your first kiss with a boy...or girl?

                         BECKY
                (refusing to take the old bait)

I've enjoyed our little chat, Jack.

As Becky leaves, Jack whirls around to see where she is going, starts to get
up to follow her, thinks better of it, and sinks back in his chair. We see his
face now (CLOSE UP), infuriated beyond belief at what he considers one
more heartless rejection at the hands of his little sister.

INT. POLICE HEADQUARTERS. DAY.

Dan, utterly absorbed in what is happening, is in the process of being fingerprinted. A female police officer is carefully rolling the tip of each finger on an inky, absorbent surface, as Detective Burns closely watches him.

DAN

(ironically)

Well, at least I'm learning how the other half lives.

INT. JAMISON HOME. SAME DAY. LATE AFTERNOON.

Jack, first making sure that his mother is downstairs, is sneaking into Becky's room. He quietly closes then locks her door, all the while listening for the sound of footsteps on the stairway. He knows what he is looking for—something intimate and revealing, a diary, a journal, some personal letter—but he does not know where to look. So he searches everywhere. He goes through her drawers and carefully examines the contents. He is struck by how few, how simple are the clothes that she wears. He chuckles at the undergarments she wears. He is puzzled by the newspaper clipping on the murder of Pat McDougal, which is tucked away into the corner of the drawer. He could not be more delighted when he uncovers the box of Tampax, which he holds aloft almost as a trophy. Jack knows full well—because his mother has confided in him on a number of occasions—how Becky spent years anxiously waiting for her period to arrive. For a fleeting moment, a devilish prank takes shape in his brain...and he begins to pocket the Tampax, almost immediately thinks better of it, and returns it to its former hiding place. He accepts that his search is fruitless only after he has gone through everything, including the box on the floor and the shelves on top of her closet. Then, he puts everything as it was before and listens again for the sound of his mother's footsteps.

He goes to the framed picture on the wall, above the head of Becky's bed, and pauses to look at it. (CLOSE UP) It is Becky, balancing herself as she stands erect, her hair flying, on the back of Storm, who obviously is in motion. (It is the frame we saw in the opening credits.) Jack's eye travels downward to the lower right-hand corner of the framed picture. With the nail of his right thumb, he peels away a tiny flesh-colored piece of tape concealing a keyhole-size aperture (CLOSE UP) just a fraction of an inch from this lower right-hand corner.

Then, he quickly, stealthily, and at last leaves Becky's room. He goes into his own room, repeats the exact same procedure to a corresponding spot on his own bedroom wall, separated by a mere foot or so from his sister, and reveals a matching keyhole-size aperture (CLOSE UP). Jack puts his eye up to it (CLOSE UP). We now see, with Jack, a perfect sight line from the center of his bed to the center of Becky's bed, to the large oval mirror hanging above the dresser at the far end of her room. His work done, Jack feels considerably better about himself. He breaks out into a sadistic grin. A power grin. He removes from his back pocket a flask filled with vodka and tonic that he has lately taken to carrying around with him wherever he goes and takes a long swill. He is in the place he wants to be. He is in action. On the go. On the move—like Storm.

EXT. RANCH. LATE AFTERNOON.

Speaking of Storm, Becky is performing the trick she first taught herself to do when she was ten. And Martin, who has witnessed this numerous times, cannot help watching her do this yet again with a look of admiration, a little bit of awe, and a touch of love. So, as she dismounts, he must tell, as he always does...

MARTIN

I just don't know how you can do that.

BECKY
(pleased)

It's only a trick, Martin. It looks a lot harder that it is. The back of a horse is very strong and steady. If you trust your animal...trust your own body...have good balance... you can do it.

MARTIN
(trying to comprehend this)

They say your brother was a great wrestler when he was at Silver Oaks.

BECKY

I'll give him that... he's really a fabulous athlete.

MARTIN

And your father... you said...

BECKY
(helping him out)

Family legend has it, in the '76 Olympics he was only a sixteenth of a second away from making the track team.

MARTIN

It must be in your gene pool.

BECKY
(smiling)

Maybe, that is the one, the only good, thing I got from my parents.

MARTIN

I'm not a real athlete....

BECKY
(hurrying to defend him)

What matters in karate is execution, and nobody in the whole school executes as beautifully as you do.

They continue to walk, with Storm in tow. And now Martin decides the time has arrived, is as good as it will ever be to ask Becky the question he has been rehearsing in his mind for the past two years.

MARTIN
(very nervously)

Uh, Becky, there's a dance this Saturday night at Glenmore. I...was wondering...if you're not doing anything ...if you'd consider going with me.

BECKY
(blindsided by this and desperate to get off the hook without hurting her friend's feelings)

Well, I don't dance, Martin.

MARTIN

I could teach you...with your balance...you could pick up a few steps in a matter of minutes.

BECKY
(getting stubborn now)

I don't want to learn how to dance.

MARTIN
(just as stubborn now and determined to get an answer one way or another)

We could skip it then.... There's a movie playing.

BECKY
(trying one more time to spare his feelings)

Martin, if you really want to date someone, I happen to know that a lot of girls at Silver Oaks would love to go out with you.

MARTIN
(being sullen)

I don't like a lot of girls.

BECKY
(finally exasperated)

You're pressuring me, Martin. For two years, ever since I met you.... You've acted like we were just friends.... But you want more than that, don't you?... You drop a hint here... you drop a hint there.... You want to date me?... Then stop beating around the bush... be a man... just ask me. I'll say yes... I'll say no... and that'll be that.

Martin looks down briefly to cover his shame, more hurt by these remarks than by any he has ever received at the hands of a girl. But he has too much quiet dignity; he is too much of a fighter not to retaliate.

MARTIN

Shut up, Becky! Take your high and mighty act and show it to someone who deserves it.... Don't you ever talk to me that way again. You don't want to date?... The hell with you.... You're right, there are plenty of girls at Silver Oaks who would love to date me.

BECKY
(not only remorseful once again, but strangely
emotional and on the verge of tears)

I'm sorry, Martin.... Look... it's not you at all.... I just don't date... you may happened to have noticed that little fact about me in the two years you've known me.... I don't care if they don't think that's cool at Silver Oaks... or what they say about me.... I'm not gay... but I'm just not ready to date... now.

MARTIN
(all of a sudden feeling very sorry for Becky)

Okay...I'm really not that slow...tell me something seven, eight, nine times, and on the tenth...I get it....It's not personal...Becky Jamison doesn't date....So, all we can be is friends...for now...and maybe forever.

BECKY
(grateful)

You mean it?

MARTIN

Sure. (a beat) And don't worry...I'll let you ride Storm.

INT. DAN RAINER'S OFFICE. LATE AFTERNOON.

BECKY
(seated in her chair)

And I actually said, "Dan, Dan, Dan. Why do I act this way?"

Dan is looking at Becky, utterly absorbed in her account of her locker room confrontation with Rita Jenkins.

DAN

Well, Rita struck a nerve....You've been worrying about the development of your breasts for years now....Still do those exercises?

BECKY

Religiously. Once in the morning...once at night. Sometimes I think they're okay...once in a while I even think they're kind of nice....Most of the time, though, I wonder if they're too small and puny looking...and I keep torturing myself...can't seem to make up my mind.

DAN
(thoughtful)

Well, there's something you haven't tried.

BECKY

What?

DAN
(hesitating)

Well, you could let me take a quick peek.

BECKY
(confused, but curious)

You mean with my leotards on?

DAN

No. Without the leotards.... Look, Becky, we're more intimate than you are with your doctor ... and I'm just talking about a simple look.

BECKY
(shyly)

Okay.

Slipping her hand under her sweater, Becky slowly eases the straps of her leotards, first off one shoulder, and then the other. The CAMERA now focuses behind Becky. Dan moves from his chair and assumes a crouching position directly in front of her. Erotically, as though undressing, we see Becky, inch by inch, raise her sweater, as Dan's face gradually disappears from view. Becky's head tilts further and further back as she seems to surrender herself to Dan. Quiet rapture infuses her face. Her breathing becomes visibly more rapid. Finally, her ecstasy peaks, subsides; her head comes forward; we see her roll her sweater back down, and now Dan's face reemerges. He is misty-eyed ... awestruck ... enchanted.

DAN

Becky...they're beautiful...they're just beautiful....

CLOSE UP DAN'S FACE AS IT WAS A FEW MINUTES AGO.

He is looking in a very puzzled way at his patient.

DAN

Becky, I have to say...you seemed so lost in the world of your thoughts just then. I can't help asking, what were you thinking?

BECKY
(blushing)

Oh—I uh,...was just wondering...trying to imagine what it would be like...to be a woman who's really confident about her body. (a beat) I think you were saying there's something I haven't tried?

DAN
(trying to recapture his thoughts)

Oh, yes. Well, I think you might try dating....There's nothing I know as validating as a young man, someone you like and respect, who acts as though he finds you an attractive woman.

BECKY
(happy to get off the hook)

Are you forgetting, Dan, I haven't had my first kiss yet? (a beat) You know, Dan, I wanted to say before...I was thinking that when Rita was standing next to me with her breasts exposed...she wasn't just trying to humiliate me ...she was also getting off sexually.

DAN

Well, lots of people seem sexually interested in you, don't they?

BECKY
(annoyed)

You're saying I'm sexually provocative?

DAN

I'm saying... what you yourself have told me many times ... that you're very sexually self-conscious.... You think about sex a lot, without expressing it. People sense that. If they happen to already find you attractive, then the perception of you as struggling with thwarted sexual desire is that much more exciting.

BECKY

So, do you find me exciting?

DAN
(taken aback)

Why are you baiting me, Becky?

BECKY
(stubbornly)

Why are you answering a question with a question?

DAN
(increasingly frustrated with Becky's knowing air,
the realization that she's deliberately holding
something back that she's now using to toy with him)

You really need an answer?

BECKY

I asked the question, didn't I?

DAN

All right...I find you a very attractive young woman... but as a professional psychotherapist, I've been trained for years to sublimate whatever erotic desires I may have in order to focus on what I'm really here for.

BECKY

You're saying...when it comes to sex...you're a monk?

DAN

I never said that.

BECKY
(now worried that she's gone too far)

I really know nothing about you—whether you have a girlfriend, plan to get married. All I know for sure is that you're not gay.

DAN

How do you know that?

BECKY
(realizing she has just made a slip)

Well, I assume...I mean the girls at Silver Oaks talk about how foxy you are.

DAN

But you said you *know* I'm not gay. (a beat) Becky, have you heard something...from someone...about some sort of relationship I'm supposed to have had with some woman?

BECKY

Why, Dan, is there some relationship with a woman that you're afraid I might find out about? (a beat) (glancing at the clock) Well, time's up again.

DAN

I see you've developed the fine art of saving your most suggestive remarks until the very end of the session.

BECKY
(enjoying her one-upmanship, as she
gets up from her chair)

I guess we'll have to discuss that next week, won't we?

INT. POLICE HEADQUARTERS. EARLY NEXT MORNING.

Det. Ray Burns and Det. Joe Giminoni are discussing their favorite case.

DET. BURNS

Okay, Joe. I want to hear your take on Dan Rainer's story about Pat McDougal as a closet dominatrix.

DET. GIMINONI
(struggling to answer this)

Well...I don't know what to make of it...part of it I can believe...part of it I can't...but I just can't swallow the whole thing.

DET. BURNS

I can. Every last syllable of it.

> DET. GIMINONI
> (thoroughly confused now)

But ... why?

> DET. BURNS

Couple of reasons. Murder suspects, when they want to cover up something, they tell stupid lies, tell irrational lies, tell lies with obvious holes in them, but they don't concoct a fantastic story. That serves absolutely no purpose—that is, unless the story happens to be true. Then, the more I get to know the guy, the more real and believable he seems to me. ...But the clincher for me was his behavior yesterday, when he was being fingerprinted. He certainly must have realized there was an excellent chance that his prints would match a pair taken from the corpse. You would never have known it though if you saw how relaxed he looked.... That kind of confidence comes only from knowing that you are innocent.

> DET. GIMINONI

I've put a rush on Dan Rainer's fingerprints. Maybe they'll put him in the clear.

> DET. BURNS

I hope so, for his sake.

INT. JAMISON HOME. AFTERNOON. SAME DAY.

Jane Foley, a very sexy, upbeat young woman, and Jack are leaning against the refrigerator, making out, as Becky comes home from school.

> BECKY
> (irritated)

What are you guys doing? Working on your intervention for Sam?

JANE
(trying to break free of Jack, who
does not even turn around)

Hi, Becky. Long time, no see. Listen, I would like to talk
to you about Sam.

JACK
(pulling Jane back)

I'm not through with you yet, babe.

BECKY
(now enraged)

I'm outta here.

Becky, slamming the door behind her as she goes, but she has nowhere
really to go except back to her car.

INT. POLICE HEADQUARTERS. EVENING. SAME DAY.

Detective Giminoni, perpetually enthusiastic, is entering Detective
Burns's office.

DET. GIMINONI
(excited, waving his notebook)

I think I got something.

DET. BURNS
(smiling in a kindly way)

You're a real go-getter, aren't you, Joe?

DET. GIMINONI

Thanks. Well, first, Dan Rainer's fingerprint results are
back; and they're inconclusive.... They don't rule him in,
and they don't rule him out. (a beat) But here (looking at his

notes) so far I've gone through all the names I have, and the only one who seems to drive a Nissan Sentra is a Becky Jamison. (a beat) She's Dan Rainer's patient, whom he's been seeing for the last five years. So I did some checking, and a Mrs. Morris, she's been living across the street from the Jamisons for the past six years, remembers seeing Becky on the night of the murder, getting in her car, a Nissan Sentra, and driving off around 7:00 p.m.... She didn't see her come back... and didn't see her again until a little after 7:00 a.m. the following morning when she picked up the morning newspaper as soon as it was delivered. Listen to this, though—she remembers at the time she was struck by the fact that she had never before ever seen Becky pick up the newspaper as soon as it was delivered.

DET. BURNS

BINGO! I think we've just found our 911 caller. Great work, Joe.

DET. GIMINONI

Thanks, but do you think Dan Rainer is gonna cooperate here?

DET. BURNS

Good question. I think Dan is definitely a guy who, if there's a conflict between what the law mandates he should do and what his conscience tells him, will definitely side with what he thinks is in the best interest of the patient. (a beat) Well, I guess I have to have another go at poor Dan.

INT. JAMISON HOME. LATER IN THE EVENING. SAME DAY.

Becky, returning from hours of time killing and aimless driving, sees her mother sitting at the kitchen table having tea and toast. Suddenly she pauses, thinking she has heard some noise emanating from upstairs.

BECKY

Where's Jack?

MRS. JAMISON
(continuing to stare at her toast)

Upstairs in his room.

BECKY
(thinking she hears the same noise, but getting louder)

Is Jane gone?

MRS. JAMISON

Jane is with him.

INT. JACK'S ROOM. SAME TIME.

We see Jack, naked, who has started to have intercourse with Jane, also naked. If you only saw Jack's strained face, his wild look, you might think—instead of making love—he was engaged in some exhausting physical labor.

The CAMERA returns to Becky, who begins to identify the rhythmically escalating, mattress pounding noise for what it unmistakably is.

BECKY
(agitated)

Mom, do you hear that?

MRS. JAMISON
(still poking at her snack)

Hear what?

BECKY

That noise. Do you know what that's the sound of?

MRS. JAMISON

No, sweetheart.

BECKY

That's Jack and Jane FUCKING!

MRS. JAMISON
(putting her hands over her ears)

I won't have that kind of language in my house.

BECKY

Okay, Mom. Let me put it to you this way—are you aware
that your son is having intercourse this very moment with
Jane Foley in your sacred house?

MRS. JAMISON

I'm sure I have no idea what they're doing. And I don't
want to hear this kind of talk.

BECKY
(screaming)

And I don't want to hear that!

Enraged, Becky flies up the stairs, storms up to Jack's room, and begins to
pound furiously on the closed door with her fist.

BECKY

Jack, Jane, Mom says she doesn't want to hear you two
FUCKING EACH OTHER!

Instant silence. Then forced laughter. Then...

JACK (O.S.)

Yeah, right.

Becky, with nowhere else to go, retreats to her room, sits on her bed, and tries to think what she should do next. She is startled when, in less than a minute, the figure of Jack, who has hastily thrown on some clothes, appears in the doorway.

JACK
(face red with rage)

What I do behind closed doors is my business. What is your fucking problem anyway?

BECKY
(jumping off the bed to confront her brother
in a way she has never dared to do before)

When I hear you two going at it like baboons, then it is my problem.

JACK
(inching menacingly closer)

No, your problem is that you're sexually frustrated because you're afraid to come out of the closet.

BECKY
(not backing down)

No, my problem is that I've got a brother who has just come out of the closet...but he's a PERVERT!

For a moment, Jack, who has been wounded to the quick by this last remark, entertains the thought of cracking his sister's head against the bedpost—doing to her what he did to Bill. But he knows that if he loses control—no longer being able to restrain himself—he will move into dangerous territory. So he stops short, gives his sister a very violent "fuck you" sign, and stomps off.

INT. JACK'S ROOM. MOMENTS LATER.

Jack, still fuming, rejoins Jane in his bed, who passes him the joint she's working on. Jack greedily puffs on it, reaches for his flask on the bed stand, helps himself to a very long drink, and hands it to Jane.

> JANE
> (thoughtful)

Jack, do you really think your sister is a lesbian?

> JACK
> (pausing)

I think... she's afraid to find out... whatever she is.

> JANE
> (grinning)

Well, you're certainly not afraid.

> JACK
> (hungry for a compliment)

What do you mean?

> JANE

Jack, baby, I don't think you've ever fucked me like you have in this room.

INT. DAN'S OFFICE. AFTERNOON NEXT DAY.

Becky enters, having spent another sleepless, tortured night, but relieved she has finally made an important decision.

> DAN

I'm very eager to find out what it is that couldn't hold over the weekend.

BECKY

(long pause)

Dan, I've decided to stop therapy.

DAN

(stunned, although not that surprised)

Becky, I know that you're keeping something important from me.

BECKY

What if I am? That's my right, isn't it?

DAN

If you don't tell me, who are you going to tell?

BECKY

Did you hear me, Dan? I said I'm stopping therapy. That means I don't trust that any more good can come out of this. (a beat) Now, if I don't trust you enough to continue to see you as my therapist, why would I trust you with some terrible secret?

DAN

Because they're separate. You can decide to stop therapy and still think of me as a trustworthy person. (a beat) Now, let's say, let's agree that you are stopping therapy. But let's also say, at the same time, you happened to have witnessed, inadvertently, a terrible thing. Say you saw a friend getting raped. Or say you saw a friend raping someone. Or you learn about it. Or you discover something equally hideous. Now, even if you were stopping therapy, wouldn't it be helpful—since you trust me as a person—to get it off your chest, tell it to someone who is experienced and who cares about you as a person?

BECKY
(wearily)

No, Dan. If there were some horrible, painful, shameful secret, in order to tell you, I'd have to trust you as a person, and it's not enough to trust you—have trusted for five years as a therapist.

DAN
(trying to hide the fact he has been quite
hurt by this last remark)

Have I ever shown myself to be personally trustworthy?

BECKY

But, then, I don't really know you personally.

DAN
(a little impatiently)

Have I ever lied to you?

BECKY

No.

DAN

Have I ever betrayed you?

Only an awkward silence in which Becky refuses to answer. Then...

BECKY

You said a long time ago, I could choose to stay or to go.

DAN

That's true. But someone can also choose to squeeze the trigger of a gun, stab someone with a knife, inject heroin in their veins, or kill themselves. But that's not freedom. In my experience, people rarely act out of real freedom. They act out of ignorance, out of fear, because of pain, conflict, compulsion, obsession, and desperation. But that's not freedom.

BECKY
(very sadly)

I am desperate, Dan. But, whether I choose to fight that desperation by continuing to come here...or by some other way...is my decision.

DAN
(realizing he has gone as far as he can)

I agree.

BECKY
(getting up, choking back tears)

Good-bye, Dan.

DAN

Becky, could you do just one thing for me?

BECKY

What is it?

DAN

Could you think about coming for one last session. Not for me to try and sell you on the benefits of staying in therapy, but just to sort of wrap things up and say good-bye. I promise you, I won't even mention your secret. We'll call it X and it will be a taboo subject. You don't have to respond now. Think about it. And if you are agreeable, give me a call. Could you do that?

BECKY

I'll think about it.

But she is sure, as she leaves, she has just had her final session.

JAMISON HOME. SAME DAY. LATE NIGHT.

Becky, stripped to her waist, is doing her breast development exercises, her back to her mirror. Suddenly, we see the same view, but as though through a keyhole. The CAMERA now CUTS to Jack's room, where, crouching in his underwear, he has his eye pressed against the hole in his wall. We see Becky pause now, as though she hears a noise from the next room, quickly move to her door to make sure it is locked, then abruptly start to cover herself. We then see Jack realizing she has heard something, and he turns off the lamp on his bed stand, sinks back into the shadows of his bedroom, reaches for his flask, drinks. He stares stonily into space, brooding upon what he has just seen. Then his arm begins to move. A subtle, but unmistakable gesture that tells us—though we don't see it— that Jack is beginning to masturbate.

INT. DAN RAINER'S OFFICE. SATURDAY MORNING.

Detective Burns is seen entering, as Dan, very curious, looks at him.

DET. BURNS

Thanks for being so generous with your time. I'm going to make this as brief as I can. I frankly need your help...so I'm going to tell you something in the strictest confidence. We have just two clues concerning the identity of the 911 caller. The make of the car and a Silver Oaks school button that was found at the scene of the crime on the night Pat McDougal was murdered. (a beat) Oh, by the way...did any of your patients, as far as you know, lose a school button on the morning following the murder?

DAN

(startled at first, and then angry)

You never stop setting your little traps, do you? No matter how much you appear to be trusting someone... you just go on and lay your traps.

DET. BURNS

(for once surprised himself, then embarrassed)

That's right, Dan, as long as there's a murderer on the loose who has to be brought to justice, a victim's family who needs to be consoled, a citizenry who demand to be protected, I can never forget I'm a policeman. Just as I imagine, when you're working with a patient, no matter what your feelings may be, you can't forget you're a therapist.

DAN

(very frightened as to where this is heading)

What is it you want to tell me?

DET. BURNS

The car that was seen driving away from the scene of the crime was a Nissan Sentra. Becky Jamison drives a Nissan Sentra. She was seen by a next-door neighbor leaving her house and going out for a drive around 7:00 or thereafter on the night of the murder. She wasn't seen again until around 7:00 of the following morning when she was observed anxiously picking up her newspaper as soon as it was delivered. That fact is significant to us because this neighbor cannot recall her ever collecting her newspaper as early as that. (a beat) Now, if Becky Jamison did suddenly lose her Silver Oaks school button on the morning following the murder, that would be a rather telling connection. We probably can find that out if we have to by talking to her classmates. More importantly, if she did see anything at all in connection with the murder, we can find that out, too, rather easily by just interrogating her. This is why I'm asking for your help. If Becky Jamison was the 911 caller, which I think you have to agree is a distinct possibility, then her behavior so far is rather typical. She is scared…she doesn't want to get involved…she doesn't want to come in and talk to us. But as I said to you, California laws are pretty tough on known accessories to a capital crime. If she did see something—if she by any chance saw the actual murderer and keeps choosing to conceal it—well, then she could be in very serious trouble. (a beat) And that's where you come in. If she is the 911 caller…believe me…she's a whole lot better off if she voluntarily comes to us…if you persuade her to voluntarily come to us…than if we have to go get her.

Detetective Burns momentarily stops, removes a card from his wallet, and hands it to Dan, who has been quietly mesmerized by what he has heard.

DET. BURNS (CONT'D)

That's the card of Al Donovan, our lab technician. He has a tape of all the 911 callers on the night of the murder that includes the call telling us about Pat McDougal. That caller, by the way, was a young girl…fifteen, sixteen, maybe seventeen…the tone, the voice quality are quite good. If it is Becky Jamison you should be able to tell, quite easily. If it is her, and you'll be doing her a favor… believe me. If it is not her…you could rule her out very quickly…and help both her and us at the same time. (a beat) Now, I realize, being a therapist…your loyalty is to your patient and your personal code of ethics, and not to some legal mandate that tries to tell you what to do as a therapist. So, I ask, you, to just think about it. And, if you agree, give Al Donovan a call and set up an appointment to listen to the 911 tape. What have you got to lose? Then, if you do listen to it, and if it should turn out to be Becky

Jamison, I'll leave it to your conscience to decide what you think is best. Will you do that?

DAN

Yes. I'll think about it.

Detective Burns, having dropped his bombshell, quietly leaves. And Dan, true to his word, does indeed think about it...for about five seconds. Then, arriving at his decision we see CLOSE UP DAN'S FACE AS HE PICKS UP THE PHONE.

DAN

Hello...is Al Donovan there?

INT. JAMISON HOME. LATER THAT MORNING.

We see Mrs. Jamison, dressed and carrying a suitcase, coming down the stairs and heading for the front door. As usual, she is oblivious to her daughter, who is eating some oatmeal at the breakfast table.

BECKY
(surprised)

Where are you going?

MRS. JAMISON

To see Mae.

BECKY

You saw Mae three weeks ago.

MRS. JAMISON

She's my sister and she's very sick. She needs me.

BECKY

I need you, too.

MRS. JAMISON

I'll be back Tuesday.

BECKY
(glancing nervously upstairs)

When's Jack going back to Berkeley?

MRS. JAMISON

He has an 11 a.m. bus ticket, Monday morning.

BECKY

But that means I'll be alone with him in this house the entire weekend.

MRS. JAMISON

He's your brother, dear.

BECKY

Mom, don't you understand? I'm afraid to be alone in the house with Jack.

MRS. JAMISON

Becky, you're not a little girl anymore. I can't always protect you.

BECKY
(sadly)

You never protected me.

MRS. JAMISON
(edging toward the front door)

Look, sweetheart, if you have a problem with Jack, just talk to him about it and work it out. Remember, you have a good head on your shoulders.

BECKY
(bitterly)

Work it out, eh, Mom? Like me and Jack have always done, right? Hey, Mom, Jack just killed Bill. Work it out, dear. Hey, Mom, Jack just beat my ass until it's black and blue. Well, work it out, dear. Hey, Mom, the walls are starting to shake because Jack's fucking his brains out in the next room. Work it out, sweetheart!

MRS. JAMISON
(putting her hands over her ears)

Becky, I will not tolerate language like that in my house!

BECKY

No, Mom, but you will tolerate whatever Jack does.

INT. YWCA. AFTERNOON. SAME DAY.

We see Becky with the suitcase with which she was going to run away, at a reception desk.

BECKY

How much for a room until Monday morning?

The receptionist tells her. Becky registers, pays in advance, takes her bag, and heads for her room. And she tells herself, if only for one weekend—with her whereabouts unknown—she will be safe from her brother.

INT. POLICE LAB ROOM. LATER THAT DAY.

Dan, seated at a table, is looking at the tape recorder, and listening to Al Donovan's instructions.

AL DONOVAN

Treat it like any other tape recorder. Hit the play button when you're ready, and the 911 call about Pat McDougal will come on. It lasts a little more than ten seconds. When you're finished, if you want to hear it again, just hit rewind, and start over. Play it as many times as you need to.

Dan, looking very solemn, hits the play button as Becky's voice comes on. For the duration of the message, we hear the message with the CAMERA HOLDING on Dan's face.

BECKY (V.O.)

Hello. I want to report an accident. A woman is lying in the street in a pool of blood. Near the corner of Corona and Glover Street. She looks badly hurt, so please hurry.

Although Dan is quite certain after just one hearing, he plays it three times, hoping for a miracle. But there is none. So he shuts it off... to find Al Donovan, turned around in his chair, and curiously staring at him.

AL DONOVAN

Ring any bells?

DAN

No. But maybe it'll jog something, later on.

AL DONOVAN
(disappointed)

Sure, come back as often as you need to.

Dan, realizing he now has a terrible decision to make, drags himself from the lab. As soon as he leaves, we see (CLOSE UP) Al Donovan quickly pick up the telephone.

AL DONOVAN

Hello, Detective Burns? Yeah...he just listened to the tape.

INT. JAMISON HOUSE. MONDAY AFTERNOON.

Becky, holding her suitcase, is entering her house. To make sure her mother has not by chance come back ahead of schedule, she calls out her name once, twice. She pauses, listening hopefully for sounds.

Then, softly, advances up the staircase, still listening. Not having taken a shower for two whole days, she is anxious to take one. But she checks Jack's room, the door well ajar. She enters, searching for signs of his continuing presence, that he has not yet left, but finds none. To make sure, she opens each of his bureau drawers and ascertains that they are indeed empty. Satisfied, she heads back to the comfort of her own room. We see her leave, and then...in a QUICK CUT...

INT. JACK'S ROOM.

The CAMERA zooms in on a narrow space, between the side of the bureau and the far end of the room—a spot where Becky did not look—where we see CLOSE UP Jack's suitcase, still there. Then...

INT. SHOWER.

Becky enters the bathroom, carefully locks the door, checks and double-checks the door to be certain it is securely shut. Then, in a series of QUICK CUTS, we see: Becky, undressing. Getting into the shower, bathing, washing her hair. Then...

EXT. CAR DRIVING. SAME TIME.

CLOSE UP on Jack's face, who is in a black mood, wondering what he should do next with his life, and where he should go. He drives with one hand, periodically takes a sip from his ever ready flask with the other. Then...

INT. JAMISON HOUSE. FIVE MINUTES LATER.

Jack is entering the house. He goes straight for the kitchen, but then stops. Almost instantly, his animal instincts alert him to the gurgling noise emanating from the bathroom directly above, which indicates the shower is being run. Jack sits down at the kitchen table, occupies himself with emptying his flask, now and then glancing at the ceiling.

Suddenly he smirks with a kind of devilish, what-the-hell look and very stealthily treads up the stairs. He approaches the door, listens again for the sound of the shower, and in the manner of a cat burglar tries the doorknob. He is not surprised, of course, that it is locked shut. He reaches down, tries to peer through the keyhole, and sees—CLOSE UP of a keyhole-shaped blur—nothing. Satisfied, he has done what he could, he returns to the kitchen.

Jack begins to drink in earnest, with a passion. He drains the flask, goes to the cabinet, and refills it with a bottle of straight vodka. He continues to drink steadily, and we see that something dark and terrible that has been building up in him for many years is about to be unleashed. He tells himself he has nothing to lose; there is no longer any point in restraining himself. He drinks heavily to calm his nerves, makes his decision, goes up the stairs, and waits in his bedroom, with the lights out, the door closed, as it was before. Then...

INT. BECKY, LEAVING BATHROOM.

She is covered only with a long terry cloth bath towel. She listens one more time for telltale noises, and then, ever vigilant, returns to Jack's room, opens the door and quickly scans the room. She sees no one. Satisfied she is safely alone in the house, she leaves, closing, as before, the door behind her. And then, in a QUICK CUT...

INT. JACK'S ROOM.

In the space behind the door, in a very creepy way, his back flattened against the wall, his arms spread out, his eyes predatory, is Jack. Then...

The CAMERA returns to Becky, standing before her bedroom mirror, drying and combing out her hair, which she has temporarily set free from her ponytail. The angle is from behind Becky. The SHOT is of her reflection in the mirror. But then suddenly Jack's face weirdly joins Becky's reflection.

Terrified and startled, Becky whirls around and faces her brother. In a QUICK CUT, we see Becky as a twelve-year-old being cornered in her room by a fifteen-year-old Jack, intent on spanking her. Then...

                          BECKY

Jack, what are you doing here?

                          JACK
                (attempting some sleazy charm)

I wanted to say good-bye to you before I left (extends flask). Want a drink?

                          BECKY

No, I don't want a drink. Get out of here, Jack.

Almost instantly enraged, Jack takes his flask, greedily drinks from it, hurls it as hard as he can at the bedroom mirror, cracking it. And then, his face contorted with hate, begins mimicking his sister.

                          JACK

I don't want a drink, Jack...don't kiss me, Jack...don't touch me, Jack...don't call me Bee, Jack. You've been shitting on me since you were ten years old. But you know what you are? You're a cocktease.

BECKY

(trying desperately to stay calm in order to protect herself)

You're drunk, Jack.

JACK

(taking an unsteady step toward her)

Drunk? Or am I the only person in this fucking household who sees through you?

BECKY

(who is cornered now)

Don't be insane, Jack. Think of your college record.

JACK

(loving this moment)

I don't have a college record anymore, Becky. I was kicked out last Tuesday. Why the fuck else do you think I came back? Want to know why I was kicked out?

BECKY

No, Jack, just get out of my room.

JACK

(almost on top of her)

She called it date rape. I called it rough sex. There was no proof... so they kicked me out.

BECKY

I don't know what's gotten into you, but if you lay one finger on me, I'll tell... I'll tell Dan. You remember I did that when I was only twelve, I'll certainly do it now.

JACK

That pussy was afraid of me then, when I was only fifteen. He knows that if he goes to the cops I'll beat the living shit out of him.

BECKY

Then I'll go myself, directly to the police.

JACK

And who are they going to believe... a certified psychopath like you, or me?

BECKY

You mean an alcoholic pervert like you who's just been charged with attempted rape?

Incensed that she continues to defy him, Jack reaches for her and Becky, as hard as she can, tries to kick him in the groin. But she is hampered in her movement, as fearful of losing her scant covering as she is of missing her target, and Jack easily parries her attack. But it is really what he has been waiting for because it makes it easier for him to do what he has to do. With catlike speed, Jack slips around her and captures her in a bear hug. He pauses to enjoy her squirming body, as he once did five years ago.

JACK

So, the dyke has finally come out of the closet and wants to kick her big brother in the balls?

Jack hoists Becky in the air—again as he once did, after she had stabbed him with a pencil—and slams her as hard as he can to the mattress of her bed. Quickly, he pounces on top of her, straddling her with his legs. Becky struggles frantically, one hand trying to keep her bath towel from coming undone, the other trying to fend off Jack, who sits on top, catches her wrists and pins her arms to the bed.

JACK
(gloating down at his prisoner)

Don't you know how much stronger I am than you, that any time I want, I can overpower you physically? (a beat —then glancing down lewdly and pointedly at her now fully exposed breasts) Well, I see you've been developing nicely since you were twelve.

BECKY
(trying to plead with someone
she now believes is insane)

Jack, look, I know I have a chip on my shoulder and maybe ...I really am paranoid like they say...but I never did anything to you, I never tried to hurt you, did I?

JACK

Never did anything, Becky? Whenever I walk in the room, you look like a little piece of shit just got stuck to the bottom of your shoe, and you can't wait to scrape it off. That's nothing?

BECKY
(almost crying)

Jack, I've been in therapy twice a week for the past five years, because of you. I don't have any more pain to give you.

JACK

Keep begging, Becky. It's giving me a hard-on.

BECKY
(struggling not to take the bait)

Jack, what do you want from me? Tell me. What do you want?

JACK
(pointedly and lewdly enjoying the
sight of her bare breasts)

You don't know? Well, you can begin by sucking my cock.

Becky raises her head up and spits in the face of her brother.

BECKY

You sick freak.

More enraged than ever, Jack slaps Becky in the face, but harder than she has ever been hit, harder even than Pat McDougal hit her, almost knocking her unconscious. And finally, the fight goes out of her and she stops resisting.

BECKY
(her eyes closed, whimpering and crying softly)

Jack, don't...please. (a beat, and when there is no response) Then kill me first, Jack.

Jack, astonished, cannot remember his sister looking so helpless and child-like. Not it seems since he used to spank her. He looks down at Becky, her bath towel now completely undone, lying there, naked and beautiful, the passionate object of his incestuous fantasies, ready to be taken. But, strangely, he feels quite satisfied, and he now realizes something he has never known and will never forget. What he really wants is domination, complete power and mastery of a little sister whose spirit is crushed. He wants her to look up at him, like she once did to his father, with the same childlike wonder. He wants to be her godlike daddy, to feel her obedient, worshipful love, and can think of no other way but this to get it. And feeling this way, the thought of sexually touching her is as repulsive as it would have been to his own father.

So Jack gets off his sister. Gently, he covers her up again with her bath towel. He even tries to stroke her cheek, the way he used to after he spanked her, but Becky, her eyes still shut, instantly and instinctively shudders as though something repulsive is slithering along her face.

JACK
(standing up now)

I love you, Becky.

(a beat... then, to comfort her)

I wasn't really going to do anything, you know.

Jack moves further from the bed, spellbound by what he sees—Becky almost looking as though she is having an out-of-body experience, her spirit now no less broken and lifeless than Bill's neck was five years ago. Quietly he begins to backpedal out his sister's room, exactly as his father no doubt once did when he did not want to disturb his sleeping angel.

EXT. PAYPHONE/STREET. HALF AN HOUR LATER.

Becky looks fearfully around to see if she is being followed as she picks up the telephone. SPLIT SCREEN. BECKY AND DAN EACH HOLDING THE PHONE.

BECKY

Dan?

DAN

Becky!

BECKY

I was thinking about what you said... I'd like a last session.

DAN
(excited)

Great. When do you want to come?

BECKY

How about tonight?

DAN

You can come to my house...in an hour.

BECKY

Okay.

DAN

The address is...

BECKY

I remember.

(hangs up)

INT. DAN RAINER'S HOUSE. AN HOUR LATER. NIGHT.

Becky, pale and exhausted, is sitting on a chair, facing DAN.

DAN

Becky, I do, of course, want to hear what you have to say, but first I have something important to tell you.

BECKY
(curious)

What, Dan?

DAN
(very serious)

Last Monday night, I *know* that you were there.

BECKY

You saw me?

DAN
(confused)

Saw you?

BECKY

You saw me outside your window?

DAN

What are you talking about, Becky?

BECKY

When you were with Pat McDougal.

DAN
(stunned)

You were there ... watching us?

BECKY
(ashamed, looking down)

Yes, I was, Dan.

DAN

W-well ... how much.... What did you see?

BECKY
(in almost a whisper)

I saw everything, Dan, everything you both did.

DAN

Everything?

BECKY

From the time she came into the room until when she left.

DAN
(the horror of it sinking in)

You were watching us...oh, my God. So that's the big secret you were keeping from me! You were watching us!

BECKY
(who sees Dan's shame, but not his rage)

Don't be ashamed, Dan. I'm not mad at you anymore. I realize she forced you to have sex with her....

DAN
(his eyes on the floor, now unable
to look his patient in the face anymore)

My God! How could this happen?

BECKY
(who has slipped from her chair to comfort him)

Dan, don't be ashamed. I'm not mad at you. I love you...
I've always loved you.

A few feet from his chair, she kneels down.

CUT TO BECKY HUGGING HER FATHER WHEN SHE WAS TWELVE.

Dan does not look up until Becky is almost on top of him, her head leaning toward him.

CUT TO PAT McDOUGAL BENDING TO KISS DAN.

Becky sees only a loving daddy figure whom she means to embrace in a childlike way. But Dan, misinterpreting this, sees one of the most frightening things a good therapist can see—his patient unexpectedly making explicit sexual advances. So, ashamed, terrified, and then enraged, he grabs his patient by the arms and pushes her back, none too gently.

> DAN
>
> Becky Jamison, you disgust me! You turn my stomach, I want you to know that!

It is the worst moment of her life, a moment she will never tell Dan Rainer about. We might liken it to something that is sometimes referred to in psychiatry as soul murder.

> BECKY
> (moaning and bending over)
>
> Ohhhhhh....

She holds her stomach, backs away, stumbles, picks up steam as she reaches Dan's door.

> DAN
> (almost instantly recognizing the
> magnitude of his blunder, but it is too late)
>
> Becky... I-I'm sorry... Of course, I don't mean that....

But she is out the door, and by the time Dan goes to his window, he sees her car already is speeding away. He returns to his desk, picks up his phone, leaves a message.

CUT TO INT. JAMISON HOUSE.

Where we see in successive QUICK CUTS: Becky's phone. The empty house. Each silent room as Dan's voice seems to echo through the house, seeking his patient's forgiveness.

DAN (V.O.)

Becky, this is Dan Rainer.... You just left. That was one of the stupidest...cruelest things...I've ever done. You know that I like you....Put yourself in my shoes, imagine how you would feel if the situation were reversed....

DAN (CONT'D)

Becky, if you want to stop therapy, that's up to you....But, please let's not end it on such a horrible note....Call me, when you get this...please....

EXT. BECKY DRIVING. TWENTY MINUTES LATER.

BECKY
(trying to proudly fight back her tears)
(to herself)

So, I disgust you....You want me to know I turn your stomach....Well, maybe I really am a pig, Dan....But you were my therapist, you shouldn't have said that to me.

INT. JAMISON HOUSE. HALF AN HOUR LATER.

Becky comes in and listens for the sound of her brother, but she is no longer afraid. She is a million miles away from what just happened, from Dan Rainer, from therapy, and from everything it once meant to her. All she has left is her residue of rage, and she calls upon that to rally herself for one last fight. She goes to a kitchen drawer, finds a knife, a real knife this time and not a pencil, and starts up the stair, weapon in hand.

BECKY
(more to herself than to her brother,
in a singsong, chanting, but menacing voice)

Where are you, Jack?...
I'm ready for you this time....
Bill and I have a surprise for you...

She arrives at the top of the stairs, in time to hear Dan Rainer's voice, leaving essentially the same message as before...

BECKY
(listening as though to a distant bell, then)

Let it go, Dan.... I'm beyond help.

She checks each upstairs room, leaving Jack's room for last. She opens the door, sees only a belt hanging on a chair, is about to close it, when she notices...

CLOSE UP KEYHOLE IN JACK'S BEDROOM WALL.

Becky, fascinated in a creepy way, looks through it, finds the matching opening near the bottom corner of the framed picture of her balancing on Storm, looks through it, returns to Jack's keyhole, and suddenly putting it together, sees in her mind what Jack saw: CUT TO BECKY, HER EXERCISES DONE, APPROACHING THE WALL WITH GLEAMING BREASTS.

This final unexpected humiliation is too much to bear. Her spurt of rage evaporates as quickly as it arose. With her back to the corridor wall, her body sags forward, her knife falling to the floor. A series of images takes over her mind. In some jumbled QUICK CUTS we see: Pat McDougal spitting blood. Her body bag being zipped up. Bill's neck broken. Dan holding her by the arms. Jack, sitting on top of her. Looking at her breasts. Increasingly her brain feels like it will explode, and the music here should reflect that: something like the buildup in the famous *Psycho* shower scene, but here the horror, of course, is all from within.

BECKY
(ramming both fists to the sides of her temples, either to
exorcise the images or to keep her skull from bursting
open)

I can't stand this.

She looks to her left down the corridor, then to her right, hoping for a miracle, an angel of mercy to somehow appear. But there are none. Then, she looks back to her right, in the direction of the bathroom, and a new idea seizes hold of her. CUT TO CLOSE UP TOP RAILING OF SHOWER STALL. Then...

INT. BAR ABOUT THE SAME TIME.

Jack is sitting at the bar, nursing a beer, looking anguished. He keeps trying to distract his mind by turning to the Lakers game being shown on TV. But in a series of warring and alternating QUICK CUTS we see: Kobe Bryant and Shaquille O'Neal doing their thing, and Jack murderously slapping his little sister.

BARTENDER

Another?

Making a decision, Jack shakes his head, throws down some money, hurriedly gets back in his car, and returns to the scene of his crime.

INT. JAMISON HOUSE. FIFTEEN MINUTES LATER.

Jack enters, looking very subdued. He listens, then...

JACK
(speaking reassuringly)

Bee...I mean, Becky....It's Jack. I'm not going to hurt you. I just want to talk.

He goes upstairs, looks in Becky's room, looks in his own, vaguely noting that the belt he thought he left hanging on the chair is not there. Then, as he heads back downstairs, something catches his eye that he first thinks is a misperception, then an optical illusion, and then something real but quite odd. Along the edge of the partially opened bathroom door Jack sees what looks like a part of a human hand—the knuckle of a finger perhaps—poking out. Fascinated, he approaches, pulls open the door, to reveal a finger that is joined to a hand, joined to an arm, which belongs to...

CLOSE UP OF HIS SISTER, WHO HAS HANGED HERSELF FROM THE TOP RAILING OF THE SHOWER.

But Jack, although he instantly starts to hyperventilate, knows what to do. He lifts his sister's body, simultaneously loosening the belt, which has become a noose; carries her to the corridor; determines that she is still warm; places her on her back; and feverishly begins to apply CPR, rhythmically applying pressure with his palms to her chest, while alternately blowing in her mouth. He does not know how many agonizing minutes pass without a sign of life. What he does remember is that first stirring, the first fluttering breath as for just a moment Becky opens her eyes and seems to recognize with a quiver her brother sitting on top of her. Then, the upstairs phone on the hamper outside the bathroom rings.

DAN RAINER (V.O.)

It's Dan again, Becky. If you're there...

Jack snatches up the phone, and on A SPLIT SCREEN, we see their frantic conversation.

JACK

Dan, this is Jack. Becky just hung herself. Call 911!

DAN
(gasping for breath)

Is she... still alive?

JACK

I don't know. I'm still applying CPR. Call 911!

Jack hangs up, as we see Dan, his hand shaking, trying to dial 911.

EXT. BOBBY RODGER'S HOUSE. TWENTY-FIVE MINUTES LATER.

Bobby, who is putting out the garbage, stops to watch an ambulance speeding by his house. When he sees it stop on the same block on which his friend Becky Jamison lives, he begins to run.

EXT. JAMISON HOUSE. FIVE MINUTES LATER.

Two paramedics are carrying Becky out on a stretcher, down the porch steps, and into the back of the ambulance waiting to receive her. As they prepare to lift her and put her in, Jack, who has been anxiously watching, starts to climb in, too. But Becky, whose eyes are open, sees this, and, with a shake of her head, signals a paramedic who bars Jack from entering the back of the ambulance. Then Bobby, breathless from running, approaches the stretcher and draws a first, faint smile from his friend.

BECKY
(hoarse whisper)

Bobby, come here.

Awestruck and mute, Bobby obeys.

BECKY

Hold my hand.

Bobby does so, in the manner of a little child.

> BECKY
> (as they are putting her in the ambulance)

Stay with me.

It is probably the last thing in the world he would have thought of doing on his own, but he cannot say no to his friend. So Bobby, looking more in shock than Becky, rides with her in the ambulance. Jack watches it speed off, and then, left alone in front of his house, CLOSE UP, hangs his head in shame and rage.

INT. PSYCHIATRIC HOSPITAL. MIDNIGHT.

We see Dan, having rallied himself, earnestly and passionately talking to a head nurse, who nods in agreement.

> NURSE

All right, she's just been sedated, but you can see her. She's under restraints because she's on a twenty-four-hour suicide watch. So, just a couple of minutes.

Dan gratefully thanks her, goes to a room just down the corridor, and, not knowing what to expect, slowly opens the door. In the center of the tiny room, Becky, lying flat on her back, is strapped to a table with three heavy brown belts, looking pale and exhausted, but quite alert.

> BECKY

Hi.

> DAN

Hi.

> BECKY
> (sheepishly)

Are you mad at me?

To reassure her, Dan gently puts his hand on hers, the first physical contact they've ever had.

DAN

No, I'm disappointed, I feel awful, of course...heartbroken...about what happened tonight. It's not exactly the termination to therapy that I had in mind.

BECKY

I know I'm supposed to talk to you about these things, but somehow I didn't think you'd approve.

DAN

I guess not. But maybe we could have discussed it and come up with a realistic alternative that was a little bit more hopeful.

They exchange glances, each wondering what the other really thinks, and then Dan, who can hardly bear to see his patient tied up like an animal, gets an idea.

DAN
(first checking to see that the door is closed)

Becky, you don't look very comfortable under those restraints. I'm probably not supposed to do this, but how would it be if I took them off for just a little while? But I'd have to put them back on before I left. Okay?

BECKY
(quickly nodding)

Yes.

So Dan carefully unbuckles the straps across her legs, her midriff, and her arms. Becky sits up, stretches herself, flexes her neck, and her torso. She rolls up the sleeves of her nightgown to examine the effects of the restraints.

DAN
(watching her closely)

Becky, I'm not mad at you, but what I really wonder is, are you mad at me?

BECKY
(thoughtful)

For about an hour, I hated you, Dan. But then, as you've often encouraged me to do, I tried to put it in perspective. ...I know that if the situation had been reversed and someone had been watching me, I could never have forgiven them. So I'm not mad at you.

DAN

Did you hear my message?

BECKY

I heard it, but didn't listen at first. Then, afterward, I replayed it in my mind and it began to sink in.

DAN

Becky, are you up to telling me what happened tonight?

BECKY
(nods, but then raises her hand)

First, Dan, I have something to tell you that I haven't told you yet. It's very important and I want you to listen carefully.

Although Dan thinks he cannot imagine what this could possibly be, he notices that suddenly his heart has begun to beat violently. An agitation that only increases as Becky, step by horrible step, from the time she started to tail Pat McDougal to the time she returned home, retraces and relives her hellish night. And it is the worst chronicle of horror that Dan, in fifteen years as a therapist, has ever heard from the lips of a patient. Overwhelmed as he never has been before, he does what almost any therapist would do, he tries to make sense of it . . . to himself . . . and to his patient.

DAN
(haltingly)

Becky, I think when you saw that woman acting in such a sexually aggressive way, it reminded you of Jack. You were enraged with her and a part of you wanted to protect me like you used to try to protect Bill. . . . But another part of you was also enraged with me . . . whose job it is to protect you, for allowing this to happen and not shielding you from something that was so disturbing.

BECKY
(struggling to understand)

That's too many parts of me to digest right now, not in the condition I'm in.

DAN

There's time.

For a while, they look at one another, each of them reflecting on what the other has said. Then . . .

BECKY

It was self-defense, Dan, right?

DAN

Maybe. But the question is, will a judge or jury see it that way?

BECKY

Why wouldn't they?

DAN

(thoughtfully)

Well, she was a policewoman, for one thing. You've been a mental patient for five years, that is another thing. They're going to have to understand and believe your psychological motivation. In the final analysis, it will come down to whether they decide that, in defending yourself, you used justifiable or excessive force.

BECKY

(seeing his point)

You mean did I kick her too hard?

DAN

Remember that movie you love so much, *A Place In The Sun?*

BECKY

Sure. Montgomery Clift is in the rowboat with Shelly Winters. But he wants to get rid of her so he can marry Elizabeth Taylor. So when she falls in the lake, he lets her drown...

DAN

It's not that at the moment she fell in, unable to swim, he wanted to murder her, but he certainly wanted her to die so he could have Elizabeth Taylor.... So when she fell in the water through her own fault, you might say a window of opportunity unconsciously opened up for him. And the question is, did he really try hard enough... or hard at all ... to save her?

BECKY
(upset)

All I know, Dan, is that she was tough, she could really fight, and she had a gun. I thought she was going to really hurt me, maybe kill me. And she never, never identified herself as an officer of the court.

DAN

But, in understandably defending yourself, did you use the opportunity to release a vicious part of yourself?

BECKY
(sharply)

You mean like when I told you how I watched you and Pat McDougal and you had every right to be furious with me, maybe never to see me as a patient again, but not to say the vicious things you did?

DAN
(accepting this)

You're right, of course. And if you had been successful in your suicide attempt, I would have been no less responsible for contributing to the waste of a human life than you were....

BECKY

Oh no, Dan...no...I didn't mean that. You had nothing to do with tonight.

DAN

Becky, you have every right to be furious with me for what I said. We can talk about it another time, but before I go, tell me about tonight.

Becky does, as calmly and clearly as she can, given the circumstances, and this second shocking disclosure coming on the heels of the other makes this perhaps the worst day in Dan's life. Although he wonders how much more of this he can really stand, he also knows how much more he has to do if he is to have any chance of saving his young patient from a life in prison.

DAN
(struggling to maintain his composure)

Remember, Becky, when you had just met me, the very first thing you said was about how you were suspicious of child molesters. I think, even then, you had a premonition of what Jack had in store for you. (a beat) What were you going to do with the knife?

BECKY

I was going to tell Jack if he ever touched me again, I was going to kill him.

DAN

But he wasn't there. So your rage had to go someplace else?

BECKY
(now deep in thought)

You mean against myself? I guess. (a beat) Well, I think there was more to what happened tonight though than just Jack, or even Pat McDougal. (a beat) You see, six months ago when...(her voice dropping to barely a whisper) I first got my period, I was so happy. Now I would develop, I thought, I would become a complete, normal woman. (a beat) But then I started having these sexual feelings, fantasies, and dreams...some of which were about you... and I just couldn't handle it. I was much too embarrassed to tell you, so I ...

282 the paranoia of everyday life

(trying to help her out)

Reverted to an asexual, preteen world, to twelve-year-old Becky, who used to park outside my window whenever you were really upset.

BECKY
(now remembering)

Yes. You know, Dan, I used to think then you were about the most wonderful person in the world...my second daddy. Kinder even than him, and you understood me (beginning to cry) in a way I never thought possible. But, still, you know...with Jack always being around, always being on me, I couldn't breathe. My mother being blind to my pain, my pride, my touchiness...thoughts that I couldn't accept, that kept torturing me...

DAN

Wasn't enough. You needed more, much more, than just me in your life.

BECKY

Yes. I needed someone to protect me...and when I saw you with that woman...it was like the last hope I had in the world had died.

With no more secrets now left, Becky seems released, finally free. She sighs deeply, yawns, wonders if the medication is beginning to take effect, knows she will soon be strapped down again, so she stretches her body one more time.

Dan, lost in thought, wonders, given how emotionally gutted he feels, how he can possibly continue to fight on his patient's behalf. He does not realize that momentarily he will be giving Becky more than he has ever given her.... But then, looking up, he sees something he has not noticed before and has not wanted to think about: an ugly, swollen, purplish belt burn running along the top of her throat and seemingly still searing into her flesh. Forced to think about it, he tries to imagine what Becky must have looked like hanging by her neck. He conjures up a hangman's picture, but the picture overwhelms him.

DAN
(struggling to choke back his emotions)

I knew you were getting close to me...but I didn't know it was this close....(a beat) I should have seen this coming....

BECKY

No, Dan...you couldn't have known. I did everything I could to hide it from you.

DAN

I still should have seen it coming...

Now he really is overcome and loses his composure and his professional poise abandons him in a way it never has before. Unable to speak, to even look at his patient, he drops his head....

Startled to see a display of emotion she has never seen in five years, Becky gets off her table and approaches Dan. She wants to comfort him. She wants to give him a hug, but she is afraid of being once again misunderstood. So she pauses, a few feet from his chair, silently asking permission as they look at one another. But this time there is no confusion in Dan's mind that this is a sexual advance. He allows, welcomes, and even reciprocates as Becky places her head on his chest and in a childlike, but sweet, delicate way, gives him a hug. And to Dan's amazement, it represents a release for him, too, from anguished, pent-up emotion and almost unbearable guilt.

BECKY

What am I going to do, Dan?

It lasts only a few seconds, but during that time a world of trust and love is exchanged between them. Then—on the same wavelength as never before—they simultaneously disengage themselves. Dan, restored now and mindful of his mission, stands up.

                              DAN

          I have to go, Becky. (a beat) You know I have to report
          this...

                              BECKY

          To the police. I know. I want you to.

                              DAN

          I'll see you tomorrow, then.

He refastens the straps, as gently as he can; touches her hand; and leaves.

EXT. CORRIDOR.

Down the corridor, Dan sees Jack, talking excitedly to the head nurse. He immediately heads for him, but is interrupted by Martin, whom he intuitively recognizes.

                            MARTIN
                          (very upset)

          How is she?

                              DAN

          She's okay. Out of danger.

                            MARTIN

          Can I see her?

DAN

She's just been sedated, Martin. But afterward...I think she might like that.

He puts his hand on Martin's shoulder, who nods, thankful for what Dan has just told him, and Dan again heads for Jack, who, having spotted him, is hurrying toward him.

JACK
(agitated)

How is she?

DAN

She'll live. (a beat, as he takes Jack by the arm) Jack, come with me. We have to talk.

JACK
(suddenly exploding and getting in Dan's face)

Who the fuck do you think you're putting your hands on?

Dan steps back. "Is this worth it?" he asks himself, or should he just call it a night? But he will try one more time.

DAN

Jack, I don't want to fight, I just want to talk. Okay?

Jack reluctantly agrees and follows Dan, who quickly searches for and locates an empty room. They enter together, seat themselves in the only two chairs available, and size one another up. Dan is considering how in the limited time he has, he can make a dent on this hothead. And Jack, who, not surprisingly has miraculously recovered from his attack of guilt for what he did to his sister, now that he knows Becky is not going to die, has only one goal: to stay out of jail.

DAN

Jack, to understand what happened tonight, I think we have to go back to when you killed Becky's cat.

JACK

What! You're going to dig up that old cat shit again? It was an accident.

DAN

Becky told me a few days after her cat urinated on your bed, she discovered burns on his skin that looked as though they had been made by a lit cigarette.

JACK
(smiling sadistically)

Let's just say I wasn't much of a cat person in those days.

DAN
(now getting impatient)

You know, if Becky wants, she can press charges against you. Attempted rape is a serious charge.

JACK
(starting to leap from his chair, but restraining himself)

I never touched her, man . . . not sexually . . .

DAN

Pinning her to the bed, and lying on top of her with her naked underneath you isn't sexual?

JACK

I still never touched her.

DAN

Did you say to her when she asked you what you wanted from her, "You can start by sucking my cock?"

JACK

I was just trying to break her down.

DAN

Well, judging from the fact that a few hours later, she tried to hang herself with your belt, I'd say you succeeded pretty well.

JACK

You're not pinning that on me.

DAN

You dream about her, don't you?

JACK
(startled, then defensive about Dan's question)

Doesn't everybody dream about their family?

DAN

You have dreams about having sex with her, don't you?

JACK
(stubbornly)

No.

DAN

Tell me, Jack, when you masturbate, do you think about her?

JACK

It's none of your fucking business what I think about when I masturbate. Why do you ask? Does it get you hot?

DAN
(deciding he has gone as far as
he can in confronting Jack)

Look, incestuous feelings between brother and sister are quite common, you know.

JACK

What's this, some Freudian shit about how we all unconsciously want to sleep with our mother?

DAN

No, just some cold, scientific facts. Each year there are over two million cases of reported incest. That's actual incest, some of which are really a form of rape....

JACK

I still didn't touch her sexually.

DAN

Look, Jack, instead of being so uptight, suppose Becky had been a Lolita type? Someone who not only wanted to have sex with you, but kept coming on to you. Would you have resisted then, and if so, how hard would you have resisted?

JACK

Actually, I do think she came on to me. Ever since she was ten, whenever Dad or I came into the room, she'd immediately start wiggling her ass all over the place.

DAN

Blaming her for provoking you is a convenient way to avoid taking responsibility for your own sexual feelings, isn't it?...Jack, look, was she the one who drilled holes in your adjoining bedroom walls so she could watch you undress, or were you the one?

JACK
(completely caught off guard by the question,
and reddening for the first time)

What do you want from me?

DAN

I want you to help Becky, Jack. They could put her away for a long time for this, you know.

JACK
(puzzled)

I thought it was only a matter of days in suicide attempts.

DAN

Not with her psychiatric history. Trust me, Jack.

JACK

So what do you want?

DAN

I'd like you to tell the judge at her psychiatric hearing, something along the lines of...how after your father died, the family suffered an upheaval, in which everybody was traumatized...resulting in you becoming the de facto head of the household...and how you abused that power to dominate, bully, and humiliate your sister ever since she was twelve.... You can leave out the sexual feelings and save that for a therapist.

JACK

Well, I guess I could give my edited version.

DAN

That's all I want. I don't intend to report this to the police, and I don't think Becky is planning to press charges against you either... providing, of course, this never happens again. And, (a beat) you know, Jack, if you help her, you just might feel a lot less guilty for hating her.

They nod at one another, shake on the agreement, and for the first time Jack, who has always regarded Dan Rainer as a threat and rival to the Jamison family, wonders if he might not really be an ally.

INT. POLICE HEADQUARTERS. NEXT MORNING.

Dan stops outside the door of Detective Burns's office, takes a very deep breath, and lets himself in.

DAN

There's something I want to talk to you about.

DET. BURNS
(who has been hoping for something like this
but does not dream what Dan is about to tell him)

Sure. Come on in.

INT. CONFERENCE ROOM. THREE DAYS LATER. AFTERNOON.

Dr. Marilyn Fields, Dr. Dennis Cooper, and Mr. Marvin Shapiro, all experienced clinical psychologists, are seated at a conference table. They are gathered to determine, in the light of the sensational nature and gruesome outcome of his five-year treatment of Becky Jamison, if Dan Rainer is professionally fit to continue to see patients. They have been quietly listening for the past two hours to Dan, who is describing the history of the case.

DR. FIELDS

Mr. Rainer, you've told us quite a bit about the treatment, but so far, I haven't heard anything about your personal feelings for this unfortunate patient. Could you talk about that?

DAN

Feelings? Well, I guess, I could say that I loved her, professionally and as a person. Over the past fifteen years, there have been only three patients of whom I could say that, and she's one of them.

DR. FIELDS
(after exchanging meaningful glances with her colleagues)

Could you say more about that?

DAN

In recent years I've thought more and more of settling down and having children. And I used to think ... fantasize sometimes, that if I had a daughter it would be nice to have someone like her, without the tendency to violence, of course.... I remember, once, I had a dream about her ... something in which I received a letter saying the adoption papers for her had just been accepted.

DR. COOPER

Could you tell us, what it was about this patient in particular that elicited such strong feelings?

DAN

Well, she had an exquisitely sensitive, if damaged, self. She was basically warm and tenderhearted. She had a wonderful, ironic sense of humor....But, most of all, I was touched by her spirit, her courage, how she always seemed to be fighting valiantly in defense of her own unique, personal code of honor....Unfortunately, though, she happened to live in a paranoid world filled with tormentors who were all too real...a predatory brother—a nonmother—the entire student body at Silver Oaks, who mostly seemed to hate her.

DR. SHAPIRO
(sympathetically)

You make her sound like a very attractive person indeed, Mr. Rainer.

DR. FIELDS
(interrupting)

Were any of those feelings of love for Becky Jamison of a sexual nature?

DAN
(warily)

No. I don't think so.

DR. FIELDS

You say, as far as you know, your patient stopped spying on you when she was twelve. Is that right?

DAN

Yes.

DR. FIELDS

But it is possible isn't it, that unbeknownst to you, she had returned or regressed to spying on you?

DAN

Obviously, it is possible since it happened.

DR. FIELDS

Well, then, so it was possible that last week while you were engaging in rather bizarre sex with a dominatrix in front of your window, with the curtains not drawn, that Becky Jamison was watching you, the way she had in the past?

DAN
(now seeing where this is going)

Yes.

DR. FIELDS

All right, isn't it then also possible that the realization that perhaps Becky was secretly watching you was motivating you, and you were, if only unconsciously, sexually performing for her benefit, in order to arouse her?

DAN
(who never had remotely entertained this thought,
nevertheless carefully considers it before responding)

It's possible. But, no, I don't think so. It doesn't ring true to me in any way.

DR. COOPER

Just one more question, Mr. Rainer. You told us how you said to Becky, when you mistakenly thought she was making a sexual advance to you, that she disgusted you. In

294 the paranoia of *everyday* life

light of the fact, an hour or so later she tried to hang herself in the bathroom, do you think what you said might have been a contributing factor in her suicide attempt?

DAN

Well, unfortunately, very definitely. It was the greatest blunder of my professional life and had she succeeded, I know I would never have practiced therapy again.

DR. SHAPIRO
(quickly)

Well, of course, you had no way of knowing that Jack had just attempted to rape her. Technically she had even terminated therapy and was no longer your patient. And you certainly had no knowledge that a week before she had murdered a policewoman.

DAN
(excitedly)

That was self-defense. Not murder.

DR. SHAPIRO

I'm sorry, Dan. You're right, we're not here to prosecute your patient, just to examine your conduct.

DR. COOPER

Detective Burns has reported that you played an indispensable role in solving this case.

DAN

I did nothing, really. It was Becky who voluntarily confessed to me and voluntarily wanted me to go to the police.

DR. FIELDS
(who, like the others, cannot help but be impressed by
Dan Rainer's profound remorse, the fact he seems hardly
interested in defending and salvaging his own career)

Mr. Rainer, I think we have all that we need. If you'll step
outside now, we'd like to discuss this among ourselves.

CORRIDOR INT. THIRTY MINUTES LATER.

Dan, who has been increasingly hopeless and despairing over the
future of his patient, does not see the figure approaching, who now places
a hand on his shoulder.

DET. BURNS

How goes it?

DAN

Well, I won't know anything until her hearing tomorrow.

DET. BURNS

I mean, with you and the review board?

DAN
(shrugs)

They're still discussing it. Tell me, what do you think is
going to happen to Becky Jamison?

DET. BURNS

It depends, Dan, very much on the judge. Whether he sees
it as justifiable self-defense, as an act of temporary
insanity, or as manslaughter. (a beat) (seeing Dan's
despair) I'll do anything I can to help your patient, Dan.
Both you and she were a tremendous help in resolving
this case.

The two men shake hands, and there is no doubt that a special feeling of friendship has somehow, in spite of their very different philosophies concerning crime and punishment, sprung up between them. Alone again, Dan returns to his gloomy ruminations as the CAMERA leaves him, PANS down the corridor to the large window, passes through the window to the cloudy sky beyond, and begins to climb until it reaches a bank of pure aerial whiteness. IT HOLDS THE SHOT. Then, in the center of an all-white screen, we see: THREE MONTHS LATER.

EXT. DAY.

We see, from on high, two figures strolling in a leisurely manner along a winding walkway, fringed with grassy lawns and occasional trees. The CAMERA slowly moves in, and we recognize BECKY JAMISON AND DAN RAINER, having a conversation as they go, periodically pausing to gather their thoughts and then resuming.

BECKY

Well, how much longer do you figure I'm going to have to stay in this place?

DAN

My guess is not less than three months ... not more than six.

BECKY
(reflecting on this)

It's pretty peaceful here. (a beat) A lot more than it is outside. When I'm not doing my required activities, I read a lot, sleep, and think about things. You know (a beat, laughs) some of the residents here, I mean they're really nuts. But, for some reason, I'm a lot more well liked here than I was at Silver Oaks.

DAN

Maybe they can see your pain a lot better than other people can.

BECKY

You know, I really do feel bad that I killed another human being. But when I think of who that human being was, when I try to put a face on it, I can't. Or when I put Pat McDougal's face on it, then I think of her mocking me, slapping me, and punching me in the face and I start hating her all over again.

DAN

Well, by separating the two, maybe it's a way of not having to take responsibility for your rage.

BECKY

So what is it then, Dan? I have to live the rest of my life with the idea that I'm a murderess?

DAN

For all I know, Becky, it really was an act of self-defense, pure and simple. But that was only the last act in a complex chain of events. If you hadn't been outside my window watching me, if you hadn't tailed her, none of this would have happened. And that is something for which you are responsible.

BECKY

So until I can take responsibility and feel some empathy for Pat McDougal, I'm not really cured?

DAN

Becky, your hero Raskolnikov, whom you wrote your paper on, he murdered with an axe in cold blood an old pawnbroker woman and her pathetic sister. Now how long did it take him before he could feel genuine remorse for his victims?

BECKY

Nine years...so there's hope for me.

DAN
(looking at her in a kindly way)

There's a lot of hope for you, Becky.

BECKY

What do they say about me on the outside?

DAN

Well, you've been embraced by the feminists; currently you're their flavor of the month.

BECKY

And the kids at Silver Oaks, what do they say?

DAN

Your popularity has skyrocketed. You're the rebel who stood up to a fascist cop with a gun and took her down.

BECKY
(amused)

So, if I had been a serial killer, I might have been able to run for class president!

They stop to briefly reflect on what each of them has said. Then...

DAN

Any visitors?

BECKY

Mom has come a few times, and we had a few pretty good talks...for us. (a beat) Jack keeps trying to see me, but, honestly, I don't know if I can ever look him in the face again.

DAN

You don't have to make that decision now. (a beat) Jack's in therapy, you know.

BECKY
(anxiously)

With whom?

DAN
(reassuringly)

Not with me, Becky. That would be inappropriate to say the least. With someone I never met but hear is very good.

BECKY

God knows, he needs it even more than me. (a beat, then sadly) Bobby has been forbidden by his family to ever have anything to do with me. He comes from a long line of career policemen and to them, I'm the worst thing there is...a cop killer. (a beat, then trying to cheer herself up) But I did get a wonderful letter from him a few weeks ago. (a beat) Know who comes regularly though, each week, like clockwork?

DAN
(not wanting to spoil her surprise, but unable to resist)

I'm going to take a wild guess and say Martin.

BECKY

Sometimes he even stops by that fence. (LONG SHOT OF A HIGH FENCE several hundred feet away, enclosing the area and standing next to a busy thoroughfare.) And we just talk, sometimes for over an hour. (a beat) Next month, for my eighteenth birthday, they're considering giving me a Sunday pass...and we're supposed to celebrate by going on a picnic.

DAN
(gently teasing)

Your first date?

BECKY
(laughs)

I guess.

DAN
(remembering)

Oh, Principal Watkins has just pushed through a resolution for Silver Oaks to get its first metal detector and armed guard in its history.

BECKY

That isn't the answer.

DAN

You know, I agree.

They approach the green-domed dormitory, which marks the end of their conversation.

BECKY

My new home.

DAN

See you next week.

The CAMERA focuses on Becky as Dan's face recedes behind her, gradually going out of focus. Before going in the dorm, she scans the horizon and now finds what she is looking for. The CAMERA follows her gaze and settles on Martin, who is leaning against his car, parked on the other side of the high fence, which serves as the one boundary between the outside world and the residential hospital. When he sees his friend seemingly looking in his direction, he waves at her excitedly.

CLOSE UP BECKY'S FACE.

A weight seems to have been lifted from her. For once, her eyes seem unclouded by pain. She turns to the left, in the direction of the horizon, and waves back. Behind her are years of suffering and humiliation, Silver Oaks, Jack, Pat McDougal, even Dan. To the right is the hospital, her temporary new home. But she steps forward:

To her future.

FADE OUT.

postscript

Becky today is well liked, earnest about whatever she does, and caring of the few friends she has. Not surprisingly, she is wary of entrusting her feelings to another, finds it difficult to un-self-consciously enjoy sex, and does not like to be touched. Her episodes of rage and the violent impulses that in the past have overwhelmed her for a long time have been effectively controlled. Exceptionally verbal and introspectively insightful, she is the kind of patient almost any experienced, dedicated therapist would welcome, which is one reason I've spent the amount of time I have on her.

Becky continues to search for someone, not to protect her, but to be with her in a meaningful sense. She is very much estranged from her brother and cannot ever imagine that changing, although Jack occasionally makes what she regards as insultingly feeble efforts to repair the lasting damage he has caused. She maintains a necessarily very distant relationship with her mother, whom she regards now as more pathetic than cruelly indifferent, but who every once in a while is still capable of wounding her daughter to the quick. She still suffers from what she describes as inexplicably "creepy feelings" that seem to take her over and, she thinks, are linked to her hypersensitivity to having her body violated by sensations of intrusive touching. She is aware that she harbors buried feelings of self-loathing that emerge in dreams and nightmares and that she describes as "weirdly revolting."

Although obsessively deliberate in what she thinks, feels, and does, she knows she is forever battling impulses that seem alien to her, that seem to represent the wishes of a person whom she does not recognize and whom she could not possibly allow herself to become. While she is extremely intelligent, she nevertheless will often express a kind of childlike naiveté at the lack of common decency that she sees constantly displayed around her: that is, "How can people treat one another that way!" Finally, she continues to search for love, knowing that on some level she is seeking a personal salvation for the sense of psychic desolation that still torments her.

In sum, Becky's story is a cautionary showcase for the urgency of the true self's need to be affirmed—the toxic consequences that can ensue when this fundamental need is systematically thwarted by a brutally indifferent, loveless family.

conclusion

I n the book, I explore as graphically, narratively, and profoundly as I can the many faces of everyday paranoia.

Why everyday paranoia? Because the subject needs to be liberated from the chains of clinical diagnosis and psychiatric classification in which it has been safely incarcerated. I do not deny such syndromes exist. But I point out syndromes begin, take root, and grow up some place, and that place is the real, mundane, everyday world.

A paranoid point of view develops when our natural desire to protect ourselves crosses an invisible line, which varies greatly from one person to another, and begins to become unconsciously irrational. It is characterized by a kind of runaway vigilance, an increasingly pointless and draining around-the-clock guardedness that can only be maintained at a steep psychological price.

The concept of the paranoid trigger is introduced, and the crucial distinction is made between personal, social, and cultural triggers.

In the first chapter, the paranoid explosions of such pop culture icons as *The Sopranos* are contrasted with the realities of ordinary, everyday paranoia, where it will be the tiny details in our lives that seem most to torment us. Here there is precious little real-life drama. Here we move from fighting crime families and the federal authorities to fighting something that can even be as small and unheroic as a mouse.

In the second chapter, in a series of telling vignettes, the basic dynamics of everyday paranoia are explored. It is shown how, through the mechanism of projective identification, an unbearable, anxious field of unspecific threat becomes personified. What before was maddeningly amorphous has been magically made concrete and precisely located in space-time. What before was in dynamic flux has now been prematurely frozen. But the paranoid solution is a shaky one, characterized by a profound ambivalence over whether to stand one's ground or run.

In the third chapter, the deep connection between paranoia and the dread of being powerless is developed. It is shown how this gives rise to myriad power plays, power games, and strategies of control designed to fend off such fears. Yet, in a final irony, it is our unconscious recognition that power plays are games no one can win that continue to make them fertile soil for what we are calling the paranoia of everyday life.

And, in the fourth chapter, I conclude with a major clinical study of a patient (whom I call Becky Jamison) who dramatically personifies my central themes.

references

Alper, G. 1992. *Portrait of the Artist as a Young Patient.* New York: Insight/Plenum.
———. 1994. *The Singles Scene.* San Francisco: International Scholars Publications.
———. 1996. *The Dark Side of the Analytic Moon.* Bethesda, MD: International Scholars Publications.
———. 1999. *The Puppeteers.* Bethesda, MD: International Scholars Publications.
———. 2004. *Like a Movie: Contemporary Relationships without the Popcorn.* St. Paul, MN: Paragon House.
Bion, W. R. 1992. *Cogitations.* London: H. Karnac Books.
Bollas, C. 1987. *The Shadow of the Object.* New York: Columbia University Press.
———. 1995. *Cracking Up.* New York: Hill and Wang.
Erikson, E. 1950. *Childhood and Society.* New York: W. W. Norton.
Fairbairn, W. R. D. 1994. *Psychoanalytic Studies of the Personality.* New York: Routledge.
Freud, S. 1911. *Psychoanalytic Notes on an Autobiographical Account of a Case of Paranoia.* London: Hogarth Press, C.P., III; 387, S.E., XII, 3.
———. 1915. *Mourning and Melancholia.* London: Hogarth Press, S.E. XIX, 239.
———. 1923. *The Ego and the Id.* Reprint, London: Hogarth Press, 1957, S.E. 14: 146–58.
Goffman, E. 1959. *The Presentation of Self in Everyday Life.* New York: Doubleday.
———. 1959. *Stigma.* New York: Simon & Schuster.
———. 1962. *Interaction Ritual.* New York: Pantheon.
Kahn, M. 1979. *Alienation in Perversion.* New York: International University Press.

Klein, M. 1946. Notes on some schizoid mechanisms in *Developments in Psychoanalysis.* Edited by J. Riviére. London: Hogarth Press.

Laing, R. D. 1961. *Self and Others.* London: Tavistock Publications.

Lorenz, K. 1970. *Studies in Animal and Human Behavior,* vol. 1. Translated by Robert Martin. Cambridge, MA: Harvard University Press.

Miller, A. 1949. *Death of a Salesman.* New York: Viking Penguin.

Phillips, A. 1993. *On Kissing, Tickling and Being Bored.* Cambridge, MA: Harvard University Press.

———. 1996. *Terrors and Experts.* Cambridge, MA: Harvard University Press.

Rapaport, D. 1967. Principles Underlying Projective Techniques in *The Collected Papers of David Rapaport,* edited by Merton M. Gill. New York: Basic Books.

Salinger, J. D. 1951. *The Catcher in the Rye.* New York: Little, Brown.

Shapiro, D. 1965. *Neurotic Styles.* New York: Basic Books.

Winnicott, D. W. 1965. *The Maturational Processes and the Facilitating Environment.* New York: International Universities Press.

Wolfe, T. 1976. *Mauve Gloves, and Madmen, Clutter and Vine.* New York: Farrar, Straus and Giroux.

index